THE
PSYCHEDELIC
CEO

An Explorer's Journey into Psychedelics and
a New Era of Business Leadership

W. MURRAY RODGERS

Cover Illustration by Ariel Davis | arielrdavis.com
Interior Design & Cover Typography by Andrew Bell | andrewbelldesigns.co.uk

Book Edited & Produced by Raab & Co. | raabandco.com

Additional Art Design by Andrea Rodgers

Printed in Canada

First Print Edition
10 9 8 7 6 5 4 3 2 1

ISBN: 978-1-7331334-3-2

Dedicated to the leaders of the 21st Century.
We can all be CEOs: Conscious. Empathetic. Open.

CONTENTS

PREFACE

Hundreds of billions of dollars are spent globally on contemporary leadership development training. These training initiatives generally comprise coaching, team building programs, and seminars accompanied by a seemingly endless stream of business books and courses.

I used to occasionally attend these sorts of events. We would all leave feeling "self-improvement" rushing through our veins; we were emboldened with hope for ourselves and the people we wanted to serve. This excitement, however, wore off like any cheap drug, the confidence was mostly transitory, and we were left with the same habits and behavioral patterns that we set out to "fix."

Throughout my career as a geologist, executive, company founder, and CEO in the energy sector, I feel I have created tremendous value for stakeholders, employees, shareholders, and many local communities and economies. But I also feel that my own unconscious and, at times, destructive beliefs and behaviors have contributed to business and personal losses that dragged down many innocent souls around me. For I toiled away without realizing, like many of those around me, that I was a wounded leader.

WHY?

In my experience, the litany of leadership development tools routinely sold to companies around the world share one thing in common: They overlook *the wound*.

They simply cannot—or choose not to—account for the personal and often buried wounds, doubts, fears, and traumas that affect our everyday lives. These wounds often reveal themselves through egocentric, narcissistic, and sociopathic tendencies that pervade the human psyche and lead us to make disastrous personal and professional decisions. I too was blindly burdened by these "frailties," and now I can observe them freely in myself and others.

In 2009, leadership researcher Malcolm Higgs[1] outlined the following characteristics of bad leadership:

a) Abuse of power

b) Inflicting damage on others

c) Overexercise of control to satisfy personal needs

d) Rule breaking to serve own purposes

Can you imagine a leadership coach really grilling a businessperson about these behaviors? They would be out of a job in a heartbeat. This might as well be a list called "How to Become a Ruthless and Effective Leader in Modern Business." The leadership industry artfully focuses on "good" leadership qualities, while carefully skating around the deeper, uglier aspects of power and ego that are rife in all humans but particularly harmful in business and organizational leaders whose psyches affect many people's livelihoods. The leadership industry in itself is a result of these wounds; it's a Band-Aid that CEOs and managers created to satiate their urge to somehow improve and even heal, without actually getting to the source of the issue. While this brand of self-improvement is fundamentally flawed and ineffective, it is however seductive and marketable because it is easy and does not require true self-reflection. Inspirational posters on the wall, running meetings more efficiently, sitting through some seminars, and bean bags and ping-pong tables are merely superficial antidotes.

The leadership industry—like much of the wellness industry—preys on people's false belief that there is an easy way to become a more prosperous, healthier, happier, and even more exceptional human being. We have become conditioned, I daresay addicted, to the idea that we must strive for more than we need, and that we can become more than we actually are. This is the myth of exceptionalism. We perpetuate this myth because we have a distorted view of the relationship between ourselves and the world around us.

The good news is that a simple reframing, or rewiring, otherwise known as a change in consciousness, is readily available from Mother Earth.

SO WHAT?

My purpose in writing this book is twofold. The first is to highlight the healing that can occur from the use of the psychedelic plant medicine known as Ayahuasca—when conducted in a sacred, protected setting under the guidance of ethical shamans or other trained therapeutic practitioners.

The second and equally important purpose is to answer a question I asked myself soon after my first Ayahuasca ceremony: Could psychedelics become an effective leadership tool for the modern businessperson?

Real leadership is rooted in a deep and honest self-awareness that is rare and usually arises only out of one or more deeply personal and profound healing experiences. These reckonings issue from deep spiritual or therapeutic work, but they can also occur—rather traumatically—when people hit "rock bottom." Whether these events are triggered by death, disease, divorce, addiction, or financial loss, no one seeks out these experiences because they are painful. To come out having learned something rather than only lost something requires ruthless self-examination and personal work. It is well documented that a large number of people around the world who have had near-death experiences report life-changing transformations. I'm not saying all of these people are suddenly healed and have no more psychological issues or could be perfect leaders, but I am saying that whatever the path to awareness, it shouldn't be as easy as a leadership seminar; it should be dramatic, heart-wrenching, and soul-searching.

CAN I SPEAK TO THE MANAGER?

True leadership first and foremost means leading oneself before leading another. Who is leading you? What is leading you? Do you even know?

My experience with psychedelics suggests there may be another path to experience a powerful, life-changing transformation that does not require the random intervention of life events, and the cost, the loss, and the trauma that often goes along with them. This path is voluntary, intentional, sacred, and importantly—when shared with others in a sane, safe, communal setting—ultimately life-affirming in the deepest way I can imagine.

❝❞

The leadership industry—like much of the wellness industry—preys on people's false belief that there is an easy way

With proper guidance and integration, Ayahuasca can cause a powerful reset that allows us to know ourselves fully and crystallize our interdependent relationship with the entire world around us. This is a powerful, organic technology for helping to create Healed Leaders. Leadership is now the responsibility of each individual in society. We must empower and lead ourselves first, in order to lead and interact with communities and organizations in a compassionate, holistic, and productive way. It is time for the death of exceptionalism and the birth of humility.

I propose a new definition of CEO: **C**onscious, **E**mpathetic, **O**pen. This is not a career path, this is a life path. Let me show you.

THE PRISON PARABLE

"The best way to keep a prisoner from escaping is to make sure
he never knows he's in prison."
—Fyodor Dostoyevsky

Much about psychedelic experience eludes logic and empiricism. As a scientist, I understand that the subjectivity of psychedelic experiences can invoke skepticism and doubt in many people. Don't worry, I love science and believe in the scientific method. We'll get to the studies about psychedelics eventually, but there is still something to be said about the power of fictional storytelling. Before we get into the nitty-gritty evidence, I want to tell the following story, which—metaphorically— describes my inner world before and after Ayahuasca.

ONE

The icy wind penetrated the stone walls of my squalid, bug-infested cell—a perfect, eight-foot symmetrical cube. My feet were numb and nearly purple, like I was already dead meat. My thin cotton pajamas were a joke, unable to withstand the bone-jarring, paralyzing chill. I rolled over on my straw mat and looked at the tiny window high on the far wall. There was a glimmer of sunrise, or sunset—I couldn't tell the time, the day, or the month.

I turned over on my stomach and looked at the door. The eye level slot was closed, so it wasn't time for my meal yet. I had been in this cell for as long as I could remember. I don't know who or what was on the other side of the door, but they brought me just enough food to survive. No reason given to me as to why this sentence had been handed down; no indication of how long I had been here; and no hint of whether I would ever be released.

Usually the guard had no voice, just spindly talons pushing "food" through silently. Lately, I'd heard more breathing, and now, more words. It would ask me, "Do you know who you are and what you want?" I never answered because I didn't know the answer. Sometimes I would just scream, predictably: "Freedom!" And other times, when that was clearly not the answer, I would just say dejectedly, "I don't know." Sometimes I wondered if the Voice knew the answer, or if it was in prison too.

I searched my memory for clues—anything to recall what I had done to end up here. Whatever it was, it must have been heinous. My search led to no answers. Stories floated in my mind, a kaleidoscope of images, senses, memories, and feelings, none of which had any bearing on this incarceration.

I had clearly forgotten something very serious; I'd completely forgotten why I was in prison.

TWO

I had a dream that I met someone who seemed to hold the answer to the Voice's question. She was a shadow come to life—a ghost of the infinite—with a message for me. I was frightened, felt a burning pain in my left side, my right side was numb, and my head pounded from the thud of her power.

Oh, God! I begged inside, *take me from this place, let this power go, and release me from the heat of my anger and torture. Allow me to go free.*

Her voice was like a scalpel, cutting my defenses with deft surgical artistry. I could only stand, a sodden statue witnessing my own death sentence.

"Are you ready to listen to my message?" she asked.

Her eyes seared me with heat—unrelenting, all-seeing, all-knowing. She released the message before I could respond. It was a message from the eternal Mother—the one businesspeople like me were taught to laugh at and ignore. She didn't have to cut too deep to expose the pain of my existence; it wasn't hidden far beneath the surface.

"Your six decades on Earth might have been a waste."

"Six decades?" I asked. "Is that how long I have been here?"

"You've been living in three dimensions, but there is no room for you there anymore. You can no longer fit in those constraints. You must escape from within if you ever hope to escape without. Don't be afraid—you *know* why you're here, and you *know* how to get out. The life force you carry is scary because it's powerful, but it's yours, and trusting it will set you free."

"But, how do I escape from within?"

"It's simple," she said. "Kill the guard."

THREE

I awoke with a rush of ideas and hope that warmed me and the prison cell. The ghost was still in me. I could feel her.

The guard must have felt warmth emanating from my cell. The small door slid open but no food came through. I felt I was being watched. Instead of fear, I felt seductive. I felt my newfound feminine warmth to be more powerful than words and

THE PSYCHEDELIC CEO

swords and violence and "please." My presence was sharp.

The door slid closed again and I had the distinct sensation that I had just dismembered the guard and left it to rot.

I turned and looked up at the sodden stained ceiling of the cell. I felt an ancient blacksmith working inside my heart and my head, pounding and hammering, honing and tempering, fine-tuning and polishing.

I felt a curious mix of elation, dread, fear, and hope. My new awareness was percolating. I heard the lock tick open and echo in the quiet cell. The heavy metal door creeped open and I could sense that freedom was near.

INTRODUCTION

"Even today we hear people ask in surprise: What is the use of these voyages of exploration? What good do they do us? Little brains, I always answer to myself, have only room for thoughts of bread and butter."
—Roald Amundsen, the South Pole

When I was fifty-nine years old, I was ejected from the company I founded, and then from my marriage soon after. On my sixtieth birthday, I found myself alone in a big house in the Canadian Rockies drinking boxed *cardbordeaux* wine while watching *The Rewrite* starring Hugh Grant.

While it wasn't clear to me at the time, this all would lead to the personal healing journey on which I was about to embark. Over the next few years, I would attend eight psychedelic ceremonies using Ayahuasca, the sacred plant medicine of the Amazon.

As a former CEO, and a practicing professional geologist in the energy industry, I have explored for oil and gas in many countries around the world. I have led small and large teams from highly diverse cultural and spiritual backgrounds over a career spanning more than three decades. Along the way I have been instrumental in raising over a billion dollars in capital. While I have lived a reasonably successful and interesting life outwardly, inwardly it has been a much different journey.

Over the years, I have attended a rather broad sampling of workshops and retreats. Spiritual practices to which I have been introduced in my adult life have included Christian, Buddhist, Hindu meditation and prayer, yoga, non-psychedelic shamanic prayer, drumming and song rituals, and Canadian First Nations sweat ceremonies. I was highly engaged in Jungian analysis and dreamwork during my thirties and explored non-psychedelic altered consciousness through sound and breathwork.

As a part-time professional musician, songwriter, photographer, and artist, with a deep love of the mountains and nature, it would seem that my inner life should have reached a state of coherence by my sixties.

But no. I had reached a point of despair, unable to unravel and reconcile regrets, business failures, disappointment with myself, a failed marriage due to my infidelity, binge drinking, and unreconciled feelings of grief, hopelessness, and suicidal ideation. I finally had to confront the Voice on the other side of the door—which had always presented itself to me as the deep, nagging sadness and low-grade depression that had followed me most of my life. It couldn't be ignored any longer.

I was unable to find a convenient, rational, tidy explanation for why my life had gone the way it had. All the while, I knew I was blessed to have two daughters with whom I have a deep, loving relationship, many strong friendships that have lasted over several decades, and wide-ranging and meaningful relationships with my extended family.

By all outward appearances, I was cognitively and spiritually "normal"—advanced even. I had never been medically diagnosed with a mental disorder. In fact, my demons, or variations of them, seem rather pervasive among the many so-called successful people I know, and many of those people are leaders.

At one point, my closest friend commented, "Murray, I'll never understand why, with everything you have, you're still not happy." At the time, it didn't even occur to me to ask myself whether I was happy or not. I just wanted to be *successful*—whatever that meant—and, of course, I was never successful *enough*.

❝❞

I was unable to find a convenient, rational, tidy explanation for why my life had gone the way it had

My desperation centered around the fact that I couldn't seem to get rid of my underlying sense that something was missing, something beyond the grasp of my rational mind. Every time I tried to peek in, all I could see was darkness.

I spent much of my adult life exploring: looking for minerals from basecamps in Northern Canada, Yukon; discovering the interior of southern British Columbia as a summer student; searching for oil in Pakistan, Albania, Austria, Canada, and the United States; drilling high-risk wells in different parts of the world; always trying somehow to uncover the mysteries of Mother Nature.

But what was I *really* looking for?

The search started even earlier. In what is now basically a rite of passage for young Westerners, I took a year off school in my twenties to travel throughout Southeast Asia and India. I was trying to ... *find myself* of course.

At that age, finding myself looked like ingesting hash brownies to deal with my aversion to crowds, trying to find favorable currency exchange rates, and finding ways to stay within my self-allotted budget of $2 per day. This all led to ultimately finding myself trying to find a clean toilet to relieve my amoebic dysentery and explosive giardia. I found myself alright—crapping in a gutter on a side street in Calcutta.

Despite the partying and episodes of debauchery, there was an underlying current driving this trip. I also sat for days in the vast colonial library of the Sri

Aurobindo Ashram in Pondicherry, India, reading from the great works of the world's philosophers and spiritual teachers. I ate meals served by white-robed Westerners who worked in the kitchens and gardens immersed in some sort of rarefied bliss. As a short-term guest of the ashram, I was allowed to read, think, and learn to meditate. But while there was an intriguing quality to it all, to me it also felt mildly creepy, cultish even. There would be no enlightenment for me on this trip.

Still, a strong sense of possibility awoke in me, and it has never left me. I understand there is much—perhaps more—beyond what we consider reality. There is a place of joy, grace, peace, and inner serenity. It appears to me like some other terrain—an inner geography waiting to be explored, mapped, and drilled down into. There I go thinking like an oil man again. I can't help but feel that deep down there is the source of our own wealth, a source of infinite energy, a realm, and a kingdom where sanity rules.

After my travels ended, I returned to law school with a sense of doom. I loved what I was learning, what I was experiencing, but, but, but, I didn't care about the *real* world. After a disastrous second year, during which I spent an inordinate amount of time skipping classes and copping guitar licks from my vinyl collection, I flunked out of law school and headed West for a life in the oil business, bouncing along the Prairies in my mother's old Corolla, just another pioneer seeking his fortune. That was me for the next thirty-five years.

BUT HOW?

Throughout my career, I continued to develop my spiritual life, for better or worse depending whom you talk to. I am no stranger to healing modalities that contain elements of mystery, unquantifiable in the scientific sense, yet profoundly impactful with practical outcomes in both my personal and professional life. The intersection of logical and intuitive thought has been an ongoing theme for most of my adult life.

My experience with Jungian analysis over a ten-year period beginning in my late thirties was a dramatic descent into the realm of dreams and the unconscious, and it benefited my leadership skills as I began to see that everyone is fueled by their unconscious drives. It allowed me to develop into a leader who could meet my people where they were, not where I was. This was a burgeoning form of empathy, I was to later learn. The most positive outcome of my work with Jungian analysis was that I was able to work well with all types of personalities.

On a personal level, I learned to mine my dream content for meaning, for messages, for understanding, for my health. My subjective experiences made me aware that energies within my mind-body system percolate, mutate, and lodge, and can be relieved, and shifted through catharsis, which usually resulted in a new perspective of some kind.

At this time, the concepts of the divine feminine and masculine were introduced but remained largely intellectual constructs for which I had no means to understand their practical application in daily life. I abandoned analysis at a point where I felt it had become lodged in an intellectual framework that kept me trapped in man-made ideas rather than actually addressing the amorphous spiritual issues I suffered from.

My sporadic practice of meditation over many years occasionally achieved satisfying results in terms of peace of mind, slowing down my heartbeat and breath, and occasionally deepening my awareness. More often than not, I fell asleep in weird positions, leading to chronic neck pain. While mindfulness is now a common term, companies have yet to fully embrace the power of the practice as a helpful tool.

My lifelong interest in yoga led me to undertake a teacher training course to further explore the interplay between the physical and emotional bodies, and to explore the depths of yoga knowledge.

❝ ❞

The intersection of logical and intuitive thought has been an ongoing theme for most of my adult life

However, for all my exploration, none of the methods went far enough to crystallize a new way of being and none of them relieved my depression.

My search led me to *learn* about psychedelics, but I had no interest in trying them. I, like many of my peers, had fallen prey to the negative bias so often promulgated by the media and the scientific communities. I was afraid of losing control, afraid of flashbacks, afraid of psychotic breaks, and afraid of all sorts of things that are no more a required part of psychedelic journeys than they are a required part of chewing bubble gum. Still, many people I met through the yoga, shamanic, and even business communities had spoken positively about Ayahuasca. They reported nearly identical stories—stories of transformational experiences.

But how? That was always the question for me, and the answers were not always satisfactory. In many cases, I could not find a tangible articulation of *why* the experience was impactful, and so I ended up dismissing much of it as voodoo. Whatever the case, it was impossible not to notice what all of these people had in common. They all shared an affect I had been searching for; they appeared less troubled by day-to-day life than me—less neurotic—and held the weight of people who had glimpsed into another realm.

I began voraciously reading about shamanism and ceremonial psychedelics. I was curious, but still operating from my logical (and skeptical) mind. Esteemed writers and shamanic teachers Michael Harner and Sandra Ingerman seemed uncommonly lucid, sane, and rational, and I was further convinced there was something to this shamanic business. *Could this be a way out of my lifelong malaise?* At my age, being in my sixties, I felt I really had nothing to lose at this point. And yet—there was still fear.

This fear was not only unrealistic, it was not even a fear of the medicine itself. I see now it was a fear of receptivity, a fear of losing my *manly* control over the world. It was a fear of, even momentarily, allowing myself to *receive*—in a word, to be feminine.

THE DIVINE

It turns out that the most impactful group experiences in spiritual settings that I have participated in have been predominantly attended by women: shamanic workshops, yoga teacher training, Ayahuasca ceremonies, and Monroe Institute consciousness retreats, to name a few. I often found myself questioning, "Where are the guys?" I knew the answer: this is not something guys typically do because it requires the courage to be vulnerable—a type of courage not exactly valuable in the world of external achievement.

Standing at the headwaters of Lake Louise on a cold August morning, I was one of three men encircled by a group of nine women. They stood arm in arm, singing a prayer in which the feminine was caring for the masculine. I hoped no hikers or climbers were watching this spectacle—my fear of ridicule stopped me from fully embracing the ceremony. As the singing progressed in feeling and intensity, the sincerity, caring, and power of this group of women left me trying to cover tears rolling down my cheeks. It felt like an overwhelming opening to the truth of real feminine power. At the end of the ceremony, after a peaceful moment of silence, I was compelled to make a joke. A sure sign that my frail masculine veneer was about to shatter. "I guess this really is a womb with a view," I said, to uproarious laughter.

This event, my first foray into South American shamanic beliefs, involved no psychedelics; it was purely ceremonial prayer, singing and chanting, and meditation. I was apprehensive. In fact, I confided to one of the male attendees that I thought I was on the edge of an anxiety attack in anticipation of this. I know now that this fear was not of the event, but of the unknown inside me.

The leader was American therapist and shaman Karen Duncan, who had traveled over a two-decade period to Peru to study shamanism. In her mid-seventies, a mother and grandmother, powerful and wise, she led us through a series of rituals in several locations around Field and Lake Louise, with the intention of activating the energy of the magnificent mountains in the area. Karen had been guided to this place by her Peruvian teachers, whose visions showed them that the Canadian Rockies were not being treated with sacred respect, unlike the Andes in Peru, which are sacred, divine gods in the spiritual lives of the locals. And while the Andes also attract throngs of deeply motivated spiritual seekers, in Canada, these mountains are only tourist magnets, and little else. The vast majority of the tourist population do not travel into our mountains for sacred reasons, nor do the majority of locals venerate them for anything other than the infinite outdoor adventure opportunities they provide.

It was in this setting that I was introduced to the concept, and the experience, of what is known in many traditions as the *divine feminine*. I had long ago dismissed this as New Age mumbo jumbo, for I had not met anyone who could actually tell me what it meant.

In the period following my experience in the Rockies, I began to notice a change in my perceptions. I began to observe that in all the endeavors that pulled my interest, in addition to the fact there were relatively few men, it seemed that many of these women, regardless of age, race, socioeconomic status, and education, were simply smarter than me. While I joke that I finished at the bottom of my yoga teacher training class, it is in fact true. In hindsight, I was guided to this particular training program for a specific purpose. It was unique in that it was taught jointly by a husband-and-wife team. I observed in real time the balance of the masculine and feminine, both between them and their different approaches to teaching, the masculine being focused on knowledge, teachings, physical principles of alignment, and the feminine being embracing, intuitive, nurturing, but no less powerful. And yet each teacher carried a beautiful blend of all energies within themselves. They seemed to have achieved a marriage that balanced beautifully the masculine and feminine, between them, and within them.

Meanwhile, the big-time CEO had been reduced to the dunce in the class. I was often singled out as a physical example of what a misaligned body looks like, a corporate Quasimodo, lurking in the shadows of power, squinting in the light. In contrast, an angelic former gymnast, all power and grace, was used as an example of what an aligned, harmonious body looks like. While this was always done with kindness, and endless humor, the message was not lost on me. This was humbling, but at the same time, a great relief. My ego continued to take a beating until I began to develop a deep respect and appreciation for my fellow yoga students, all of whom were women. This was new for me. I come from a hyper-masculine world, and by the end of the training program, my deep unconscious bias and sense of superiority vis-à-vis women erupted in a molten mass of nauseating shame and disgust. At the closing ceremony, while looking around the room at these incredible women, I found myself choking back tears. What had happened to me?

With apologies to that annoying bird, and that annoying band, I ate crow and humble pie.

This continued in my daily life. I could not help but notice the extraordinarily capable, *interesting*, and inspiring women in my life. It was, frankly, intimidating. Conversely, I began to notice that many men I met, both personally and in business, seemed lost, unhappy, and frankly, boring.

And nature. She began to show up differently. In hikes in the mountains and on the west coast, rocks, trees, and landscapes began to adopt animated forms, with human forms appearing in the ice in the river, or along a rock face on a mountainside, or in the sand formed by oscillating tides on a beach. I began to wonder if my experience with the shamanic group in the Rockies a year earlier had really opened up some new awareness in me.

𝟔𝟔 𝟑𝟑
I had long ago dismissed the divine feminine as New Age mumbo jumbo

Some eighteen months later, in what seemed to be the divine feminine telling me it was time to release all fear, I bumped into an old friend at the local coffee shop. I had not seen her for many months, and I asked her what she was up to. She rather cautiously looked around, leaned over with her hand over her mouth, and whispered that she was going to Costa Rica to do an Ayahuasca ceremony. This is what either Carl Jung—or was it Sting—termed *synchronicity*.

"Excuse me?" I mumbled with milky froth leaking down the side of my mouth from my latte. Like a rabid dog, I blurted out I had just been reading about Rythmia, an Ayahuasca retreat in Costa Rica. I confided, bravely, that it scared me to contemplate doing psychedelics, but that I was seriously intrigued. She promised me that she would let me know how it went. A month later, I received a text from her that simply said, "Go."

It is said that this plant medicine calls out to you when you are ready. While this can be easily dismissed as magical thinking, or a conceit of spiritual superiority, in my experience, it is not. The realm of consciousness that beckons us to go deeper is real and should not be ignored. This is where the magic occurs. What holds us back is our fear.

It was finally through my Ayahuasca journeys that the light bulb flickered, then stayed on. It is said that the spirit of the plant medicine, Ayahuasca, is a divine feminine spirit. She is referred to as The Mother, or Mother Aya. What she does is strip bare our masculine landscape and regenerate new life, infused by the feminine— the sense of humility, empathy, connectedness to and reverence for the Earth. A renewed empathy for our fellow humans is an outcome described by generations of participants in the ceremony. The frequency and similarity of these experiences is so grand it runs the risk of cliché. This medicine performed a miracle of alchemy for me and many others. The masculine and feminine are now swirling tides, ebbing and flowing according to the dictates of my daily challenges.

CHAPTER 1

THE SINKING LEADER SHIP

"The crisis of leadership today is the mediocrity and irresponsibility of so many of the men and women in power ... Leadership is one of the most observed and least understood phenomena on earth."

—James MacGregor Burns

n a mid-career moment of questionable judgment, I worked at an investment bank before being fired in under a year. The leader of the company was unduly kind, and I am eternally grateful for his wise counsel. He said, in all sincerity, "You keep challenging the clients, and they don't like you. You really should consider starting your own company."

In the investment banking business, client relationships are paramount, and the truth was, I didn't like a lot of the arrogance that permeated our industry. The master and servant dynamic brought out a combative streak in me that I admit was unattractive.

One day prior to my exit, the managing director and I hustled over to the office of the CEO of a very large oil and gas company in Calgary. This company had just taken over another highly regarded company in a blockbuster transaction. We were to present a new business idea to the CEO of the acquiring company. We were escorted into a gigantic boardroom and we ... waited. The door suddenly burst open and in loped the CEO, sweating, tie askew. Flopping into the enormous leather chair across an airport runway of a boardroom table, he exclaimed, "I just came from the convention center where I had to talk to all 1,500 employees of a company we just bought." Then he shook his head, and said, "I couldn't get away! All they kept asking me was, 'What about the company culture, what's the culture going to be?' It drove me crazy!"

He looked at us proudly, a gleam in his eye and blurted out, "Finally, I just said, 'Forget about the company culture, it's just a bunch of bullshit! We're here to make money!' " And with that, our meeting commenced.

WHAT IS CULTURE?

It turns out this particular CEO, in a paradoxically Trumpian way, may have been correct.

In 1961, critic and theorist Raymond Williams suggested that *culture* has three divergent meanings. Williams maintained that the three meanings are not only different, but actually compete with one another. The first, or ideal, is the "state or process of human perfection." The second, is "documentary ... the body of intellectual or imaginative work," or a record of "human thought and experience." Third is the most commonly understood definition, a "description of a particular way of life." It is into this third definition that we have attempted to shoehorn the leadership mantra of "corporate culture."[2]

Confusion around meaning has not lessened in today's increasingly divided world. In a 2014 article in *The New Yorker* entitled "The Meaning of 'Culture,'" Joshua Rothman points out that the Merriam-Webster dictionary has six definitions of the noun *culture*, and that the word *culture* was the most searched word in their database that year.

In today's leadership industry, *culture* is generally defined as a set of shared attitudes, values, goals, and practices. Leaders try valiantly to frame their mission statements, values, and purpose in mostly sincere, well-intentioned language. This language is essential, helpful, and provides a frame of reference for how people conduct themselves in our organizations. So, it's a good start, but it just does not go deep enough.

In microbiology, *culture* is a verb that simply means "to grow" or, less succinctly, "the propagation of microorganisms in a growth medium." Like bacteria and all living things, companies exist to grow—profit motive. In this book, the question is: Are we creating a growth medium for humans? Does our petri dish (corporate culture) look like a beautiful forest or a cancerous overgrowth?

For over twenty-five years, Jan Eden, a highly experienced executive development specialist, worked nationally and internationally with hundreds of executives. She observed why the majority of leadership training programs are ineffective. She saw that after executives or leaders participate in training programs, there is typically no clear plan for how the leaders can then implement and integrate what they have learned in their organizations. They are effectively cast adrift, alone, in an ocean of entrenched mindsets and behaviors, a culture of infertility.

In Eden's view, the issue is that hired gun CEOs in public corporations are "outward looking"—focused primarily on pleasing shareholders and their boards. Typically, their mandate is to directly impact the bottom line and shareholder value. Company culture and employee well-being is not their primary focus. It's likely not their secondary focus either. However, without loyal, productive, and happy employees, both the shareholder value and the executive team are vulnerable.

❝❞

Like bacteria and all living things, companies exist to grow—profit motive. Are we creating a growth medium for humans?

In contrast, CEOs and owners of private companies with their own "skin in the game" are "internally focused" on their own ideas, egos, technologies. While they may start their companies with the best of intentions regarding employee culture and employee well-being, they ultimately succumb to a singular focus on profit growth.

In both public and private companies, neither is looking up and out at the inevitable change and disruption in their respective industries, all the while ignoring the internal realities of the company and their people. The fear of being knocked off the competitive game board more often than not distorts the good intentions, and ultimately, the true purpose of leadership for many executives and business owners.

Eden's solution is that an internal and external CEO be assigned. Both CEOs are equal and effective. The externally focused CEO (shareholders) aligns with the internally focused CEO (people) to ensure no balls are dropped and that one side is communicating with the other, keeping the corporate, financial, and human aspects of the company sustainable.

ARE LEADERS BORN OR RAISED?

In Jan Eden's experience, corporate culture is created from consciously living the corporate values from the top down. Self-aware executives and leaders can infuse the culture with the humanity that employees crave, while less self-aware and wholly self-interested leaders infuse the company culture with mistrust, suspicion, and pernicious self-interest. The cognitive dissonance in much of the corporate world today stems from the competing—and perhaps paradoxical—objectives of (a) better financial performance in a brutal market and (b) developing one's self and others into better, more socially responsible leaders. While we assume that the title of "senior" or "executive" implies leadership skills and self-awareness, it often doesn't, and good people are left with their well-being in the hands of wounded, inept, and uninterested leaders.

❝❞

Forget about the company culture, it's just a bunch of bullshit! We're here to make money!

The true fault of this dynamic is illustrated in a story Eden tells about one of her clients, a popular middle manager from a large, international public company. He'd been selected, along with another ninety-nine employees out of thousands, to partake in a $5 million leadership training program. There was no clear reason why this particular group of employees had been chosen—and no details were shared with them prior to being picked. It was just another mindless action and directive by senior management. Still, they felt special, anointed, and many believed they were perhaps being groomed for illustrious senior or executive roles.

This select group of candidates developed a perceptible sense of superiority and entitlement versus those who were not chosen—most truly believed there was a secret and gleaming agenda for their working future at this company. Meanwhile, senior management displayed little or no interest in the program or their development. Shortly after completion of the training program, Eden's client was abruptly fired. As were many others. No reason given. No performance feedback. Nothing. To Eden's knowledge, few, if any of the participants in the program ever reached a level of influence in the company. It appears there was no correlation between the people chosen for the program and the actual enriching of their careers and the company culture. If anything, one could cynically assume the company put only people in the program who they didn't think had bright futures, so as not to hinder the productivity of other employees. Whatever the case, it's clear this $5 million investment was mere lip service to say they embraced leadership development.

As the above example illustrates, in attempting to improve, or develop, leaders within corporate culture, often the leaders have no idea what culture actually is, how to nurture it, and how it could one day help them achieve their business goals. Today's leadership development endeavors are just a glossy paint job on a rusted-out sculpture of a dinosaur.

WHO'S NEXT?

Another common theme Eden observed among executive teams was a deep reticence to consider executive succession planning. While executives did name certain employees who they felt might have executive capabilities, they kept it private, never telling a possible successor what they were thinking. Therefore, rather inevitably, those strong candidates and exceptional producers eventually left the company to be hired by a competitor as senior leaders or executives.

This type of deep-seated insecurity among leaders can further manifest in the inability, or unwillingness, to know when to pass the baton. In a healthy culture, leaders would be developed, grown organically, and imbued with the DNA of the organization. But this is predicated on the CEO being self-aware, but not self-critical, and secure enough to nurture the future leaders of the company. Good leaders know their end is inevitable—much like dying is inevitable. Neither topic is popular around the water cooler. The idea of hiring a top performer to apprentice under the guidance of the current CEO or executive would ensure a conscious and seamless transition. This might mitigate the executive's fear of passing the reins—and also any paranoia that candidates are lurking the halls plotting their demise.

As a former CEO, I can attest to the fact that we all like to believe we are indispensable. This is because, deep down, we fear irrelevance, fear being exposed as weak, ineffective, or aging, and so the idea of a successor is an undermining factor in our already chaotic minds. Given this type of insecurity, it is little wonder that we don't really support leadership development programs. To some degree, I'm sure the half-hearted leadership programs are ineffective by design: most executives have little interest in training their replacements and planning their own demise.

HOW DO YOU DEVELOP LEADERS?

Throughout my career, I've observed a proliferation of people who identify as *executive coaches, leadership consultants, wellness experts, human potential guides,* and many other cockamamie titles. People in *the leadership industry*—as it's called—traffic mainly in acronyms and loosely defined "professional" designations, jargon, and credibility by mere association. Terms such as *change agent, executive performance expert, thought leader, influencer* all amount to the vapid worldview that leadership is broken, but not to worry because it can be fixed with some motivational quotes. There seem to be more people advising on how we should lead than there are actually leading. The truth is, very few leadership and business consultants have built or lead an organization, or even a team, from scratch, nor have they sufficiently healed, or at least explored deeply, their own wounds, such that lasting and effective changes can be brought to bear in their practices.

❝❞

While we assume that the title of "senior" or "executive" implies leadership skills and self-awareness, it often doesn't

Oddly, this seems similar to the music business, where whom you've met often eclipses what you have actually done. A typical interaction between two unknown musicians involves a type of verbal swordplay that goes along the lines of "I played with so-and-so," or even, "My cousin played with so-and-so." This is a way of vicariously validating a lifetime spent on a skill with very little to show for it— credibility by association only. A useful reply to this is, "I haven't played with any famous people, but I have played with myself a lot."

And so it goes in the leadership industry: "I trained with so and so," or "I attended a weekend retreat and am now a graduate of 'The Big Name' Master Class in Awesomeness." The leadership industry is a self-sustaining economic fantasy, the efficacy of which yet remains alarmingly opaque.

Recently, professor Gianpiero Petriglieri wrote that "leadership development is one of very few industries that can chastise its own product and continue producing it!"[3] The invisible hypocrisy of the leadership industry is that most practitioners know it is not effective, at least in any lasting sense, yet there is a near-messianic zeal in promoting its virtues.

EMPTY SUITS

In one instance, a company a female friend of mine worked for hired a leadership development group to guide their exclusively male executive team on a yearlong mission to improve their leadership skills. The thought was that this would result in greater harmony, transparency, and trust, among many other attributes that these sorts of consultants love to throw around.

Following one of these workshops, the whiteboard in the meeting room was littered with traits that oscillated between commonsensical, meaningless, and traits that only a deity would possess:

- Take advice with a grain of salt.
- Ask 4 second opinions.
- Don't add noise/static to decisions.
- Don't take your team for granted.
- Surround yourself with diverse opinions.
- Leverage your peer talent fully.
- Develop my own appreciation and understanding of leadership.
- Value the experience.
- Trust shows up in new, different ways; support, communication, asking for support.
- Manage different personalities.
- Resilience exists at the company.
- Humanizing executives; be yourself. We are learning to manage /deal w/ change, together
- Winging it is no longer an option.
- We have a say in how things evolve.
- I don't know what the culture is.
- We have grown as a team (TRUST)
- We need a space to express our concerns.
- We need clear direction and decision-making from financial, board, exec, team.

With more technical and executive experience in the industry than anyone in the company, and quite capable of running the show, my friend was not included in this program, which she somewhat facetiously referred to as "charm school." The reason she was given is that she was only a consultant, and therefore not part of the core staff. Keep in mind it's a small company, twenty-five people, and she had been a key technical expert in their entire growth over a four-year period. The senior team chosen for the program were all male. Typically, upon returning from a workshop, the language and tone of emails changed, indicating a newly found enlightenment among the attendees. This usually lasted for a week or so, then it was back to business. After a year of these power sessions that promised to elevate the executives to master-level leaders and ensure operational harmony, the CEO and another senior executive were fired for lying to the board of directors.

My view of leadership was always hardwired around the idea that if you can't figure it out on your own, you're probably a loser. This type of leadership is fueled by pride, ego, and their odd sister, insecurity. Like many leaders, in fear of being exposed as a fraud, I had a closet full of these psychic suits. Custom-made to my needs.

Successes were invariably due to being saved by the collective wisdom and talent of those around me, which I am happy to acknowledge. But the failures were deeply personal, and painful, leaving me stuck in a lonely vortex. Would it have been helpful to have someone to talk to who truly understood my situational distress? Absolutely. But I could not risk the vulnerability of exposure—whether to a therapist or to a leadership coach—out of fear of being exposed as a fraud. This is what I term the dinosaur mindset: a rapacious desire to "eat what you kill," to dominate, to show power and strength, yet unwittingly headed for extinction.

So, after the failure of my last venture, in which I was fired from the company I had founded by a board led by ethically questionable shareholders and their minions, I naturally began to wonder if I could transition from being an entrepreneur to becoming an executive coach. It seemed to be the thing to do. I had certainly experienced almost everything a businessperson could experience, and I love helping others succeed. Perhaps I could assist others in avoiding the mistakes I had made along the way.

My prevailing shortcoming, however, was that I did not have a "professional designation" from the likes of a prestigious institution like the Academy of Godlike & Immaculate Business Leaders. I have always been severely averse to formal designations, having dropped out of not one, but two MBA programs. In each case I was faced with spending my nights slaving over pointless case studies and group projects instead of playing guitar in a hard-drinking blues band six nights a week while also working a day job.

Despite having managed and led people for most of my life, I felt I likely didn't have the skills to coach or advise anyone because I hadn't been coached on how to lead. In retrospect, it turns out this was completely misguided, as the issue lay much deeper than that.

In my effort to gain some sort of credibility in this realm, I decided to talk to the director of one of the recognized executive leadership programs in Canada. I made an appointment with one of the program directors. I felt a lot of sincerity from the director, who was fairly young—as most are now, relative to me—but I could not help but feel there was some sort of naiveté; a lack of real-world business and life experience underlying the basic tenets of the program and those entrusted with administering the program. Most importantly, there did not seem to be firm follow-up on how this training impacted the graduates' professional lives following graduation. My guess is the results wouldn't be too impressive.

It seemed the vast majority of participants in the course came from middle management in large organizations, and that this course was a way to jump up the corporate management ladder. This goal lies at the heart of the leadership industry: telling people that some certification suddenly makes them more valuable employees—deserving of more responsibility, and more money.

❝ ❞

But I could not risk the vulnerability of exposure— whether to a therapist or to a leadership coach— out of fear of being exposed as a fraud

When I asked the director of the program to give me some examples of graduates from the program who had successfully built a leadership training business from scratch after graduating the program, she became deathly silent.

I do know one entrepreneur who attended this program after having built a private company worth many millions and wanted to transition into coaching. He was fifty-fifty on whether the program had helped him to any meaningful extent. Despite his highly successful business track record and having a gold star coaching certification, he quickly become frustrated in being unable to build up a successful coaching business. His failure wasn't because he lacked real experience and leadership abilities; he simply wasn't a branding and marketing expert—which is all many successful coaches are. It turns out that those who can, do, and those who can't, coach.

I decided this type of program was not for me.

THE ABILITY TO ASCEND

After my first two ceremonies with Ayahuasca, a cacophony of emotions, images, ideas competed for primacy in my mind. The powerful shamanic belief that humans are wounded, and that the medicine can heal the wound, presented me with a series of questions that tumbled out of my reinvigorated mind.

I wondered if I would have been a better business leader if I had done plant medicine earlier in my life. *Would I have been a better husband and father? Would I have been a better human being?* All of the answers were clearly *yes*.

I met a group of businessmen who had traveled to Costa Rica to experience Ayahuasca together. Outwardly they were successful, athletic, and confident, the types of guys who might have graduated from name-brand business schools and ended up working in finance for investment banks or running their own companies. Aside from the cursory smell-test of one another to see where each fit in the subtle power structures of men, we didn't talk business. I didn't inquire further; they didn't volunteer nor did they inquire. What set them apart from the typical hard-driving business types who head off on beer-soaked golf trips to "clear their head" was that while not knowing what to expect, the general consensus among them was that Ayahuasca was a cool thing to do. To these men, it was because it was outside their comfort zones, and because it required them to receive intelligence rather than impart and assert it—like leaders are *supposed* to do.

❝❞
A week of psychedelic ceremonies is akin to a psychic form of skydiving—without knowing who packed your chute

A week of psychedelic ceremonies is akin to a psychic form of skydiving—without knowing who packed your chute. It looks cool, the pictures will be great, your friends will admire you, and you can, for the rest of your life, say you did it. But, when you are hanging on the wing strut of the aircraft, one foot on the wheel, one foot dangling a mile above the ground, and you are humbled beyond belief by your paralytic fear, the experience transmutes into something completely unexpected. And when the jump master tells you to let go, you truly fall into an abyss where you might approach death (though rest assured both skydiving and Ayahuasca are generally safe).

The power of this medicine is that once you are confronted with the stark and often shocking reality of your own egoic mind, it is very easy to spot those same traits in others. Ayahuasca gives you eagle eyes for hubris, judgment, self-protection, and other traits we try to hide. Suddenly, you're able to spot those who are able to ascend, and those who are stuck to the ground.

DON'T TAKE IT FROM ME

On Rythmia's online forums, I conducted a survey asking participants how Ayahuasca impacted their lives and their views on leadership: almost everyone answered that they experienced improvements in self-development and self-awareness. Most people said they had some form of spiritual awakening.

As most of these survey participants hold leadership roles within their community—CEOs, CFOs, bankers, founders, property developers, entrepreneurs, bodyworkers, and counselors—I asked if they felt Ayahuasca was beneficial for their leadership development. The participants responded nearly unanimously by saying Ayahuasca could facilitate a wider lens of connection and responsibility by helping leaders see their greater connection to the natural world. They reported that their experience helped them see the bigger picture and what could potentially be missing from their perspective. They also said Ayahuasca could help open leaders' minds, supporting the internal balance of a leader's work and personal life, helping leaders process their anger, supporting the dissolution of their ego, leading to greater humility, empathy, and care in their daily actions.

Scott S., Finance, CFO, Texas

Ayahuasca has had a profound impact on my life. I'm one of the few people in my cohort that did not have a specific intention going into the ceremonies. I limited my intentions to learning about myself and the universe. The plant medicine and accompanying ceremony did exactly that. Trust and faith would allow the medicine to work its magic. The medicine kicked in with a central focus on me. She seemed to say, "Okay, you have a long list of baggage to address; where do you want to start? Let's start at the top." The rest of the ceremony was a difficult process of addressing all the material weights I have been both consciously and subconsciously carrying around. The weights that have been weighing me down in life and impacting both my professional and personal decisions and relationships. By addressing each issue presented by the medicine, that issue would be forever put to rest.

The overall impact this experience has had on my life includes increased humility, enhanced empathy. a heightened sense of well-being, an insatiable desire for self-improvement, and the recognition that this powerful experience is curative and needs to find a respectful place in our society.

Ayahuasca is unequivocally useful in leadership training. The ego is the single biggest barrier to effective leadership, and so deconstructing the ego, a natural effect of Ayahuasca, is arguably the single most important thing a leader can do to increase their effectiveness.

Corrin T., Interior Designer and Creative Project Manager, New Jersey

What brought me the most peace from the Ayahuasca experience was receiving confirmation that my purpose is to simply be me. I was reminded in a visceral way that all life is connected and equally valued yet within that connection is beautiful diversity and unconditional love. The experiences at Rythmia reminded me that life is best lived in ceremony of its gifts which can be accessed at any moment through our full attention to the present moment.

Life is a sacred expression and exploration of infinite possibilities; to fear is to forget.

What the spirit of Ayahuasca can teach leaders is that we are all connected through nature and the only separations are those that we create inside ourselves through nonacceptance. In order to be helpful to others we have to stop seeing them as others; as outside of ourselves. We are reflections of the whole. If people are to feel valued, heard and safe to be themselves, the opportunity to co-create anything with depth and brilliant uniqueness is available.

Alysa L., Event Planner, Los Angeles

I quit my job within the week of returning from Rythmia and have had the courage to bring myself back to a lifestyle of happiness and health. I knew I had a complete imbalance of mind, body, and spirit and all the traumas of my life had to be interrogated and investigated. With the help of plant medicine, I have been able to dismantle a lot of pain, resentment, and traumas in my life.

I lost over fifty pounds and feel better than I did in my twenties! Spiritually, it has connected me to the truth of my soul's desires and has kept me on a direct path of being unabashedly me. I live with more compassion and understanding of others while coming to peace with mortality we all share.

While I see much good intention in human beings, so many leaders lead from fear, doubt, and misplaced energy. Leaders can benefit from this medicine by realizing their true nature and directing love into their companies. They might be able to dismantle the theory that "work life" must be separate from your "personal life." They will have the ability to create a healthy culture that supports the quality of life for employees and will be interested in their personal growth *as well as* professional goals. A shift could happen where leaders can feel free to show up as much as possible as their true selves. They would keep a safer environment without pretense or judgment. Egg shells would not feel stepped on and manipulation would be at an all-time low. It could be a revolutionary step.

Avril L., Creative Director and Designer, San Francisco

I feel as though there are profound changes within me. I have been able to live with a more open heart (less ego), heal some deep wounds, and forgive myself and others for things that no longer serve me. All this with being able to go back and see that everything that happened, good or bad, was perfect as it led me to where I am today. I am more in the present moment and able to surrender to situations that in the past I would have tried to have more control over. Overall, I have a deeper sense of peace and connection to spirit, Mother Nature, and all beings.

I know the medicine continues to work on me and have even experienced dreams (I hesitate to use that words as it feels like more of a real experience) that take me right back into ceremony.

I believe it would enable leaders to do their work without ego and therefore with more inclusivity. To be truly open to exploring ideas that may not have been the "norm" and outside the box. Most importantly, to able to lead with an open heart, to not judge others, and from there the magic of empowering others can happen.

Darren M., Property Developer, United Kingdom

My whole perspective on what life is has completely shifted to a new way of thinking. A much more desirable, less pressured way of living. My outlook on life and the future now includes goodwill, forgiveness, growth, compassion, and progression. I feel less controlled by the noise that once was and more focused on delivering what really matters: a life of love and happiness.

I feel that Ayahuasca would allow you to see things from more dimensions, allowing you a greater understanding of how others operate and the most profound way to deal with them. I feel the medicine could empower leaders to better manage others from a more compassionate perspective so as to get a better response that once may not have been obtainable with a fixed mindset.

Sharon B., Entrepreneur, Alberta, Canada

My experience with Ayahuasca allowed me to experience just how infinite our influence and energy fields are, and how interconnected everything is. I truly know now that all sentient beings are my "relations" and that we truly are "one"—created from the same Source energy. The outcome of this has been deep gratitude and profound reverence for all beings, and especially Pachamama, from whom all things flow to us.

As far as leadership goes, any experience—including Ayahuasca—that effectively exposes the ego as the hindrance/death knell most often leads to right thinking, right action, and right living—the critical components of right leadership—would be invaluable in leadership development.

Pitzy F., Entrepreneur, Melbourne, Australia

Ayahuasca has taken my ego away and I am far more open to exploring new opportunities. I also go into meetings with no strategies or expectations—and it is incredible how positive the outcomes of this mentality have been. My personal life feels much more accepting and judgment-free than before and has opened many relationships in a far more honest way.

Mike M., Retired Firefighter, Lake Tahoe, Nevada

The first trip to Rythmia was to assist me with some severe depression I was suffering from post-concussion syndrome. The four days of ceremony helped to alleviate the depression but also opened me up to how vast and interconnected everything is! The Ayahuasca experience validated my beliefs that everything on the planet and universe is connected ... how little we know!

Because of the positive end result of my first trip to Rythmia, I rebooked nine months later and brought my youngest daughter with me this time. Once again, the ceremonies did not disappoint. We both left after a week feeling refreshed. The Ayahuasca experiences have given me a greater awareness of everything that occurs in my daily life and especially thought patterns. While the highs and lows of everyday life have not changed, the way I react and perceive them has changed.

In terms of leadership, the Ayahuasca experience helps with viewing situations, especially ones dealing with other people, from several different perspectives. Because the medicine assists in erasing one's ego, it allows the participant to look at opposing viewpoints and personalities with an open mind and heart.

MAD WORLD

I began to wonder if the shamanic view of the "wound" underpinned much of what was commonly touted as business acumen: headstrong independence, answers for everything, oleaginous confidence, and the sense that one was anointed to the position by the creator themself. In the extreme, I felt like this behavior might constitute some sort of mental illness.

In 2006, I was in the middle of a critically important conversation with a major shareholder who had invested around $4 million of seed capital into a new energy company that was on the leading edge of a new sector in the natural gas industry in Canada, a company that over a six-year period went from a standing start of zero to a multibillion-dollar valuation. This wealthy, successful businessman—a good man by most standards and someone whom I liked—had a blind spot that would turn out to be fatal for the company. I needed his vote on a merger that would have valued our company at $2.7 billion, and importantly would have placed the value of his shareholding at $400 million.

He would not vote for the deal.

I sat him down in my office and, one on one, simply asked, "Why won't you support this deal? Your stake is now one hundred times your original investment, and there is nobody else on this planet that will come close to this number. *And* the company will be bulletproof if we complete this deal."

66 99
The "wound" underpinned much of what was commonly touted as business acumen

He looked me in the eye, and said simply, "Well, Murray, I want to be a billionaire."

Our valuation had been vetted by top-tier, independent third-party engineering firms and multiple investment banks. These valuations had been presented to the board in painstaking detail. By all objective measures, this deal was a no-brainer. The absurdity of his position left me speechless, and not just a bit depressed. It was a light bulb moment for me. This incredible company was being destroyed by a mindset that was impermeable to reason, logic, data, and most importantly, the well-being of stakeholders, which included hundreds of employees, service providers, joint venture partners, shareholders, and debt holders. This sort of behavior, often couched as being that of a "tough negotiator," is what we have been taught to believe is evidence of strong leadership skills. I couldn't get him to budge.

Later that same year, we were positioning the company for an initial public offering (IPO) on the New York Stock Exchange. All filings were complete and the founders were licking their chops at the prospect of cashing out. It was a risky play because, by now, the company's burn rate was perilous and without an IPO it would be running on fumes. Again, against the recommendations of management, the board rejected the idea of a rights offering to offer us some protection in case *something* prevented the IPO from being successful. Basically a rights offering is a safety net that gives existing stockholders the opportunity to buy more shares in the company, often at a discount to market. It can be an efficient method to quickly bring more cash into the company.

That *something* turned out to be a precipitous drop in gas prices. The IPO was canceled, with the lead banker on the deal telling our major shareholder he could "not rely on hope as a strategy."

Our only option in the estimation of management was to find a buyer for the company. Which we did. I spent two months meeting my counterpart in a local coffee shop in downtown Calgary, negotiating price and terms. Eventually, we managed to agree on a $1.8 billion valuation, up from the original offer of $1.675 billion.

With a deal firmly in hand—one that was negotiated to preserve jobs for the entire staff and provide positive financial returns to all parties in the capital structure—we had found the magic bullet.

One day prior to closing, while sitting in a team meeting, I received a terse call from our lead banker. The buyer wanted to meet with me right away. This type of call is stomach-churning. Bad news has a way of reaching out even before a single word is spoken. In the corporate enactment of a dead man walking, I shuffled to the meeting. Turns out someone had leaked false information to a national newspaper, and with rumors now afloat of a minority shareholder lawsuit, the buyer was spooked and the deal was dead.

That same major shareholder, whose equity earlier in the year would have been worth $400 million, and who, with the sale of the company would have made $40 million in cash, now held a completely worthless investment. His equity value would never recover above zero.

He called me frantically upon hearing the news, begging me to resurrect the deal. I simply said, "You don't get it. It's over."

The conference call the next day was unusually silent and brief. It was an eclectic group comprised of conservative, clinically analytical, household-name blue-chip institutions representing the preferred share and second-lien holders, as well as the junk-bond hedge fund upstarts with eyes on huge bonuses and management fees. The first group was endowed with a degree of professional respect and behavior— theirs being a world where masking one's emotions in a public forum was correlated to a rise in professional status. The second group was the young, cookie-cutter hedge-fund MBAs whom we jokingly termed "the skateboard crowd." Identical haircuts and suits, full of business school jargon, a surplus of self-confidence, and an annoying habit of explaining our business to us.

Unlike the more seasoned professionals, the skateboard crowd didn't take news like this so well. Unable to contain their tantrums, they were close to tears.

There is no amount of leadership training that can prepare an executive for this type of circumstance. No recipe. No formula. Equanimity? Cold rationality? Dark humor? Soapbox speech about living to fight another day? Pick one. Grief is personal, individual; it pervades business failures, shadowing you for years to come.

Only one question was asked: "What happened?!"

And I could offer only one simple answer: "It's called greed. That's what killed this company."

Within another twelve months, the company was headed for a Chapter 11 restructuring, as we had predicted, and by then I had resigned.

I had spent over three decades in this very challenging, competitive, ego-driven, male-dominated business. I saw firsthand the mad world we create for ourselves with rigid, narrow, self-focused mindsets—including my own. It was the lower-frequency human traits such as fear of rejection and failure coupled with greed and self-interest that ultimately led to poor decisions, most noticeably at the highest corporate levels.

❝ ❞

There is no amount of leadership training that can prepare an executive for this type of circumstance

I'm not being hyperbolic when I assert that our corporate system is such where the well-being of many is commonly subjugated to the interests of the few. And if those few are wounded, their behavior can have drastic repercussions.

In my experience, an entire team of leaders can be aligned around a common goal, or purpose, yet it only takes one outlier to steer everyone in a destructive direction. An individual, a team, a company are one and the same; they are delicate, dynamically interdependent ecosystems.

Another way of saying this is that the well-being and functionality of the whole is dependent on a collective belief system that originates within each individual. This belief system doesn't have to be conscious; in fact, I'd venture to say that more often than not, it is the individual's unconscious belief systems that permeate and mutate the agreed-upon objective corporate missions, goals, targets, and exit strategies. These beliefs often undermine the very well-intentioned constructs of the group.

One of my favorite sayings—which I overheard one of my board advisers use in an intense disagreement—is, "I believe *you* believe that, but I don't believe that."

This summarizes the challenges of bringing a group into a common vision.

INSPIRING BUT INCOMPETENT

While the study of leadership has been around since the times of Plato and Confucius, the leadership industry emerged as a *legitimate* realm of academic research and study during the mid-twentieth century, and now, in the twenty-first century, it occupies an enormous segment of the business world. Forbes estimated the global expenditures on leadership development in 2018 at over $300 billion! While this confirms there is an incredible appetite for *real* leaders, it also goes to show there is no end-all-be-all "cure" to bad leadership. With this sort of budget, you'd expect there to be more great leaders walking around. I do think they exist in many places, but are typically in societal roles that are overlooked as being not glamorous, or inspiring—in realms that are tough, dirty, unseemly—like an oil rig, or motherhood for that matter. Leadership also exists broadly in the so-called lower echelons of the corporate hierarchy, but is often not recognized as such.

In 1991, San Diego State's Joseph Rost completed a comprehensive review of the century's writings on leadership; he found over two hundred definitions of leadership. The closest they came to a consensus definition of leadership was the idea that it was "good management." In practice, Rost wrote, "*leadership* is a word that has come to mean all things to all people."

Two decades later, Barbara Kellerman of the Harvard Kennedy School's Center for Public Leadership wrote a book entitled *The End of Leadership*. She breaks Rost's record by pointing out over forty theories of leadership and as many as 1,500 definitions of leadership.

Kellerman found that "As a whole the leadership industry is self-satisfied, self-perpetuating, and poorly policed [...] leadership programs tend to proliferate without objective assessment; [...] leadership as an area of intellectual inquiry remains thin; and [...] little original thought has been given to what leader learning in the second decade of the twenty-first century should look like."[4]

Regardless of its scientific flimsiness, one can be sure that the leadership industry provides an endless array of networking events and career opportunities that all distract from the uselessness of any particular leadership theory or definition. The most successful of leadership gurus command six figures for one-hour cheerleading extravaganzas at annual corporate gatherings while basking in rock star status. There is little to differentiate the experience of these events from highly staged, ephemeral entertainment.

Relationship sociologists assert that if people would stop looking for a soulmate who checks every one of their boxes and makes their heart sing, and look instead for someone with whom they could be at peace then people might experience love and happiness much sooner in life, and maintain it for longer. Similarly, I would personally much rather work for a competent leader than an inspiring one. Of course, the leadership industry has since cleverly pivoted over the past thirty years to emphasize "process oriented" and more "human" leaders, rather than the "charismatic" types. And yet the hunger for the inspirational, or charismatic, leader has not disappeared.

In 2015, in his book *Leadership BS*, Joseph Pfeffer of Stanford University bluntly states, "There's all this mythologizing that besets leadership, as people try to generalize and learn from exceptional cases. But that has resulted in this enormous disconnect between what actually makes individuals successful and what we think makes them successful."

To take it even further, Pfeffer argues that one reason the leadership industry has not been successful is that its recommendations are based on an ideal world, rather than on the real world. Among the prescriptions for better leadership, for example, is that leaders need to be truthful, when in reality, the ability to lie can be very useful for getting ahead. Skill at manipulation, writes Pfeffer, "is a foundation of social power." In fact, he says, there is a reciprocal relationship between power and lying: the powerful deceive more often, and the ability to deceive effectively creates social power.

❝ ❞

The most successful of leadership gurus command six figures for one-hour cheerleading extravaganzas at annual corporate gatherings while basking in rock star status

In a *Harvard Business Review* article, Gianpiero Petriglieri observes, "This enchantment with vision, I believe, is the manifestation of a bigger problem: a disembodied conception of leadership. Visions hold our imagination captive, but they rarely have a positive effect on our bodies [....] Visions work the same way whether mystics or leaders have them: They promise a future and demand our life. In some cases, that sacrifice is worth it. In others, it is not. Just as it can ignite us, a vision can burn us out."[5]

Even these esteemed scholars admit that the leadership industry—of which they are key participants—is predicated on an idealized version of a leader. I would further add that we all carry within us an image, or belief, or vision, of what this leader would look like, and it is subjective, rooted in our subconscious, and often unrealistic or even unattainable.

A recent discussion I had with a successful finance executive working in private equity illuminated the issues beautifully. Over a fifteen-year period, in addition to his own company, he experienced the implementation of leadership development programs in over thirty leading institutions and corporations that spared no expense in developing their executives and high achievers.

The menu of personality tests reads like the list of brand names for an amazing new drug, while the results of the assessments often turn out to have multiple side effects:

- Myers–Briggs Personality Test
- True Colors
- The Attentional and Interpersonal Style Assessment
- DISC Personality Test
- Gallup StrengthsFinder
- OCEAN Personality Test

Reflecting back upon these programs and their results, he realized that these types of tests need to be handled with care. Test results often change over time, meaning you can take the same test a day, week, or years later, and the results are different. It's difficult to determine if these changes are due to mood, health, or shifting values. Or an emotional, mental health, or life circumstance event that is not addressed within the paradigm of creating traditional moneymaking machines.

He expressed caution with regard to how the tests were used. Test results risk pigeon-holing of individuals into certain roles. He acknowledged that in some cases it felt like there was manipulation, where more politically inclined individuals attempted to use the gray areas and the labels arising from the testing to maintain or gain advantage over others.

❝ ❞

Even these esteemed scholars admit that the leadership industry is predicated on an idealized version of a leader

Recently, he shared with me that he has had more success unraveling his own complexities looking within and allowing himself to pursue things that bring him peace and joy. Simple things like playing sports, getting outdoors, exploring various artistic endeavors, journaling, and meditation. For him, many of the personality tests and leadership development programs missed an emotional and perhaps spiritual dimension of being a human. So, while these tests can be useful for self-discovery and growth, they are only a snapshot from one angle and a single point in time. Moreover, the results need to be interpreted in the context of the political and monetary framework at stake.

While the thought of being superhuman in productivity and leadership skills might be exciting for a young corporate employee, the fact that we are teaching people they can and should be *superhuman*—i.e., more than human—is pointing us in the wrong direction and perhaps even doing damage to our psyches, our communities, and the Earth. Instead, we should be teaching young leaders to accept their humanity rather than rise above it—exceptionalism and the striving toward endless goals and targets works for only a few people who tend to be as lucky as they are exceptional. For the rest of us, we're left insecure, stubborn, ego-driven, and unfulfilled as we try to prove to the world that we are the next Steve Jobs, laboring under the delusion that Steve Jobs was in fact a perfect leader.

CHAPTER 2

THE PILL

Conventional Medicine

Con·ven·tion·al Med·i·cine /kən'ven(t)SH(ə)n(ə)l/ 'medəsən/ noun
A system in which medical doctors and other healthcare
professionals (such as nurses, pharmacists, and therapists) treat
symptoms and diseases using drugs, radiation, or surgery. Also
called allopathic medicine, biomedicine, conventional medicine,
mainstream medicine, and orthodox medicine.

"Indigenous medicine is the sum of the knowledge, skills, and practices
based on the theories, beliefs, and experiences indigenous to native
cultures, whether explicable or not, used in the maintenance of health
as well as in the prevention, diagnosis, improvement, or treatment of
physical and mental illness including, but not limited to, alternative,
complementary, holistic,and integrative approaches"

—Alvin Not Afraid Jr., Tribal Chairman, Crow Nation

After my company and my marriage blew up, I was anchorless and depressed. For the first time in my life, I made an appointment to go to a medical doctor and to tell him I was depressed and see what he could offer me. The World Health Organization estimates that as of January 2020—pre-COVID-19—over 264 million people worldwide suffered from depression. Given my own experience of keeping it well hidden, I wonder how many undiagnosed cases of depression abound in the world today? If I typified men and women in any type of leadership role, carrying on the façade of well-being, I expect the numbers would be shocking.

It was one thing for me to talk to a therapist, but it was another to talk to an MD. Why? We go to a doctor when we are sick and by going to my doctor, I was admitting I was sick. But I ran up against a wall of my own making, and this was not due to any lack on my doctor's part. In this context, vulnerability felt highly dangerous and the prospect of being honest about my feelings produced huge anxiety in me. My competitiveness and ego-drive kicked in, and although I offhandedly commented that I was a "bit depressed," I defaulted to a businesslike, mechanistic mindset. I was stuck in my old pattern of trying to look good. I felt like I was talking to a business colleague, and although I knew I was deceiving myself, and my doctor, it was a familiar and safe place. If you were to open up to a business colleague about your deep pain and emotional blockages, the ones you deal with every day but rarely talk about, would you feel nervous and scared or excited and ready to heal? If you're like most people, you'd probably feel nervous and scared, and you'd likely shut down.

My value system regarding myself and others was completely out of whack. A doctor deals with sick people all day, every day, and yet I could not admit how sick I really felt. My family doctor has had a long career working in large regional health organizations around Calgary. He now works in a small, rural clinic near his home where he can also care for his chronically ill wife, who is housebound with MS. All the men I know who see this doctor love him. He has a keen, sincere interest in his patients as people, and he frequently runs thirty to sixty minutes late because of this. I have come to learn this is not out of disrespect for the patients waiting, but out of respect for the patients he sees. He takes the time to talk, to show you data on his computer, to explain what's going on, and most importantly, to listen.

"You sure don't present as depressed," he said. To which I replied, "Looks can be deceiving, doc." I *was* depressed, I had just developed such a shell of protection around myself that it was almost impossible for anyone to read the truth.

He asked, "What sorts of things have you been doing? Do you have hobbies?"

I listed a dozen things I love to do regularly.

"Relationships with your kids?" he asked.

"Excellent," I replied truthfully.

He asked, "Do you have good male friends?"

"Yes, many. I have friends I've known for forty years, and we are close. I couldn't be more fortunate than to have the buddies I have."

"Well," he said, "compared to most guys like you that I see, you have a lot of very good things in your life."

"Really?" I was perplexed.

He said, "Let me tell you the typical profile of professionals who struggle with depression. They have sat in a car driving to and from the office for thirty years, they sit at desks staring at computers all day, they work in their heads all the time, and when they are out of the system, they have no idea how to build a meaningful life. The thing is, they don't actually have any meaningful connections to anyone; even their wives are frustrated."

I asked him what he did for them, and he said most of them need some sort of antidepressant.

I told him I don't even take Tylenol unless I have a nasty hangover.

He said, "You know, Type A guys like you suffer the most from depression. Over 40 percent of the male doctors in Calgary are on antidepressants. All of them are super high achievers who live in their heads most of the time. And carry around lots of ego."

❝❞

My value system regarding myself and others was completely out of whack

This took me aback. *Hmmmm. Is that me? I have music, art, yoga, friends, great family relationships, so what the hell is wrong with me? Why do I feel this way?* I was outwardly *normal*, but inwardly I felt terrible. This realization crystallized for me the idea that there may be a lot of people in positions of authority, power, and control who carry similar burdens, yet no one feels safe admitting it. This is the great façade of leadership: the inability to be vulnerable about our wounds.

He said, "I can prescribe a medication for you, an antidepressant, and you can give it a try. Some experience side effects but give it a month or so and see if it helps."

With a lot of hesitation, I filled the prescription and took my first pill.

The next day, my mouth was cotton, I felt like crap—worse than a hangover. My head hurt and my vision felt messed up. I was worried and called my sister, who is a nurse. I love her dearly, but we are very different. She sees life in a *clear* light; hardcore, linear, life or death, black and white, I'm right, you're not. She's been an ER nurse for thirty-five years, and her training is: if it ain't dead, give it a drug and it'll be okay in the morning. Her personal awareness falls at the far end of the pragmatic scale.

"Damn right I've got PTSD," she said, "and my pill is right here," laughing as she threw back another glass of white wine. I know what she suffered during her long career taking care of others. I've heard the stories over the dinner table, and they invariably elicit my gag reflex or evoke tears. No therapists for her though. She relies on her band of fellow nurses for support, and an outrageous sense of humor.

When her kids were small and whenever one of them fell and skinned a knee, she tossed the kid over her knee like a blacksmith trying to shoe an unruly mare, hauled out the toothbrush, and gave that wound a quick scrubbing with a vigorous modified tooth brushing movement, causing much hysterical screaming and tears. The sediment would get cleaned out, the knee would get some ointment and bandage, and then she'd say to her traumatized tyke: "You'll thank me later 'cause you won't have scar."

❝❞
With a lot of hesitation, I filled the prescription and took my first pill

This is a family cure that will be passed down through the generations, but she's wrong about the scars. Her counsel to me was similar when I told her how I felt taking the antidepressants. "Keep taking it. You'll eventually get used to it and you'll feel better." I felt the toothbrush scraping against me under the guise of love, care, and support.

This is the modern medicine world's answer: just let the pill do its thing. But, having meditated for years and done much research on health, habits, the body, the mind, I had a general aversion to this way of thinking.

I hung up the phone and vowed: There is no way I'm taking this crap. I'd rather stay depressed for the rest of my life if that's the way it needs to be, but I'm not going to make it worse by bringing into my system a chemical treatment plant full of artificial sewage.

I should have—but didn't—suddenly become open and vulnerable about my mental health, which might have actually helped. Instead, I tried to keep up the façade. In Calgary, there's a mania around appearing to be doing something significant, groundbreaking, or at least moneymaking. When I'd meet someone from the industry, the usual greeting was a very deliberate sniff test pioneered by dogs. This may be all too familiar to anyone who has lost a job.

A standard conversation goes like this: "Hey, Murray what are you up to these days?" While outwardly a simple pleasantry, the subtext is less so, typically translated to, "Are you up to anything important? Are you making money? Can I make money off of anything you're doing?" Or darker yet, "Man, I'm sure glad I'm not you."

Now, in the past, I'd have ample replies that were true, or at least, I made them out to sound true. I always admired the temerity of an American senior executive I once knew who had been caught in what is laughably and euphemistically known as a corporate "right-sizing" episode. He was fired, but when asked what had happened, he proudly declared in that uniquely American form of exceptionalism, "I've gone independent."

But since my job and marriage had fallen apart, I wore a sense of failure, and although my suit was nice, it felt like it no longer fit me and definitely didn't give me the protection I needed. So, after many lame replies laying out a linear set of accomplishments-to-be, I started saying, "Nothing." Now, if you want to experience a pregnant pause, try answering this way with the next businessperson you meet.

Despite the off-putting reply, it is invariably met with one of two responses. One is simply some version of "Well okay then, take care, see you around." And the other is, "What do you mean nothing? No one does nothing."

I always want to answer this second one metaphysically, "Well, the way I understand it, I am no one, and no one is doing anything."

I vowed to dig deeper into why I felt the way I did. I began to read and reread much of what I had explored over the years on psychology, the brain, the mind, the body, yoga, meditation, prayer, and quantum theory—most of which is far beyond my reach. The realm of psychedelics at this point was beyond my scope of interest, or more precisely, my comfort zone. Like the proverbial lonely bull, I was confined to my familiar pasture, ceaselessly retreading old territory, unable to jump the fence. And all the while I noted, with some curiosity but minimal real interest, the seemingly endless preponderance of business and leadership books and branding that dominated the publishing landscape.

66 99
I should have—but didn't—suddenly become open and vulnerable about my mental health

The so-called crisis in leadership seemed out of control, as did the quest for greater "wellness." It was not lost on me that this could also easily describe my own state of being at the time. I became obsessed with the idea that we can't rely on anyone else to cure our ills, that we have to become our own "guru," or our own CEO. I continued this line of inquiry for a long time as I pretended to work on various oil and gas projects, never being fully committed, meeting each opportunity with immense internal resistance. I wanted life to "return to normal," much as we do today in the realm of the coronavirus. After an accumulation of wounds, individually or collectively, I've since learned that once an event of paradigm-shifting impact is introduced into society, or our singular consciousness, returning to normalcy is neither possible nor can it be the goal. The real goal is to understand the deeper meaning of the event, and to allow a reframing of our definition of "normal." This is the evolution of consciousness.

In my quest to find answers, I stepped back to look at both leadership and wellness as commercial realms, as industries in their own right. My industry, oil and gas, is singled out as the culprit for much of the world's ills today, but it was clear to me it wasn't the industry, it was the humans. Our behavior. Our consumption. Our entitlement. Our endless quest for something more.

I began to question the broader idea that if there was a hunger for an idealized leader in the business world, was this a simulacrum for something else? Did it represent some other greater need that was being unmet in the broader population?

WHAT IS WELLNESS, ANYWAY?

These days, the concept of *wellness* permeates our culture and parlance. I had long ago lost track of what it really meant, so I started to dig into the wellness industry. For many years I have been deeply engaged in learning about the yoga world, its origins, its teachings, its purpose, and its effectiveness, and it technically belongs to the wellness industry.

In 2018, the Global Wellness Forum (GWF) published statistics on the worldwide wellness industry. The numbers were staggering. The worldwide wellness industry was estimated at $4.5 trillion in 2018. Trillion. That is a number only Jeff Bezos can comprehend.

Of that, for example, the mindfulness movement subset is around $30 billion, not a small number, and largely comprising various styles of yoga. What really stuck out for me though, was the amount of spending on what is termed workplace wellness: $48 billion. This is less than 2 percent of the entire wellness industry.

If the annual wellness industry is a $4.5 trillion market, more than half the $7.8 trillion global health expenditures, and the leadership industry is estimated at over $300 billion, why are workplace wellness expenditures so low? From $48 billion in 2017 and projected to be $66 billion in 2022, even in a pre-COVID world, these numbers are low. More alarming is that only 10 percent of the world's workers have access to workplace wellness programs and services, concentrated unsurprisingly in North America and Europe.

Aren't the leaders the ones who authorize the spending in the first place? Why are leaders spending so much on becoming better leaders while underfunding

50

THE PSYCHEDELIC CEO

workplace wellness spending in their organizations? It's almost as if they are trying to keep the wellness for themselves. The GWF also estimates that in a pre-COVID world in 2018, $2 trillion a year was *lost* due to unwell workers suffering from a vast array of issues from depression, anxiety, stress-related illness, poor physical health, or simply, *I'm-sick-today-because-my-boss-is-a-jackass syndrome*—which is very prevalent although not usually couched in such unscientific terms.

❝❞

I vowed to dig deeper into why I felt the way I did

This allocation of attention and funds seems like a variation of a term used in the engineering world: *non-terminating loop* (NTL). In the context of this book, I define an NTL to mean going around in circles. It causes me to wonder, based on my own experiences, whether the term *wellness* is fundamentally misunderstood, and if leaders themselves remain as unwell as the rest of the workforce. Another way to say this is the wounded are leading the wounded.

GURUS, THOUGHT LEADERS, AND BRANDING . . . OH MY!

The spiritual industry, which in my definition includes religions and any other form of belief in a power greater than oneself, has always had its leaders and followers.

The hunger for a truly "enlightened" leader is as old as humanity itself. The term *guru* in its essence means (in Hinduism and Buddhism) a spiritual teacher, especially one who imparts initiation. But initiation into what? Normalcy?

The word *guru* has now infiltrated our common lexicon to mean almost anyone who has done anything that a group of people think is noteworthy—or anyone who has pontificated about anything slightly deeper than a typical news broadcast. There is also its slightly less presumptuous but equally misleading cousin, the *thought leader.*

The Western world has co-opted the meaning of the word *guru* and it is now routinely used in business to describe a person of uncommon knowledge, gifts, and often, wealth. It connotes expertise, and more often than not carries a strong dose of ego, skill at making money, and a high level of public visibility via expert branding strategies. There is even an organization entitled Global Gurus, working with speakers who operate exclusively *within* the business leadership industry. An industry of gurus who help facilitate yet another industry of gurus. With all these gurus you'd think utopia would have finally been achieved.

Instead, they have just created enormous confusion in the mixing of jargon from the worlds of business, spirituality, and religion, resulting in a brew that, when ingested, leads the participant into a never-ending, addictive cycle of seeking but not finding. As the clichéd freshman philosophy professor advises his young and eager students, "When you feel yourself looking endlessly for an answer, you've probably forgotten what the question is."

When I look at the myriad angles taken by the most successful thought leaders, the trend has been migrating in the past decade more toward principles typically found within the spiritual movement. The "heroic, charismatic" leader type is slowly giving way to one who embodies more "human" qualities, such as empathy, service, humility, and morality. Of course, these attributes are always paired with substantial management or business skills. In other words, a business guru is simply a skilled manager with a lot of positive human traits who knows how to market. It seems the two industries—spiritual wellness and corporate leadership development—are beginning to overlap. And yet in business, *spirituality* is still a dirty word. And in the spirituality industry, *business* is the dirty word. So now we have these silos of commerce symbiotically feeding off one another yet pretending not to notice.

❝❞

The word *guru* has now infiltrated our common lexicon to mean almost anyone who has done anything that a group of people think is noteworthy

Confusion abounds in the messaging of the spiritual segment of the wellness industry, and increasingly, the leadership industry. Dominant parts of the wellness industry emphasize spirituality-based practices to "get what you intend, what you deserve," to manifest! In the words of Jesus-like musician Alex Ebert, "It's pretty obvious that the New Age movement's notion of a sovereign manifestation creates a Super-Capitalism state, in which not only is selfishness a virtue, but the poverty of others is now unrelated to our accumulation of wealth." The end goal of enlightenment, in the realm of business gurus, is usually financial reward. But therein lies the irreconcilable difference between the two industries; one is based on finding value internally, while the other is based on finding value externally. If thought leadership really had anything to do with spirituality, we'd probably see more entrepreneurs quitting their jobs to follow their actual dreams as whole people instead of following the dreams of their parents and the market as fragmented people.

In any case, what both industries share is their exploitation of our wounds while using highly manipulative marketing techniques to get our attention, our money, and our admiration. So, how do we stop going around in circles?

CHAPTER 3

EXITING THE CIRCLE OF MADNESS

"To tell you the truth, it's my sixth marriage—
I'm starting to think it's me."

—Gregg Allman

What do psychedelics have to do with leadership? Maybe nothing. Maybe everything.

Through my personal experiences, and also through my experience with psychedelics, I can see that all humans suffer a primary wound—birth and separation from the mother—and various subsequent wounds that are different for each person. It's important that we stop to reflect what effect these wounds might have on how we conduct ourselves and how we lead others. What exactly are we chasing when we chase *success*? Or when we venture to *make the world a better place*?

I see now that the so-called crisis in leadership—as extolled by the bleating hordes in the media and business literature—is actually the symptom of a much deeper issue. The issue is the feeling inside each of us that we really only have two options: to become a savior or to follow a savior. In actuality, you don't have to be either, you can just be you. As a collective, we are wounded and looking for help.

This woundedness, whether intentional or not, is then exploited by a cynical leadership industry that preys upon equally cynical business leaders, who then pay egregious amounts of money in furtherance of an idealized, but illusory, notion of leadership. We're given this sense that some affirmations will actually heal our wounds and lead us to *success*.

My shaman-led psychedelic experiences reveal this symbiosis to be a "circle of madness." In this chapter, and several subsequent chapters, I'll share my story of how I personally exited this circle of madness, and how I believe a more enriching, more harmonious world is possible if leaders of all kinds took the off-ramp as well.

THE LEAF AND THE VINE

According to Western medical definitions, Ayahuasca (pronounced "eye-ah-WAH-ska") is simply a "plant-based psychedelic." Psychedelics are also known as entheogens, which induce alterations in perception, mood, consciousness, cognition, and behavior. Some are from plants, and others, such as LSD, are synthetic. They can cause a person to hallucinate—seeing or hearing things that do not materially exist or are distorted.

Ayahuasca is a decoction made by prolonged heating or boiling of the *Banisteriopsis caapi* vine with the leaves of the *Psychotria viridis* shrub, although there can be a variety of other plants included in the decoction for different traditional purposes. The active chemical in Ayahuasca is DMT (dimethyltryptamine).

Ayahuasca has been used for centuries by indigenous peoples from contemporary Peru, Brazil, Colombia, and Ecuador for religious ritual and therapeutic purposes. Other names include Huasca, Yagé, Kamarampi, Huni, brew, daime, the tea, la purga.[6]

In its original form, Ayahuasca is the Quechua name for the tea that is derived from the vine and the plant. It is traditionally experienced as sacred, divine plant medicine that manifests as a loving feminine spirit, Mother Aya. Or simply, the "vine of the soul." Interestingly, the Quechua also discovered the Cinchona tree, from which quinine—the leading malaria medication—was derived. Other notable drugs derived from plants include aspirin—from the bark of a willow tree—and OxyContin, morphine, and codeine, which are derived from the poppy flower. More recently, as publicly and privately funded research and acceptance accelerates, psilocybin, from the fungi, or mushroom, is likely to be the first psychedelic to permeate the mainstream medical realms within the next five years. The ease of cultivation and prevalence of fungi in many geographic localities will naturally lead to its widespread utility. In 2020, Oregon legalized psilocybin therapy. It's presumed that other US states will follow suit.

Whereas Western medicine now seeks to standardize, sterilize, and monetize the usage of these naturally occurring medicines, the indigenous people who discovered them believe that these plants have a sacred purpose that goes much deeper than simply acting as a "medicine" in the Western sense. The current chase within the commercial marketplace to isolate the molecules to create a repeatable medical product with no "disturbing hallucinogenic effects and visions" may have already begun to negate some of the traditional deeper healing properties of the medicine.

Imagine staring up at a humble willow tree with the reverence it deserves, understanding that it has the ability to heal everything from acne (salicylic acid) to heart complications (aspirin). We might well regard the plants of Ayahuasca and the fungi of psilocybin with the same reverence, embracing the mystery by asking: How might they heal us?

COSTA RICA

Costa Rica is a magnet for spiritual seekers from around the globe. Its reputation as one of the original blue zones on the planet has galvanized the Western imagination since the term first emerged into the public consciousness in an article in *National Geographic* in 2005. The term *blue zone*, coined by researchers Gianni Pes and Michel Poulain, and further popularized by author Dan Buettner, refers to five locations on the planet where the local populations statistically have much greater longevity than in other parts of the world.

Visions of herds of contented centenarians, sprinting ably and contentedly grazing like goats in the rainforests, making love on the beaches of the Nicoya Peninsula, have spawned a massive wellness industry. One questions whether our obsession with longevity is in itself indicative of a deeper, fundamental lack, or wound.

In Costa Rica, retreats bubble to the surface like the hot gases from the nearby volcanoes, although the famous Arenal Volcano mysteriously stopped its gaseous emanations in 2010. It has been perhaps supplanted by the abundance of Ayahuasca ceremonies and associated purgative properties.

Dominant factors influencing longevity as identified by the blue zone researchers include family relationships, plant-based diet, exercise, strong social networks, and not smoking, among other factors.

❝ ❞

The indigenous people who discovered them believe that these plants have a sacred purpose

These somewhat mundane conclusions do not radically differ from the advice for healthy living that comprises the endless self-help, diet, and spiritual books that litter our cognitive landscape. My simple observation of a few people whom I met who had excavated their lives to move to a better life in the blue zone share a common absence: family. Where are the aged relatives? Usually in a care home back in Milwaukee. Where are the siblings? Spread across the globe. Children? Nowhere to be found. Warm weather and feel-good ceremonies seem to have provided an intoxicating illusion for a better life. Geography alone is not a cure, however, as I have learned. But it can be a pathway to another level of consciousness.

Deciding to join in the fun, I'm now sitting in a *casa* in Tamarindo, a coastal town on the Nicoya Peninsula, if not in the blue zone, certainly close enough to envision a bright future. While killing time before leaving for the retreat center, which is a short taxi ride away, a video pops up on my phone entitled "Modern Masculinity." The description reads: "Men need spaces where they create community. Men need men. Guys helping guys. You're not the man you think you are." *Strange,* I think, likely a Facebook algorithm tracking me around the globe. That Zuckerberg knows me better than I know myself, but I hope that's about to change.

For this adventure, I chose Rythmia—an Ayahuasca retreat center two hours from the northern city of Liberia. I was attracted to this location as there appeared to be deep commitment to creating a safe, controlled, and coherent context for Ayahuasca. It is a medical clinic licensed by the government of Costa Rica. Advance medical screening is mandatory, with medical histories both physical and psychological undertaken prior to admission into the program.

Prescriptions are examined, and various drugs and medical and mental conditions are cause for exclusion from experiencing the ceremonies. Certain preconditions may permit an attenuated ceremony with smaller doses or a tincture being ingested with astute care and guidance from one of the shamans. A licensed MD and psychiatrist are on site, as is trained nursing staff.

A medical clinic of high standard is part of the complex and is open and available to all attendees. Having gathered anecdotal, experiential data from over seven thousand participants over the past five years, the team has a very broad sampling that underpins their practices and protocols. The experiences of the participants comprise a credible, reasonably broad demographic sampling, with participants ranging from under twenty years old to well above seventy.

Participants come from countries on all continents, spanning a vast array of professions, educational levels, and life stories. Combined with the deep knowledge and guidance of the shamans who regularly conduct the ceremonies, this creates a body of knowledge and understanding of the primary purposes of the ceremonies. Some of the documented cures reported by the center include herpes, certain types of cancer, borderline personality disorder, narcissistic personality disorder, attention deficit disorders, Lyme disease, antisocial personality disorder, as well as lasting reductions in alcohol and drug abuse.

It's the edge of summer, and it's burning hot in the taxi. Despite my due diligence, years of reading about Ayahuasca, and following up on the positive recommendation from my friend who had just recently attended a week at this retreat, I'm wondering what I have gotten myself into. And yet I feel a quiet elation at the prospect of delving into the unknown realms of my own being. I see a gated community, a few high-end hotels, a protected enclave, and a security gate as I roll up to the main reception area. I see people hugging, coming and going, everyone seems like they are friends. I feel strange, displaced, out of whack, alone.

It seems everyone is tanned, radiant, and shiny, and the overt demonstrations of affection trigger an old, manly, and familiar feeling of resistance, judgment, and cynicism. I'm already beginning to notice this reaction as foreign—not an innate or true part of me.

❝❞

Despite my due diligence, years of reading about Ayahuasca, I'm wondering what I have gotten myself into

A radiant young woman comes over, asks my name, and consults her clipboard. Immediately, I feel a bit more relaxed and welcome. There is something calming about the cool lime drink she offers along with her guileless, friendly manner. As I look around, the departing guests seem openly delighted with something. What that is, I don't know, but assume I am soon to find out.

I am given my room number and sign up for the wellness sessions included with my package: workshops, massage, and ... colonics. Three sessions. *Oh man, here we go.*

If you don't know, for colonics you lie on a sanitary bed with your legs in the air, much like a woman would in giving a hospital birth, and you insert a sanitary little tube into your own rectum. You turn on the water, and a gentle warm flushing flow of water begins to circulate through the tube, washing through the lower realm of your colon, and flushing out the "debris" into the sink below. This goes on for the preset forty minutes, by which time you find yourself thinking you'd rather work in a meatpacking plant or as a sorter in a large urban landfill. When finished, you clean up, stand up, and man up—not wanting to make eye contact with the staff, who are without exception unbearably cheerful and kind, as though they were working in a bakery that makes the best cinnamon buns in the world. Something smells off about these pastries though.

I am given some beads on a string and told to take a walk in the labyrinth out in the lawn. It is said that the labyrinth is a symbol of a life, and that by walking it while counting the beads you imbue them with things you want to get rid of or change. The beads now represent my intention. As I walk the maze, I'm having a hard time thinking of what it is I really want to change. *How could this be? Why am I here?* My overall disquiet gives way to confusion and the inability to articulate what is *wrong* with me. I feel inhibited, uncertain, and exposed. I settle on love, compassion for myself and others, understanding, various issues with success and failure, my depression and sadness—*Okay, that's enough for one trip,* I think to myself.

It's amazing to me that in our minds we carry a list of complaints, but when put to the test to actually articulate them, the question immediately comes up: *Am I making this stuff up?* It all tends to sound trite, phony, self-absorbed, and pathetic.

I jump in a golf cart there to shuttle me to my room, and an older guy like me is sitting in the cart. An affable American, he is happy to talk about himself, which is a pleasant distraction for me. He's feeling pretty confident about the whole experience, and he's eager to tell me he did acid as a younger man. He clearly feels he has a handle on psychedelic experiences and doesn't really expect to get much out of this one. He seems quite happy to see this as an all-inclusive Club Head for trippy explorers, or a Sandals for well-off hippies. I go along with his story, although I'm thinking it sounds like a bit of protective posturing. One thing I've learned is that if someone is talking nonstop about how unafraid they are of trying something, most likely, there is a streak of terror in there somewhere.

The rooms aren't ready yet, so we are encouraged to walk about, sit by the pool, go to the dining area for a cold, nonalcoholic beverage. There is no alcohol allowed on the premises, a stark contrast from Club Med. I sit down beside a tattooed, brawny man in his late thirties. I ask him if he's just starting the week, and he says, "No, I just finished a week and am waiting for my ride to the airport." He is animated and immediately tells me about his week. There is an aura of enthusiasm and kindness emanating as he tells me about his divorce, his issues with his small children, and his alcohol abuse. This open, unfiltered disclosure coupled with his joy, humility, and honesty touches me and opens me up a bit. He tells me he is determined to return home a better father, a better ex-husband, and a better businessman, full of optimism that something within him has actually been healed. I don't know what I was expecting from someone who just encountered plant medicine for the first time, but it makes me very excited for what lies ahead.

WORKSHOPPING THE WOUNDED

In workshops—where attendance is highly encouraged, for good reason—it is explained in clear, unambiguous language that the shamans believe that all humans are wounded. While the wounding usually happens early on in life, generally at some point between birth to around seven years old, the actual age is not particularly relevant. Nor is the nature of the wounding relevant; rather, it's the outcome of the wounding that is the focus.

The wounding need not be heinous either, such as physical, emotional, sexual abuse, although these are sadly all too prevalent the world over. A wounding can occur simply by a momentary fright like a nightmare or falling off a swing in the backyard when there was no one around to help or protect us. According to the shamanic view, the instantaneous terror creates a momentary loss of soul, or *a split*, and leaves us brokenhearted. We are no longer a complete, divine being, but rather a human who has set aside a vital part of their being in order to protect themselves.

❝❞

He seems quite happy to see this as an all-inclusive Club Head for trippy explorers, or a Sandals for well-off hippies

Wounding can also be due to the systemic stifling of creativity. In a NASA study focusing on creativity, researchers George Land and Beth Jarman tested 1,600 children between the ages of four and five years old. The stunning result was that 98 percent scored at genius level. Equally stunning, and depressingly so, by grade school only 30 percent met the genius threshold, and by high school it had dropped to 12 percent. Explanations for this predictably lay the blame on the "education system." But what is the education system? It is an industry that devolves from a scientific, mechanistic mindset. And it is failing. The school system is just a reflection of the corporate mindset, which fancies itself a meritocracy without any introspection about the true value—or faults—of the *merit*.

Much of the Western education system has historically focused on developing critical thinking, the determination of whether something is true or not. This arises primarily out of convergent thinking, in which logic is paramount. The opposite of this is divergent thinking, in which imagination prevails. The challenge for modern educators is fusing these two modes into something useful, lateral thinking. This concept, originated by the Maltese physician and psychologist Edward de Bono, has been widely adopted in school systems and companies worldwide. While often termed "outside the box" thinking, and highly prized, it is still somewhat of a rare commodity in most companies. In light of the work cited above by Land and Jarman, one might postulate that efforts to superimpose objective "techniques" to improve thinking are inherently limited by our underlying wounds.

❝❞

A wounding can occur simply by a momentary fright like a nightmare or falling off a swing in the backyard

Psychedelics, breathwork, yoga, meditation, sound, all act as a circuit breaker, interrupting this loop and providing relief from the noise. I use this metaphor in my yoga class, as many of my students have engineering and scientific backgrounds. I sometimes have to clarify the difference between *om*, the sacred sound, and *ohm*, the electrical term. The former implies lack of resistance, while the latter is the opposite.

Is it possible that the mindset that created our education system springs from a collectively wounded perspective?

As a matter of fact, my journey with psychedelics elucidated an aspect of my own education. While always a slightly above average student, I nevertheless struggled with organized education systems. I flunked out of law school and dropped out of two MBA programs. I dropped out of jazz guitar lessons for the same reason: too much structure. By my mid-twenties, I was convinced I was simply stupid, but also resisted this judgment, so I decided to take the test for Mensa. I fully expected never to get the results back. I imagined the genius staff at Mensa headquarters, with their giant brains propped up with structural supports on their desks, unable to shake their heads and laugh like normal people due to these cranial constrictions, simply fluttering their eyelids with derision and pity at my test score.

But I made the grade, at the lower end of their scale, likely just skipping across the threshold as a statistical anomaly. Still, I proved to myself I wasn't stupid, at least within this one narrow definition.

I attended one Mensa cocktail party, and I felt extraordinary pressure to say smart things. In fact, I had a relapse of self-doubt, believing that everyone in the room was suffering from spinal disc compression due to the weight of their oversize noggins.

My thin attempts at humor were met with blank stares and I never went back.

My wounded perspective had for so long been that I was stupid—and I had built my life from this incomplete state. I might never have even been in Mensa—or at that cocktail party—if I had accepted rather than rejected myself. My striving for validation might very well have been supplanted by a deeper, more confident mission in life. Instead, layer upon layer of behaviors, drives, goals, accomplishments were used to avoid or forcefully bandage the wound. This bandaging of the wound then re-damaging with perpetually desperate decisions—instead of just accepting, listening to, and embracing the wound—is, again, the circle of madness.

In the workshops, we are told that Ayahuasca is not just a brew, it is sacred plant medicine. It is a divine feminine spirit from the earth; she is Mother. She can manifest as a snake, as a beautiful goddess, as tentacles of a beautiful plant, and she will decide what form she needs to take for your healing to occur.

We are forewarned that purging—also known as "vomiting your guts out" in Canadian Prairie parlance—is a key part of the entire experience. The Mother Ayahuasca spirit enters us as we drink the dense, acrid, black "tea," known locally as Yagé (pronounced "yah-hey"). While euphemistically called a tea, it's really sludge, or more accurately, medicine. Unlike the ceremonial, non-psychedelic, sugar-sweet ceremonial teas I've shared with local villagers during my work in many countries, from the Swat Valley in Northwest Pakistan to the Accursed Mountains of Albania, this is truly an accursed tea, according to the initial taste. But its far-reaching curative power is sacred and blessed.

❝❞

Is it possible that the mindset that created our education system springs from a collectively wounded perspective?

We learn that in our first journey, the Mother infuses us with her healing spirit, she seeks out where we need healing, insight, and light, and she takes us there whether we want to go or not. We are *not* in control of the journey. She leads us into the dark corners of our subconscious, beyond our rational minds and egos, and takes us on a psychic journey of snakes and ladders.

The purge—*la purga*—is a way for the body to release stored energy, emotions, experiences. Up to this point in my life, I had seen many examples of the body's ability to carry and release stored traumas, but I had a feeling this was about to launch me into a new universe. The list of possible purge effects is varied and can include vomiting, shitting, sweating, crying, shaking, groaning, yelling, singing, and laughing. I direct my intentions to the last two and hope they are the only I experience. I wonder if this resistance is breaking a sacred vow even before the first ceremony. We are told not to eat past lunchtime and to drink only a moderate amount of water.

We are to wear loose clothing, preferably white, as this is a sign of our pure intentions. Previous shamanic workshops I attended in the Canadian Rockies carried a very similar ethos, couching these instructions in a deeply spiritual context. We are respecting the spirits by wearing white, and if they are pleased, they will grace us with their wisdom and healing light. While this dress code may appear cultish or overtly New Age, every realm of reality has its costume. Think of the corporate costume, the suit and tie, intended to invoke the power of the commercial spirits. Nonetheless, I didn't wear white mainly because there was a good chance I would shit myself during the ceremony.

66 99
We are *not* in control of the journey

There are around sixty people attending the first week. I wonder whether it would be possible for a group this large to be safely guided through an entire ceremony which could last anywhere from eight to twelve hours. Who would look out for us? What if someone went crazy? More to the point, what if *I* went crazy? Even more importantly, there were only six toilets! I did the math and it didn't work out! I begin envisioning people lined up in front of each bathroom, completely zonked, muttering and moaning, with the sartorial splendor of their pristine white clothing now sullied by vertical patterns of purge-driven earth tones while they waited for the next person to emerge from the now sacred restroom. It would be like a Costco checkout for freaky, loose-boweled hippies.

My first Ayahuasca ceremony would be on Monday, but on Sunday we partook in breathwork classes that we were told would create similarly profound experiences to the plant medicine. My experience with breathwork goes back a long way. Almost all "spiritual" training including meditation, yoga, and kundalini exercises focuses on breathing techniques. For many years, as a yoga student, I heard various instructions around the idea of creating "space," moving the breath to "heal"—and generally, I just felt angry and impatient. Phrases like "There is no perfect pose, you were born perfect" would cause me to hold my breath, lapse into a high-cortisol-laden fight-or-flight response, and replace my deeply personal sacred mantra with the more colloquial "f*&k!" I could not understand what the hell it all meant. Space for *what*? Heal *what*? Finally, after taking a basic yoga teacher training course, I realized for myself what it meant.

Breathing exercises act as a circuit breaker between the busy, everyday mind and the more inward levels of self. The "space" that's created is another level of awareness, somewhat imaginary, where an expansiveness sets in, and the busy mind takes a back seat to a larger aspect of "mind." When the busybody mind is in charge, I feel like a deflated balloon. When the space is created, I feel like a hot air balloon ready to fill up and take off. Larger, lighter, more spacious.

And healing. Healing what? How on earth would the breath heal? Well, it creates space or room for other forms of awareness to appear, and these can include old emotions, memories, thought patterns. By focusing only on the breath, our anxious mind gradually settles, as the task at hand is so simple and usually automatic. No matter where you are psychologically, emotionally, or physically, a well-executed breathwork practice will at minimum leave you relaxed and possibly even permanently transformed.

We are given precise instructions on how to breathe rapidly and fully while lying on blankets and pillows. This goes on for an hour. For brief periods we are encouraged to shake our limbs, yell, scream, cry, and move our energy. I feel a bit inhibited doing this, it seems a bit forced, but I have to admit, it feels pretty good. The room emits a din that sounds like an oncoming tornado of lunatics. Surely people are faking this, I think, as my resistant mind kicks in to gain control of the situation—despite the feeling of the breath moving through my body. I feel like I might begin to cry. I overpower it with my fear. I see vivid colors—it's hard work, this rapid breathing—I begin to sweat, and suddenly, I disappear. Where? I have no idea. The instructor tells us to come back into our bodies, and to slowly return to our seated positions. I look around the room. Sixty people have been reduced to disheveled, unkempt wraiths. Tears are streaming, laughter abounds, some are in deep silence with heads in hands. It is a bouillabaisse of global emotion.

❝❞

Breathing exercises act as a circuit breaker between the busy, everyday mind and the more inward levels of self

I realize here that these sorts of transcendent experiences, unaltered by any chemicals, are possible in even a workplace setting, if only our business leaders were able to hold space for them. What sorts of different leadership and business decisions would we be making if our workplaces had just a bit more room for meaningful and healing collective experiences?

WHAT EXACTLY *IS* "HOLDING SPACE"?

"When I ask managers to reflect a bit more on the leaders whose visions they
find most compelling and enduring, they usually realize that none of those
leaders started from a vision or stopped there. Instead the leader started with a
sincere concern for a group of people, and as they **held** those people and their
concerns, a vision emerged. They then **held** people through the change it took
to realize that vision, together. Their vision may be how we remember leaders
because it can hold us captive. But it is their **hold** that truly sets us free."

—Gianpiero Petriglieri

Even though this is a quote from contemporary management thinker and teacher
Gianpiero Petriglieri[7], a former psychiatrist, it brings a deeper understanding of the
human psyche to bear on leadership in the workplace. Having "sincere concern"
for a group of people and holding space for a unified vision could be a description
of my Ayahuasca ceremony or any of the workshops I attended at Rythmia. My
shaman, Taita Juanito, and the other instructors hold the well-being of the
individuals *and* the group—together—in a sacred healing space. Juanito's singular
focus on working for the highest good for all was unwavering and powerful. It
seems to me that the purpose and requirements for a highly skilled shaman and a
highly evolved leader are essentially the same.

This concept of holding space is not new, but it is essential that leaders
understand its true meaning. It was originally conceived by the British
pediatrician and psychoanalyst Donald Winnicott and simply means creating a
supportive environment. The term is routinely applied in many types of healing or
psychological forums such as therapy, group meditation, or yoga. It is, however,
rarely used in business, where almost anything remotely suggestive of an element
of personal vulnerability, emotion, psychology, or spirituality is cause for suspicion
that perhaps this person is not up to the task at hand. This judgment is a symptom

of our wounded view of ourselves; we actually believe that *strength* is being dishonest with ourselves and others about how broken we feel. Unless you want to drive your company or your team into the ground, a powerful, intentional display of empathy and care for those around you is an essential tenet of leadership.

This empathy comes in different forms ranging from the mundane to the profound. A mundane example with which many business people will be familiar is the amount of time and energy wasted by meetings. Whoever is leading a meeting *should* hold space for the attendees. This means having real empathy and understanding of the time and pressure constraints that everyone is under, as well as what they need in order to get value out of the meeting.

It's now Monday and we are lined up outside the large hall where the ceremonies take place. It is 5:30 in the afternoon, and most are wearing white. People are talking nervously, not knowing what to expect. There is a sense of anxiety, nervousness, and it feels a bit like waiting to be let in to a concert where there is only rush seating and you haven't been told who the headliner is but it's someone you absolutely must see. The building is spotless and spacious. There are single mattresses spread out in neatly arrayed patterns. Each mattress is about six inches from the next one, which leads to even more anxiety, as I begin to wonder whether I can count on the people around me not to erupt, either physically or emotionally. We have been advised to stay within our own experience and to ignore what is happening with the people around us, which leads me to suspect this single mattress may be no more safe than an air mattress on an ocean.

It seems most attendees are in similar states of uncertainty. The doors open and we file in with our digital key fobs registering our attendance. This modern approach to an ancient ceremonial practice is evidence to me of a very rational, intelligent way of providing an overall business framework that is designed to offer maximum safety and support for the participants, as well as to gather data to further demonstrate the profound healing aspects of Ayahuasca in such a setting.

But, on another level, I feel like I'm walking into the aforementioned concert unsure whether I should be close to the stage or at the back. It might get loud, I fear.

There's a scramble to find the right mattress, whatever *right* means. I later learn it's irrelevant where you place yourself. Each ceremony drops you into a realm within which your physical location is commonly independent from the experience. In some rare cases, a highly skilled shaman will choose to place a participant in closer proximity to the shaman if it is determined that additional care and vigilance needs to be maintained for that person. I pick a mattress that is away from the front, where the shamans gather to deliver the medicine and sing, pray, and guide the ceremony.

I choose an area that is close to a large sliding glass door, which in turn is close to two toilets. I feel as though my obsessive desire for fresh air and toilet access will offset any future loss of *control*. I feel in charge of the experience; I can manage this. I'm ready.

After we are settled, we are reminded by one of the shamans that this is a sacred ceremony, and talking with one another is discouraged so that we can begin to drop into a more sacred mindset. This works quickly and the room takes on an aura of focused presence. The shamans begin to prepare for the ceremony at the front of the room, praying, singing together, bringing forward the spirits who will guide us on our journey. We are told that we can stand up and walk to one of several shamans who are sitting in different areas of the room and partake of the preliminary ceremonial clearing by inhaling Rapé (pronounced "raa-pay"). Rapé, or snuff, is a fine powder comprised of ground tobacco and ashes from medicinal trees. Each tribe creates their own mixture. One by one we approach a shaman, who dips a long hollow reed called a Tepi into a tobacco-heavy powder, tells us to hold our breath and then quickly blows the powder into our nostrils. We hold our breath for thirty seconds and turn to walk toward our mats. The world tips over, my eyes water, the back of my throat becomes parched, I feel a bit dizzy, slightly nauseous, and I start to sweat. I feel as though I've just jumped into another dimension, albeit I'm completely aware of my surroundings. It's all vaguely unnerving.

❝ ❞

I feel as though I've just jumped into another dimension, albeit I'm completely aware of my surroundings

We are told to sit or lie for an hour and let our resistance drop away. Then comes the call to take the medicine. We slowly get to our feet and line up in two long single file lines. Men in one line. Women in another. This, we are told, symbolizes a balance between the masculine and feminine. We take our medicine in a small glass of a few ounces. The shamans look closely at each person to determine how much medicine to provide, and it seems they have an innate sense of what we need. I certainly don't know how much I need.

Each person is given a blessing, we say our intentions silently, and choke back the brew.

It's seems akin to various vile remedies we were given for colds and fever as children growing up on the Canadian Prairies. I have some experience with this, which I invoke with confidence. I hold my breath, close my eyes, and gulp it down. I turn to walk back to my mattress and the room appears askew as my stomach begins to rumble.

It is axiomatic in many ancient spiritual traditions that the practice of life is preparing for death. The final resting pose in a typical yoga class for instance, is known as *savasana*, meaning "corpse pose." As I lay back down on my mattress, I realize this particular journey is the culmination of all of my spiritual searching—the therapy, the drinking, the traveling, and the business ambition. I remind myself I have trained for this. It's time to trust myself and Mother Aya; it's time to let go.

CHAPTER 4

THE THREE INTENTIONS

"No work or love will flourish out of guilt, fear, or hollowness of heart, just as no valid plans for the future can be made by those who have no capacity for living now."

—Alan Watts

On the whiteboard in the seminar room someone has drawn a simple, spontaneous, childlike but crystal-clear image. It is almost an Egyptian ankh, only it has been split, with a heart in the middle of the split. The ankh, when in its restored form, is an ancient symbol of life, of wholeness, and this form appears in many shamanic realms. We are told that the drawing on the whiteboard symbolizes the split of the soul, and the wounded, broken heart that results.

While many of us have preconceived ideas about what we will experience in our ceremonies, it will later become clear that these ideas are shaped by our conscious, controlling ego-minds, which really have no idea what is going on deep within us. To assist in bypassing these egoic limitations, we are encouraged to set three intentions, which are the distillation of thousands of ceremonies conducted by shamanic practitioners. By setting these intentions, we assist the medicine and the shaman in their healing work. The shamans believe these intentions are fundamental elements for humans to be healed.

The three intentions are framed as questions that we ask of the medicine:
- Show me who I have become.
- Merge me with my soul at all costs.
- Heal my heart.

My reactions to these intentions are varied, and generally riddled with resistance and no small measure of confusion. *Show me who I have become?* At this point I have real trepidation; I'm not sure I want to see this, or more accurately, that I can bear to see this. This, it turns out, is a deep fear carried by many. It manifests as denial, an entrenched reluctance to own our ugly truths and acknowledge our weaknesses as humans.

Interestingly, lack of self-awareness is a fundamental limitation of ineffective leaders in the world today.

Merge me with my soul at all costs? What are the costs for this to occur? What if I can't pay the price? What is my soul anyway? The concept of loss of soul is not new, having pervaded diverse spiritual teachings from ancient shamans, the Bible, Carl Jung, and Google. It might be synonymous with loss of faith in some circles, although the eternal question of "faith in what?" looms large. I am reeling with questions, and this is a big one for me. My nagging sense that something has been wrong in my life originates from this terrain. It's from this place of "lack" that I developed dysfunctional appetites and behaviors. It is the wound. And behind the wound lies the soul, a place I am about to learn is comprised of infinite beauty, mystery, and peace.

Finally, *what does it mean for my heart to be healed?* Of course I carry various levels of sadness, grief, regret, all arising from failures, disappointments, my shitty behavior, and the general sense that I am bumbling along on the track of my life with no real understanding of any of it, past, present, or future, but isn't this simply a part of being human? If our hearts are indeed broken, how can we be expected to be great leaders?

GREAT EXPECTORATIONS: THE FIRST CEREMONY

The Mother enters me as a plant, vines and tentacles reaching into the darkest realms of my being. I am unnerved and delighted. I am not in control, but also feel that, maybe, possibly, and finally, I don't need to be the one in charge.

The first hour is relatively uneventful. I feel queasy, expectant, uncertain. The room is silent and sacred. The feeling hits me with the force of a tsunami as I drop quickly into some dark container. I am aware of the tentacles of vines moving through my entire body; I can see them in bright, lush tropical colors as they wind their way throughout my being. It's as though I have become the plant, overcome by the natural forces of Mother Earth as she moves at will throughout my being.

And then there is the noise in the room around me. It's as though we are all being led by an invisible conductor, and all variations of human sound erupt from every corner of the ceremony room. I am hearing retching and heaving, moaning, laughter, and sobs. Music begins to play, beautiful serene chanting, drumming, and the shamans sing their prayers, reaching a cascading din that is warmly reassuring. It's as if we are collectively descending into a subterranean opera with crescendos followed by dynamic releases of tension and mood, all the while being conducted by the invisible but present hand of the shaman.

❝❞
What does it mean for my heart to be healed?

I fall into a deep chronological journey—from childhood to present—with no sense of how long this lasts in the *real* world. It turns out to be hours. I sweat, I cry, and I face my own weaknesses head-on. I am shown the colors and sides of many life experiences, some I once defined as positive, others I once defined as negative. It is a life's performance review, and it is a jarring kaleidoscope of emotions both painful and elated, events, memories, and insights. My inner landscape is scraped bare, eroded by the forces of nature, by this plant and this undeniable spirit.

Concepts I thought I knew and understood are being wiped away cleanly again and again as I approach the truth of myself. It reminds me of a workshop I organized for a business team in Vienna. We were discussing how one geological term—unconformity, which just means a surface of the earth after natural erosion—had almost fifty different synonyms. (The most outrageous one was *substrate recannibalization*.) It's clear to me that humans have a propensity to make a myriad excuses not to just address simple truths. In the same way we come up with numerous words for a simple concept, we also automatically contrive endless behaviors, habits, and reactions to avoid the simple truth that we are wounded. Mother Aya scrapes these synonyms away one by one so we can actually experience what *is*.

The power of this experience is that I am shown that all events of my life are exactly as they were supposed to be. My behaviors have simply been reflected back to me, as I reflect back the behaviors of others. I am shown that many events had nothing to do with me, but that I was merely a tool to facilitate another person's journey. There is a deep sense of a guiding force, a soul, that carries me along in my life. And importantly, there is the sense that there is nothing to fear or question because the sensation is of experiencing (rather than simply understanding) the capital-T Truth. Time ceases to have a linearity. It is vertical, happening at once, or not at all. There is suddenly no I anymore.

I am confronted with my shame for betraying my former wife—the knowledge of my own lack of morality. I am shown viscerally the pain I caused her. I am grief-stricken for both of us. I am sickened, the emotions are black, but I don't vomit. I stay with the pain as I sob uncontrollably.

❝❞

Concepts I thought I knew and understood are being wiped away cleanly again and again as I approach the truth of myself

Mother Aya takes me into a loving, graceful state where she shows me that my former wife and I had agreed as souls that we would play out these roles—perpetrator and victim—to learn and understand betrayal. My ego and conscious mind are trying to resist this message; I tell myself this all is nonsense. It feels like I'm just trying to justify my behavior, but I am not. It is not something for which I wished to be forgiven because it was wrong and I knew it. But this confusing sensation is what it means to be grateful for your wound and where it leads you. The truth of this had led me to the end of the road. At one point, I felt taking my life was the only real solution. Not that I actually intended to commit suicide, but I felt there was simply no way to live with my grief and continue forward.

I roll over, exhausted, and slowly rise to my feet, muttering and gurgling like a new-world Gollum. A campfire rages outside the building, and several people sit quietly in their internal voyages. I stand by the fire and think about my father and why I had lied so many times in my life. The thought of how I lied to many of the important women in my life haunts me. I know I was a coward. I also know in my essence I was a good, loving man, but I could not reconcile the two.

I become lightheaded and nearly collapse. I double over with a searing pain in my abdomen as though I have been shot. I am on the edge of vomiting, but I do not. The voice of the Mother says, "This is how you got your power, starting as a small child where your truth was unacceptable to both your parents. So, you developed the clever ability to lie for protection, but also power."

Suddenly, I descend again into another realm, an ancient realm of medieval torture, a nostalgic trip back into my parable's prison. I see knights being brutally tortured into confession; I can feel death hovering. It seems as though an ancestral trauma has carried through my father's side as well. I am in a deep sweat, nauseated by these revelations. I stagger back inside to my mattress, and slump into an exhausted heap. I fall asleep fully understanding that the past and present are healed, and that authentic power can come only in accepting truth.

In my dreams I recall selling my family home, which I had lived in for twenty-eight years. There was no longer a family in it. I sold it in an instant, one text to a real estate agent, and within two days the deal was done. I was terrified. What had I done? More importantly, why had I done it? A deep sense of having to move, but not wanting to, had underlain this decision. Since the sale I had a deep yearning to return home.

Mother Aya takes me on a journey over the foothills west of Calgary where I lived. I fly over the front ranges and she shows me all the local areas that have dark energy, or in her words "sick energy." She shows me that Bragg Creek has sick, limiting energy for me and for others. My regret over having sold the home is revealed to me as a vestige of my old psychic structure, an old version of myself. I am in a gap—wanting to go back to the familiar, afraid of the unknown, no clear path ahead. Mother shows me that my new self cannot develop in the old house. I am reassured it is okay to let the old psychic structures crumble to make room for a new structure.

Just like that, some grief I had previously barely dignified floats away from my body, never to return.

I'm taught that decisions are made from a place of peace and fullness, not lack, not fear, not need. She tells me to listen clearly to her voice, and to do what she directs, even if it seems objectively a bit crazy, or uncertain. This is not recklessness. This is her spirit working within its fullest capacity to guide me in this life's journey to become my best self. And not the self-improvement leadership skills kind of *best*, but best as in most truthful and peaceful. In hindsight, the speed and simplicity with which the house deal unfolded showed me that another force was working in my life, one that transcended my hesitant, doubting, and wounded self. And yet as I write this, I realize the journey is never really over—old chordal melodies of doubt, fear, mistrust still loom into my mind. The difference now is that when I experience these feelings, I have my time with Mother Aya as a grounding reference point. *This* is one of the best ways psychedelics can improve our lives: by forging new thought patterns that help us escape non-terminating loops of negative feelings.

As improbable as it sounds, I feel as if am giving birth to myself. I meet my divine parents. My father is a warrior king and my mother is saintly. I am saintly and regal too.

I see brilliant white and turquoise blue and I recognize it all as my soul. I give birth to a perfect baby boy—I can start anew. I experience the perfect union of male and female, and the result is perfect balance. I feel healing energy coursing throughout my body, in my hips, and up through my back.

❝❞

I roll over, exhausted, and slowly rise to my feet, muttering and gurgling like a new-world Gollum

It is around this time I become cognizant of the fact that I'm undergoing a near-death experience. Through the darkness, an initially subtle, graceful light arises from within? Below? Around? This force of maternal grace gently wraps me and my cosmic sludge in a loving embrace, and for once, I feel safe.

In a 2018 study published in *Frontiers in Psychology*[8], researchers found a "significant relationship" between near-death experiences and "DMT-induced ego-dissolution." Regardless of language, culture, sex, age, or religious belief, near-death experiences and the effects of DMT—Ayahuasca's active ingredient—clearly have a lot in common. It shouldn't come as a surprise that our relationship with and anxiety around death and pain have a lot of bearing on the way we live and operate in the world. If we can remove the anxiety around death, and instead approach it from a place of safety, we'll find ourselves making decisions from a place of excitement instead of fear.

No less profound are the striking similarities between near-death experiences and DMT in their impact on individual and world views among participants. This should give any skeptic pause.

Near-death experiences = greater concern for others, increased appreciation for nature, reduced interest in social status and possessions, as well as increased self-worth. Psychedelics = pro-ecological behavior and nature relatedness, significant clinical improvements in depressed patients and recovering addicts and lasting improvements in psychological well-being in healthy populations.

A muffled voice far, far away penetrates my visions. I hear people in the room begin to move, and the lights are coming on in the hall as the shaman signals the end of the ceremony. He beckons us all to gather in a semicircle around him so he can close the ceremony with us. It is dawn and there is a brilliant deep orange hue emerging just beyond the treetops. I sit up, groggy, unsure of where I've been. The shamans are gathered in a semicircle at the front of the room, and people are walking up to sit or lie around them, while many remain sprawled on their mattresses in a dream state, all of us unceremoniously disheveled. Pails are filled with dark brownish vomit, bedding is twisted, a patina of exhaustion and sweat pervades the space.

The shamans invite those who are present to share anything of note, but most refrain. Brief comments on colors or emotional experiences are punctuated by a sonic boom from the back of the room: "I have something to say." Like giant plants turning to the sun, we all look back in unison. It is a former race car driver who arrived at the retreat walking with two canes, painfully hobbled by traumatic injuries.

Clearly struggling for mobility, he was facing a double amputation of his legs below the knees, due to nerve and circulation damage. Ayahuasca was truly his last resort, a final attempt to avoid a catastrophic medical event. He stands up from his mattress, raises his canes overhead, and walks to the front of the room unsupported. He is jubilant and says to the shaman, "These are for you, I won't be needing them any longer." And so it was. I didn't need to see a miracle to trust the power of Mother Aya, but she delivered one anyway.

He continues to improve during the rest of the week with no canes in sight. I checked in with him recently and he reports that he can now walk up ten flights of stairs and is almost entirely free of the depression and anger that had arisen from his dire medical condition. With this emotional closing to the ceremony, the shamans guide us back into the reality of the day.

I walk slowly back to my bungalow, still reeling from the effects of the medicine. I wonder what parts of me that were paralyzed are now able to walk again.

THE DARK STUFF: THE CEREMONIES CONTINUE

Prior to the ceremonies, we were cautioned about "the dark stuff." The terrifying stuff, the fearful stuff, the death stuff. They tell us that when we encounter something terrifying, we should go right into it, and meet it with faith and courage. Do not try to run from it. In psychedelic therapies it is often said that when you feel you are about to die, you should release all fear and die. These are your fears, these are not bodily death. I knew that the Mother could manifest as a giant anaconda, or a beautiful goddess, or any other form she decides to take in a journey. I had intentionally opted for the goddess prior to the ceremony, for obvious reasons. But more to the point: I hate snakes.

With increasing amounts of medicine in my system, and no vomiting, my ability to control my experience progressively weakens until I am emptied of resistance. Mother takes me deeper and deeper each night.

During my second ceremony I journey into other realms of awareness with kaleidoscopes of geometric shapes, colors, movement, patterns alternately merging with hysterically funny cartoonlike characters that I have never before seen or imagined. There is an *Alice in Wonderland* sequence full of laughing, joking characters of indescribable jocularity. If this is madness, I'll take it. All day long.

As my laughter eventually subsides, I emerge from this cavernous mental state. The shamans immediately issue an invitation for anyone who wishes another round of medicine. Many people elect to do this, and many don't. Some are comatose, some are hugging their white pails like teddy bears—la purga still wreaking havoc.

Those in line for another round are now looking zombies. The room is replete with incense and music, filled with bodies splayed on mattresses in every pose imaginable. The shaman looks at me carefully and asks if I've vomited yet. I say no. He smiles gently and fills my glass a bit fuller than last time. I drink it down and stumble back to my mat.

The tentacles of the beautiful plant have vaporized as a large snake begins to writhe within me once again and I feel increasingly queasy. I recall the instructions to breathe, relax, and surrender, and so I do. There is a sudden change in shape and a giant spider descends, a hideous spider. I trust that what I was told is true, so I let it eat me. I give up. I can't fight it. And the Mother appears, in the form of a beautiful loving white light, and I no longer feel sick. I feel relief. Joy. A crocodile then rages out of a swamp and I am eaten again, and again, a beautiful loving energy emerges, and I am transformed. This cycle of dark and light, death and life, continues while old and unconscious fears are one by one confronted and transformed into love.

❝❞

Our resistant, egoic mind is insidious in its ability to cheat us out of the experience that is really needed to achieve a true transformation

This experience is pure spiritual teaching. Endless literature has been created over the centuries attesting to the power of facing one's fears, meeting them head-on, and finding some sort of redemptive element on the other side. In my experience, until the fears are truly experienced, confronted, digested, and transformed in a visceral, experiential way, that real transformation does not occur. This is a reckoning. Our resistant, egoic mind is insidious in its ability to cheat us out of the experience that is really needed to achieve a true transformation. It is protecting itself, but it's not protecting us. This is the difference between simply knowing it was bad to lie to my wife and *feeling* deep inside the grief of lying to my wife.

During the second part of this ceremony, I am taken back again into ancient times, to the medieval Crusades. This part of the journey is confounding to me, and not something I feel capable of inventing. I have to confess that my skeptical, controlling mind is working overtime here. In my everyday life and mind, I typically become quietly cynical when I hear someone describing a past life experience in which they adamantly declare they were once Joan of Arc, or Nefertiti, or the King of Siam. I often wondered, was no one a peasant, a murderer, a psychopath, or just another harmless schmuck in a former life? I've never met one of those people. The descriptions are invariably grand.

I see knights and crusaders, and I'm shown I originate from a family of warriors who were crucified, locked up, tortured. I don't know if it is my mother's side or my father's. Maybe these are euphemisms, disguising the fact that my ancient ancestors were just foot soldiers, working stiffs in the context of the time, trudging along muddy roads with spears in hand, marching directly into their next life after a violently abrupt exit from this one. Here, I see no glamour in the term knight or warrior. I see faces etched in steel-plated walls and floors of ancient crypt-like vaults, eyes peering through visors on battle-scarred helmets. I stare at the eyes, the dust clears, and the faces become animated and the knights come back to life, slowly emerging from lifetimes of purgatory.

The knights come alive, and reluctantly I am guided into a dungeon similar to my prison, but this time it's a torture chamber. The knights are being tortured in a vicious, merciless froth of madness. I feel sick, I feel the horror, I feel the pain of the knights. Frightened. Terrorized. I black out. Or disappear. Do I fall asleep? I don't know.

Part of the reason these visions puzzle me is because for much of my life I have had an aversion to movies that have vivid scenes of torture and psychopathic horrors being perpetrated by humans on other human beings. These types of scenes shake me to my core, and I have nightmares. I simply will walk out of a room if such a movie is shown. And yet, action-adventure movies, with highly stylized shooting, killing, and random violence are immensely entertaining to me.

Later in the week during one of our workshops, someone asks what happens when we black out. "Are we asleep? Is anything happening? What if we aren't getting any benefit from the medicine? Is this a waste of time?" The shamans say that we are taken to other realms, other times, other dimensions, where healing is being done before returning us. It is beyond our conscious experience. We are told that when the past and present are healed, the family lineages are healed, and our future generations are no longer plagued by ancestral issues.

The shamans believe we carry the wounds of our ancestors, and that by healing the past wounds, we not only heal the present, but also the future wounds and traumas. This blows my mind wide open and may explain my visceral reaction to certain types of violence—I'm uneasy with what follows when people survive this kind of experience because I myself am likely the result of that survival.

I stay in this blackness for what seems like an eternity, but it could easily have been a few minutes. A corridor of blinding light penetrates the void and I am catapulted into a realm of immense space, a celestial galaxy, only somehow, I'm part of the vastness.

I can see the Earth, and the planets of our solar system, but at the same time, I disappear into the infinite beyond. Suddenly, an immense, geometrically complex being appears in front of me, floating in space. It looks like a floating Lego toy, but at the same time human, a childlike version of a spaceship. It seems to have the energy of a plant, but it's fluid, it subtly changes shape and texture. I know She is source, the divine source, and she tells me divine beings are here in this space. Jesus is here. Muhammad is here. The Buddha is here. I look into the void and ask, "Where are the divine beings?" I am told they are there—"just look." So, I look more intently and all I can see are used car parts, floating in a vast black void of nothingness.

In my Earthly, questioning mind I ask, "Why don't I get to see the beautiful goddess Mother Aya?"

I think I'm having a conversation with higher consciousness.

She says, "Who do you want to see?"

I say, "I'd like to meet a Dalai Lama." She tells me to look over to my left.

I tell her that all I can see is a floating bent hubcap from an old car.

She says, "That's him. Go and see for yourself."

I move my awareness in that direction and instantly a Dalai Lama appears in voice. He tells me he's not dead yet but that he lives in this consciousness much of the time. Now, I'm thinking I must be hallucinating, this can't be real. So, I test it further. I ask to see Paramahansa Yogananda, a spiritual teacher who wrote *Autobiography of a Yogi*, which had a huge impact on me as a young man.

She says, "Look to the right." I do so, and I see only a floating carburetor. It seems I'm in a floating junkyard, not the celestial heaven I intended on visiting.

She says, "That's him. Go and talk to him." I move toward the floating car part, and there he is, not a physical form, but a loving divine presence. This feels correct in my heart.

I ask again, desperately, "Why am I seeing used car parts instead of the forms I am looking for?"

❝❞

The shamans believe we carry the wounds of our ancestors, and that by healing the past wounds, we not only heal the present, but also the future wounds and traumas

She tells me my beliefs are limited and based on second-hand accounts and imagination. They are not real; they are hallucinations, but *this is real*.

She explains that divine entities take on any form they choose. In this case, the purpose of this experience is to bypass my skeptical mind and place me directly in divine consciousness. My notion of spiritual or divine entities is limited by what others have described, or have imagined, and what has been in our spiritual literature. But the divine is everywhere, it is in everything, and the form it takes is irrelevant. The yearning to see robed figures and celestial beings is often merely our ego wanting to feel special, but they might as well be car parts.

These visions seem purposefully designed to give me faith that these other realms of spirit are real, far outside my egoic mind. I emerge from this ceremony with the clear sense that all my doubts about the spirit world have been erased. The divine is special, and it is nothing. And it is everywhere.

After the ceremony, a participant asks, "Why does the voice of Aya sound like mine?" The shaman answers that the medicine adopts a language that is familiar to you, a voice that is relatable. I think to myself, "Is that voice the real me?".

CHAPTER 5

THE EAGLE

"The medicine is the principal pillar of the study of man and the art of life."

**—Taita Juanito Guillermo Chindoy Chindoy,
Colombian Ingano shaman/doctor**

After a full week of activities and four ceremonies, I think I have been opened up as much as I can open up. I am tired, fuzzy-minded, shaken up, not entirely my "old" self, but not entirely a "new" self yet either. I am scheduled to check out on Saturday, but for some reason, even in my disoriented state, something tells me to stay because my work is not done. I pack my bag anyway and walk up to the reception hall to settle my bill. As I'm paying, I blurt out a question to the young woman at the front desk. I ask if there are any cancellations for the upcoming week. I know that Taita Juanito—one of a long line of respected shamans in Colombia—is coming to lead two ceremonies later that week. Juanito has a wide following, and a stellar reputation as a true healer.

He was designated "Taita" at the age of sixteen, and is now in his early thirties. Taita means Father, much like a priest, who is granted the right to not only serve the medicine, but to hold the ceremonies in the most sacred levels of integrity and care. Remarkably, most do not reach the level of Taita until they are in their forties or fifties.

I had heard stories of his miraculous healing powers, and the fact that his ceremony was sold out months in advance led me to think of him as the Jimi Hendrix of shamans. As far as holding space, he was renowned for his ability to absorb the negative energies of large groups and simultaneously guide each individual into the depths of her own personal healing journey. He was able to emerge from a twelve-hour ceremony with warmth, kindness, and a highly refined sense of humor.

I heard a story from one of the attendees that he had once held ceremony for a particularly large group of people with abundant traumas floating in the ether. Juanito absorbed this energy within his seemingly endless reservoirs of healing power, but being human, it was still too much for even him. He erupted, overcome by frightening spasms of energy so strong that his fellow shamans tied him to a tree for his own safety until the energies finally vacated his being. For this reason, I had wanted to experience his ceremonies from the start, but the week had been sold out months in advance.

To my surprise, when I inquire about cancellations, the receptionist tells me there is one opening. It feels destined but my low-level mind fights me and presents all sorts of unimportant reasons why I should turn it down: *It's more money. It's more time. I'm tired.* I ask for a few minutes to think about it and turn around only to run into Gerry, the owner of Rythmia. He looks at me and says simply, "You need to stay." He has an acute belief that when the medicine calls you, you have no choice but to follow the message. Gerry has done the medicine over 250 times, and he has a depth of experience with plant medicine that I find profoundly reassuring. Although Gerry is a uniquely gifted businessman, he is first and foremost a deeply caring, empathetic, and intuitive human being. His level of commitment to helping each person achieve a profoundly healing result from the ceremonies was not in question.

But nevertheless, being a businessperson myself, I decide to test him. I ask him if he'll give me a discount if I stay. He looks at me, assumes what I call the "negotiating pause," then agrees to shave off a few hundred dollars. Not too much, not too little, just enough of a symbolic gesture to tell me that the language of business can work in parallel with transcendent experience. This minor transaction allows me to feel I've at least maintained some connection to my former world.

The breathwork session that kicks off the second week seems easier for me. I find less resistance. I drop into a deep breathing state, and I disappear. In one session, I can still feel the medicine working within me and I am unable to discern which effect— the medicine or the breathing—is dominant. I feel a sudden jolt. My body twitches and although I feel as though I'm asleep, I am acutely aware of a bright white light appearing in the center of my vision. It's so bright I feel as though I need to look away, but I don't. A little boy emerges from the light and Taita Juanito appears alongside. He takes the boy by the hand, they turn and begin walking into the light, away from me. Juanito becomes an eagle and disappears into the light. This cryptic thought floats through my head: *I have merged with my soul.*

66 99
The fact that his ceremony was sold out months in advance led me to think of him as the Jimi Hendrix of shamans

Upon waking from this session, I feel completely transformed. Lighter, less troubled, peaceful, serene. At the deepest level of my being, far beyond my rational mind, something has changed and I know it's forever. It feels like a bone has been removed. A sensation of complete wholeness has emerged. It feels new and unlike anything I've experienced before. This is a startling outcome considering I haven't even met Taita Juanito yet. He is scheduled to hold the ceremonies on Wednesday and Thursday. He has not seen me, nor have I seen him—he hasn't even arrived at the center yet. The experience is profoundly moving for me and I don't know what to make of it. It seems his energy has already arrived and is beginning to make itself known.

In my mind, the voice of my thoughts seems to have changed. It feels familiar, yet I don't recognize it. It speaks the way I speak, and while old thought forms still percolate, the quality and nature of those thoughts are not the same. It is as if a new set of underlying tracks has been substituted in a familiar song. The song is familiar, but I can't pinpoint what is different.

The first two Ayahuasca ceremonies of the second week confirm what I have heard from many of the shamans: you can always go deeper. At this point, I haven't yet vomited in any ceremony, nor have I had any bowel issues, much to my relief. I have, however, cried, sweat, shook, hummed, and sung.

The routine is familiar by now: I inhale the Rapé, I ingest the medicine, and I drop into my journeys.

The giant eagle appears immediately, as if it had been waiting. Its eyes, beak, feathers, talons are now my own. I feel its breath, its heartbeat, its intense gaze, its heat. I am its blood, its organs, its pulse. I feel the power of the eagle and in my conscious mind, and I know the symbolism of the eagle totem: it is merciless in providing for its family, and in seeking its prey the eagle can be vicious and cruel. This is a deep survival skill, allowing it moments of great, elegant, peaceful reveries as it soars high above the land while remaining vigilant and dominant.

I am now flying above a tropical forest, powerful, vigilant, and searching. The sky darkens. I gain elevation as I fly toward somber mountains in the distance. The power of my flight accelerates, and I soar and drop into a steep, dark canyon, navigating by instinct, hurling into ever darker, tighter fractures in the rock, never colliding, unerring in my intent and capacity to avoid destruction. I disappear into the black.

I recognize this place; I was told that all things in the material world can be manifest from this consciousness. It's so beautiful here.

I am told the Mother is here for me and this is the form she chooses to take for me. The power of her love is sublime. It is all-consuming. Delicious. I don't want to leave, but the Mother says I can stay here only a short time, to experience where we go when we die. If I stay too long, I will not want to return to my material existence.

I am told rather matter-of-factly that my ego is bullshit, just a faulty limited structure. My old ego is destroyed, I die into this darkness and I am not afraid. I am relieved. I am shown my ego, a small, limited black hole. There is no light.

She hands me a new ego structure and tells me it will become manifest only after I leave the retreat: "It will not happen immediately." I will drop back into my more earthy consciousness and I will need to work actively to rebuild my ego.

I am shown my new ego. As I look upward I see a beautiful lattice-like structure instead of the blackness I expected. The lattice structure is strong, made of some sort of high alloy material, but through the spaces I see stars, planets, and infinite beauty lying just beyond the outline of the latticework.

I hear a voice. Distinct. Clear. "Your new ego will be strong enough to do what you need to do in this life, but you will also have unencumbered access to the divine."

THE SEVENTH CEREMONY

The afternoon workshop on Wednesday is replete with nervous anticipation. Juanito and his team of four male shamans and one female are scheduled to spend a couple of hours with the group in a setting where anyone can ask questions about the ceremonies. Many questions around the nature of the ceremonies and the plant experience are answered through Juanito's interpreter, who is highly gifted and articulate in translating the somewhat esoteric answers from the shaman. They use language that make powerful sense to Western minds.

A silence comes over the room once all the questions are answered, and at that point Juanito asks whether anyone wishes to come up to the front of the room where he will administer his own Rapé in advance of the evening's ceremony. A line quickly forms, and Juanito smiles, opening his tobacco pouch, and proceeds to blow the acrid powder in the eagerly awaiting nostrils. As I watch from the middle of the line, it's clear to me from the reactions of the participants that something different is going on here. I don't know if the Rapé is stronger, the doses are higher, or Juanito himself is putting some sort of energy into the process, but the impact on everyone is immediate, powerful, and not a little unnerving. People take in the Rapé, and variously begin to weave their way out of the room into the sunshine. Some are sweating, some are flushed, some look as though they've seen a ghost. My turn comes. Juanito looks at me and smiles in a way that is knowing, compassionate, and challenging. He blows a nuclear-powered dose of Rapé into my nostrils and my world fractures.

" "
Something has changed and I know it's forever. It feels like a bone has been removed

On the spot I feel as though I have been assaulted by a large force of energy that obliterates my resistance. I reel backward, grabbing the edge of a chair. I am sweating, dazed, unsteady as I stumble toward the door. I push the door open, emerging into the pounding Costa Rican sunshine, and I collapse on a small patch of grass along the edge of the sidewalk. I vomit. Again, and again. I had not vomited in six ceremonies so far. And now I am purging on the lawn in the middle of the day after an innocuous workshop.

I feel like I might never return from this purgatory—I am sweating, gasping, sobbing. I see that many others are reeling, lying on the ground, vomiting, walking like zombies. Laughing. A kindly woman from the US sits beside me, flushed, and in a moment of pure kindness places her hand on my shoulder, with a reassurance that tells me this will pass. I am deeply grateful for this simple, human gesture.

I slowly make my way back to my bungalow. I am walking like I have just attended happy hour, but this is not actually funny. I am uncertain whether I am ready for the evening's ceremony, which is to commence in an hour. I feel I have just endured a twelve-hour ceremony within the span of a few minutes. I collapse onto my bed and fall into a deep reverie, beyond sleep.

The seventh ceremony begins much like the others, but the level of sacred energy is amplified by the presence of Juanito and his team. The Rapé has acted as a spiritual can opener, prying the lid off my grip on reality, amplifying the refrain that you can always go deeper. I have absolutely no idea what to expect in this ceremony. And that is the point of Ayahuasca.

The ritual preparations for the ceremony are intricate, deliberate, and soothing. The care, the integrity, the love among the shamans, combined with beautiful songs, known as icaros, prayers, and ritual cleansing of energy with eagle feathers, sage, tobacco, all together create a unified field of sacred power and intent.

The shamans also partake in the medicine during the ceremonies, as this allows them to connect with the spirits, and with the spirits of the individuals in the ceremony. The entire group enters a state of collective healing guided by the shamans and their spirit helpers. But each individual's journey is unique and personal.

This journey is different than the rest. It is comprised of variations of "surgeries" performed on various parts of my anatomy, in particular my heart. A "surgery" in this context is an "energetic intervention" (my words) in which the physical realm undergoes a corresponding energetic healing.

❝❞

I am shown my new ego. As I look upward I see a beautiful lattice-like structure instead of the blackness I expected

These surgeries are performed by what can only be described as "alien" entities. I acknowledge the absurdity of this description, but I don't mean little green men or UFOs, I simply mean some beings that are "other," and that stand on their own apart from my self. In the altered reality of the medicine, these aliens are visceral, tactile, and real. At different points I feel energetic surgery being performed on me by a praying mantis–like entity, and other times by minions, small, humorous beings reminiscent of Ed Grimley, an old *SNL* character.

Sharing my experience with alien surgery is not something I would usually do with rational company. Anticipating this feeling, the ceremony leaders openly address the topic in a midday workshop. In a sterile, corporate seminar room, the question is asked, "So, how many of you have had alien surgeries?" A group of ninety people take a collective breath and for a moment it seems the room is out of oxygen.

THE PSYCHEDELIC CEO

I look around the room to see if anyone else is as crazy as me. At least half the people in the room raise their hands. We are calmly assured that alien surgeries are very common during the ceremonies.

❝❞
The shamans also partake in the medicine during the ceremonies, as this allows them to connect with the spirits, and with the spirits of the individuals in the ceremony

During *my* surgery, my heart was extracted from my body and taken to another area where a group of spirit or energy forms performed elaborate procedures on various parts of the organ. Old diseased tissue was removed, new healthy tissue attached. It was placed back in my body as the healers moved to different organs. One by one, my liver, kidneys, spleen, gall bladder, bladder were worked on with a general sense of discomfort accompanying this healing, as though the surgery were real, but I was buffered by a strong anesthetic. This is to say that I could feel the very real, physical sensations of something or someone doing something to me and my body.

Bolts of energy shot through my left leg and up into my torso, electrifying my body as I involuntarily twisted from side to side. Powerful, nauseating energy pulsed through my inner organs as I was thrown from side to side; the energy seemed to know exactly where healing was needed. At my age, it was no surprise that it seemed like it was everywhere—too many psychic gunshot wounds.

I was being taught how to use shamanic powers to heal myself. I was taught to hum my own song to move energy where it needed to go. I was taught to reach into my body with my right hand, peel back the skin, and reach in with my left hand to pull out any unwanted energy. I pulled a dark, sticky black mass out of my lower back, where I had suffered a herniated disc many years prior. I placed a zipper in my right side and reached inside to pull out a messy brown liquid from my liver. I was shown how to still my physical and mental bodies and move into a level of awareness that was beyond my normal waking experience. This is the point where the higher self, the restored soul, takes over.

As the medicine performed her miracles, new difficult emotions erupted, and I had no choice but to face and own this chorus of ugliness, at which point I vomited profusely. The last bit of control was finally overcome by the power of Juanito's medicine. The other side of this purging is magnificent, beautiful, radiant, peaceful, forgiving love. My heart was acting as an engine to infuse every part of my body.

THE EIGHTH CEREMONY: MY NEW BRAIN

By Thursday, the eighth and final ceremony, I am relieved, and a bit sad at the prospect of leaving this oasis of self-discovery. But I am tired. This is a lot of medicine to ingest over this time period, and I am feeling a maddening mix of fatigue and endless energy, combined into a cosmic Red Bull experience—although I'm hopeful I won't develop a diabetic condition. I know of individuals who have had extraordinary experiences from one ceremony and never feel the need to do another. I also know others who regularly do ceremonies and have met others who have done hundreds of ceremonies. I am unsure where I will end up after this is finished, but what is clear is that integration of this information into my daily life will be no small challenge.

Before the ceremony, I reaffirm the original three intentions, although I feel my soul has been restored during the day's breathwork session, and it seems some real improvement has been made in my heart during the previous ceremonies. Without question, I have endured the discomfort of facing who I have become, but I think it can't hurt to reiterate those three intentions, just in case I've missed something.

- Show me who I have become.
- Merge me with my soul at all costs.
- Heal my heart.

My journey is joyous, calm, peaceful, and I feel my heart beating like never before. It is huge, vital, joyous, and magnanimous. I am given another surgery. This time, the top of my skull is opened up and my brain is taken out. Alien forms, humorous and childlike, remove it and take it to some unknown realm of which I am not a part. I can hear the voices debating what to do with my brain. It's surreal. I have the vague sensation of cold air entering my now abandoned cranium, and I regress to wearing a toque in –30 degree winter temperatures as a kid on the prairies.

After some indeterminable amount of time, they place my brain back into its rightful home. Except for one thing—my brain is square! I ask, "Why do I have a square brain?" The answer comes back: "So your right and left hemispheres are finally balanced." I begin to shake as though I have a fever. "And," they add, "we've reprogrammed your brain so it follows your heart now."

I see a vision of a massive log house and Juanito simultaneously flies out of the building into my line of vision, shifting first into a brilliant, incandescent white light, then morphing into an eagle, then back to the human form of Juanito himself. This occurs three times in a row. Each time I hear a voice, "Juanito is giving you his power." I purge profusely as old emotions are released, foreshadowing the emergence of a new ego, infused by the powerful light of love.

CHAPTER 6

FAMILY MATTERS

"If I get stoned and sing all night long,
it's a family tradition."

–Hank Williams Jr.

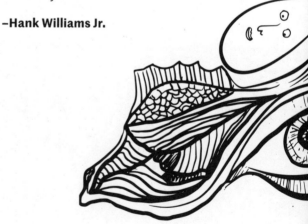

O nce the medicine calls you, very strange things begin to happen, and clues begin to appear in the most curious of ways. These clues are often personal, and they are proof that some brain chemistry has shifted, some doors have opened, and some new level of consciousness has crept in. My first clues came in the form of *Williams*: My Airbnb host in Tamarindo was William, the local clerk at a hotel was William, and the movie on the flight home was about a writer named William. My father's name was Bill (William) and my first name is also William. Strangely, my mother's maiden name is Williamson.

I had never identified with my father, despite having his name, and I couldn't imagine having anything in common with him, other than perhaps our rage. In hindsight, this entire trip was primarily about my father, the furthest thing from my mind at the time. Whereas in the past I might have never consciously chosen to think about my father when I interact with someone named William, I was no longer afraid of thinking about him, however unpalatable the thoughts might be. Once again, Mother Aya knows far more than we think we know, and she gives us the freedom to unearth and release painful memories and integrate them into our lives.

REPRESSION

"Twenty years of therapy in one night!" I have lost count of the number of times I've heard this type of comment from those who have attended an Ayahuasca ceremony. It is a powerful statement, and worth contemplating what it means practically. The term "repression" is foundational to much of modern psychoanalytical theory and practice, and widely thought to underlie most mental illness. It also occupies a large part of each human's everyday "normal" state of mind. The concept originated in the early 1800s, but was articulated by Sigmund Freud in a 1915 article in which he wrote, "The essence of repression lies simply in turning something away, and keeping it at a distance, from the conscious."[9]

Childhood traumas ("wounds") and subsequent life traumas, while largely set aside in our normal waking minds, nevertheless hover like a spectral choir, dictating our often confounding behaviors and decisions until invariably we are forced to ask the question, "Who am I and how the hell did I get here?"

An entire industry exists around the powerful idea of healing the inner child, exhuming painful memories, and reframing them in a more palatable light. Therapy, dreamwork, hypnosis, and innovative techniques such as EMDR, CBT, Holotropic Breathwork, and even yoga and meditation are shown to have a positive impact in addressing and healing repressed memories and traumas. While diagnoses of post-traumatic stress disorder (PTSD) emanated from the horrific effects of war on the mental, emotional, and physical well-being of veterans, the definition has expanded to include first responders and front-line health workers and victims of sexual and violent abuse, among others. It is not a large stretch then to include, perhaps in a milder, less obvious, but no less traumatic form for the individual, our childhood wounds.

We carry all our wounds within our being, and we suppress them so we can function in life. But they weigh on us, an invisible burden, whether we are conscious of them or not. But where are they? In our brains? In our hearts? In our bodies? Yes and no.

Modern neuroscience sheds some light on the subject of repressed memories. As opposed to a fixed file system in which memories are accurately coded and stored, research shows that memory is dynamic. We construct our memories so that we maintain "the stability and coherence of the self across situations" and that memories are "reconstructive rather than reproductive." This means we tell ourselves stories about what happened to us so that we can cope in life, but they are often not exact replicas of the traumatic event. They are our interpretation of the event. This is where psychedelics can have a profound impact in reframing these events, equivalent to defragmenting a hard drive and restoring it to optimal functionality. The authors go on to state that "memories are often stitched together into plausible—but not necessarily accurate—narratives based on beliefs, feelings, intuitions, guesses, and memory fragments."[10] Imagine revisiting your worst memories and rewriting them to be more positive.

❝❞

I couldn't imagine having anything in common with my father, other than perhaps our rage

This suggests that memories and beliefs are fluid and can be reinterpreted, reconstructed, and reframed with the right therapeutic inputs. Similarly, energy healers of all traditions maintain that our wounds and traumas reside within the consciousness of the physical body, leading to disease. A few months before leaving for Costa Rica, I was in an intense yoga class. The room was dark, crowded, hot, the practice challenging. Contorting myself in a balance pose, I was overcome with a sense of childlike anger, hopelessness, rage. I could not do the pose, and I hated myself for it.

Out of the sweat-infused ether emerged the assistant to the yoga teacher, a woman whose job it was to help us refine our poses by making gentle, tactile adjustments to our bodies. I have no idea how this expectant mother sensed my agitated state. In a very advanced state of pregnancy, she stood behind me as I rocked unstably on one leg, placed her arms around me, and said, "I've got you." Her maternal presence soothed me, I regained my balance and my internal composure, and I felt truly loved. Where had my feelings come from? Where were they stored?

In living color, this wounded child—me—was seeking a loving mother. And there she was.

While occasionally profound, most healing modalities take a long time to work. In yoga and meditation, you might only get little blips, like in this particular anecdote. But even then, they don't always go deep enough to crystallize a lasting change. I am a perfect example of this. I know my life story, I intellectually understood it, but the emotions and pain were still lodged deeply in some unknown layer in my being. I had not really healed anything and I needed something to help me go deeper, to get to the bottom of my wounding, to reframe my stories. This is where Ayahuasca has revealed herself to be a uniquely, deeply powerful, efficient, and effective therapeutic tool for healing repressed memories and wounds.

With Ayahuasca, I realized I had completely repressed my early life, and the painful and terrifying things my father did. During the ceremony, I was led to re-experience these traumas. I wept, I sweated, and then I wept some more. I shook from grief and rage. I wept again. Images of my father slapping me when I was joyful or dropping me carelessly into my crib as a baby released a torrent of inconsolable grief.

Emotional and physical trauma as a baby came roaring back into my consciousness. My mother had told me about some of the things my father had done to me, but they remained emotionally distant, theoretical events—merely topics of conversation rather than illuminating events about my psyche. I come from a pragmatic, stoic stock of prairie farmers who are not prone to dwelling on the internal complexities of human emotions. Life was hard enough trying to reach a compromise with Mother Nature so she would grace our lives with enough to live on.

66 99
Memories and beliefs are fluid and can be reinterpreted, reconstructed, and reframed with the right therapeutic inputs

For a moment, I thought I might have been sexually abused—my sexual shame and my being afraid of seeing men's penises in the changing room. No, it wasn't abuse, but there was some sort of trauma associated with men that caused me to doubt my own masculinity. I did not have any intention to revisit my childhood traumas when I embarked on my journey with Ayahuasca. I honestly felt I had dealt with and psychoanalyzed my childhood and parental issues long ago. I had spent several years in Jungian analysis, and the stories, reasons, effects of my various childhood wounds were lodged firmly within an intellectual framework that made sense to me. I felt I had reached a place of forgiveness and understanding, if not peace. Mother

Aya revealed the limitations of talk therapy because it's one thing to discuss trauma, it's another to re-experience it in your body, and in a new light.

Something miraculous occurred, and it happened many times during the ceremonies. At the deepest, darkest point of revelation of a truth, a startling, transformational shift would instantaneously occur, and a beautiful white light—or crystalline colors—would appear. I was transported into a completely different perspective about the event that had caused so much pain and grief. I found myself asking why my father and grandfather were the way they were, and what led to their alcoholism and violence. I asked to see what their reality was: *Why were they the way they were?* In an instant, I became them, revolving between each man, within his own tortured inner landscape.

❝ ❞

Emotional and physical trauma as a baby came roaring back into my consciousness

Now, I knew some of the facts of their childhoods, and had felt empathy and sadness for them at many times during my adult life. I had forgiven my father long ago, and we had a solid, stable and decent relationship for twenty-five years before his death in 2006. I had come to respect him as he overcame several bouts of "terminal" cancer—and became the longest-surviving member of a terminal cancer support group at his local hospital. Waves of people would join the group, then pass away, and he was always there to greet the next wave. Eventually, he was asked if he would give a talk to some of the cancer patients. He declined, saying simply, "What would I talk about?" With his eighth-grade education, working his whole life as a truck and bus driver, he could not imagine having anything worth contributing to the conversation, or to other people's healing.

In my experiences with Ayahuasca, I was faced with the emotional—not merely historical—realities of both my father and his father. What I saw and felt was enormous loss, guilt, and shame. My grandmother died when her three kids were under the age of six. My widowed grandfather split them up and sent them to live with different relatives. This was traumatic to each of them.

My grandfather felt shame, anger, and rage at his inability to cope. My father was sent to live with an aunt and uncle, and grew up feeling unloved and unwanted. He left school after eighth grade to work on the farm. He felt worthless, lost, and angry. He missed his mother, and in turn, any vulnerability in me—his child—enraged him because he didn't feel he had ever been allowed to be vulnerable. I knew the facts of ancestral history, and I had a basic understanding of how this trauma affected my upbringing, but I had never actually walked in their shoes, I had never felt grief for their pain.

I felt what they felt, and I wept countless hours, not for me, but for them. As I became them, my heart softened, my unresolved hatred and resentment disappeared, and I found myself amid a massive rush of love and compassion. I had been carrying the burden of their pain all this time. The outpouring of emotion left me exhausted, but the medicine does not stop until she has taken you where you need to go.

Because of my father's temperament and trauma, my fear of authority and punishment led me to routinely cave in to "stronger" or "more threatening" voices— on the board of my own company, for example. Someone else's idea could easily eclipse my own, clouding my own intuition and judgment. Fear of punishment would render me indecisive and paralyzed. When faced with an aggressive stance, I would lose my ability to think calmly, clearly, rationally and would lash out, overcome with a helpless rage.

❝❞

At the deepest, darkest point of revelation of a truth, a startling, transformational shift would instantaneously occur

The positive outcome of reconciling my paternal history was that my alcohol consumption decreased dramatically. I now feel peace and compassion for my father and grandfather, and for myself. And here I am writing this book instead of drinking. Would I have been a better leader and husband had I had the deep healings afforded by Ayahuasca? Absolutely.

During one ceremony, as I came back into my own personal—rather than universal—consciousness, I asked my father, "Who were you *really*? There must have been more to you than what I saw and experienced." This question arose from deep within my heart, which had now softened with a sense of openness I had never before experienced. Even though he had already passed, I was ready to listen.

My parents got divorced when I was fifteen years old. My mother was in no mood to say anything positive about my dad or his side of the family. So, for my whole life, I had been told the story—and told myself the story—that my musical talents and positive characteristics all came from my mother's side of the family, while my dad passed down only rage. Because of my unaddressed paternal issues, I was blocking out a whole half of my lineage. This is how shame and ancestral trauma not only wreak havoc on a child's psyche, but also perpetuate themselves down through the generations.

Mother Aya took me to visit my father, and I mean really visit him. This is not something that I could have imagined even in my most elevated state of forgiveness and wishful thinking. I was with him in a beautiful library and studio, with books on the wall, art, statues; it all felt very intellectual and sophisticated. And his mother was there, a refined and elegant soul who embodied all the attributes of an artist of rarefied intellect. My father, with his round glasses, was busy writing.

He turned to me and said, "I always was a writer, but my life didn't allow me to pursue it. I had to experience the life I did to gather more information for my next book. It's on the effects of paternalism on your planet."

The amount of joy and relief this small interaction allowed me filled my heart with gratitude and love. I had made a new and positive memory with my father, years after his death. I could see so clearly how my intellectual and artistic abilities came through *his* mother.

He said, finally, "I have always been with you, and I have always loved you."

For as long as I can remember, I have had random headaches that feel like an ice pick in my right eye. The headaches would often be accompanied by acute nausea and the feeling that I wanted to die. In parallel, these episodes would often make me think of my mother. These headaches also seemed related to the low-grade depression that had haunted me for much of my adult life, with my mornings often clouded by the thought that I just needed to make it through another day. At times I simply couldn't wait for my life to be over. I could never quite understand why I felt this way; there seemed to be no rhyme or reason to it.

And then, in one ceremony—after the visit to my ancestors' library—I found myself in the birth canal, and I could see the light of life up ahead. My head felt too big for a natural birth and I emerged with the help of huge metal forceps grabbing my head and poking into my right eye. I was shown the abrupt conclusion that these headaches were the forceps pushing into me; my body and my brain recalled them from my first experiences in this world. This was a traumatic imprint that manifested physically throughout much of my life.

My mother had told me many times that we both nearly died during my birth, and that my head was so misshapen I "looked like a little crow." That was the extent of discussion about my entry into this world, the same story, the same image of the crow, the forceps—again, and again. The discussion of anything deeper, either my mother's or my own emotions, was not a topic for further investigation. It was just another humorous war story in the family book.

I suddenly realized why my intermittent feeling of wanting to die and get it over with seemed so foreign to me. It was a feeling I *knew* did not belong to me.

That's because it was my mother's feeling, not my own. She wanted to die during childbirth, and while it seems crazy, I had internalized this feeling and it marched alongside me my entire life. At that point, we were still connected, her blood was mine, her hormones were undifferentiated from my own; I was her loyal companion in misery. It was Mother Aya who took me by the hand and showed me the truth: this dread was never mine.

❝❞

The positive outcome of reconciling my paternal history was that my alcohol consumption decreased dramatically

These familial reckonings with some of the hidden traumas in my life had an immediate and long-lasting positive impact on me. During one workshop, I shared that I no longer felt like dying. The room erupted in applause. As gratified as this made me feel, I also realized that my dread was not mine, it was shared with all humans—everyone in the room was clapping for themselves as much as they were for me. Together, we all accepted our wounds and committed to joy instead of fear.

To find paradise, we must return home to a divine state. Every religion and belief system has origin stories based on a lost paradise, and it's usually paired with an overwhelming fear of death.

Logically, if we accept that we come from a divine state, we should look forward to returning to this divine state through death. The paradox I carried throughout my life was that I held two contradictory feelings around death: the common fear of dying, and the desire to die.

After Ayahuasca, both of these feelings disappeared and were replaced by a newfound capacity for joy, for living in this world, for seeing things as they were, and for living without fear.

CHAPTER 7

THE DEATH OF EXCEPTIONALISM AND THE BIRTH OF HUMILITY

"Humility's opposite is pride. Pride's foundation is built on fear. The energy of fear is a circle too. There is abiding fear among all of us that there will not be enough. That there is judgment. That failure exists. That this life is all there is."

—Richard Wagamese, *One Drum*

With the arrival of psychedelics into the political, cultural, and scientific mainstream, we are seeing more positive media coverage. The experiences of the majority of those who have tried Ayahuasca, psilocybin, MDMA, LSD, Iboga, Bufo, mescaline, and peyote are often relatively similar, although effects can last from a few minutes, like Bufo, to several hours, like Ayahuasca. Finally, our culture sees how scientifically and spiritually interesting this "sync" of experiences is. Ego dissolution, confronting fears, and a greater sense of connection to nature and all living things are common experiences. It can be said that one's mindset, or worldview, shifts, if not permanently, certainly momentarily in a momentous way. The cynic might say, "Who cares? Once I'm back in 'reality,' it's business as usual." This line of reasoning is, however, defeatist—a cynical acceptance that humans and humanity cannot change for the better.

The fact is, the vast majority of the population suffers from some form of mental anguish or wound, or what biologist Jeremy Griffith calls a state of "psychological upset."

Buddhists believe that desire is the root of man's disease, while within the modern context of wellness, the word disease has morphed into dis-ease, aptly describing our wounded internal states. Christians believe in a loss, or wound, in the Garden of Eden. Original Sin *is* The Wound. In this way, most religious or spiritual traditions include some sort of yearning for a time or place where all of man's ills did not exist—the promised land. In secular, modern society, this is simply characterized as a "lack" of something, the feeling that we aren't good enough, and the feeling that something is missing. This explains our (secular) hunger to fill the void and avoid the wound—with products, money, and other fleeting things. We feel that the only way to deserve and achieve these things is to become truly exceptional.

The dominance of logic, rational thought, and the dependence on science as the determinant of reality has led us to where we are today. Are we happy with where we are? Where man believes in his superiority over nature, his right to take and to destroy, to use everything and everyone as he wishes for his own purposes? This doesn't sound like Nirvana or the Kingdom of Heaven on Earth.

The business world, and to some extent any large man-made organization, exists to dominate. Given that we are on planet Earth, this impetus includes domination of Earth. These organizations—corporations, nonprofits, and political, governmental, and spiritual organizations—are all established and accepted in our culture because they claim to support and enhance the well-being of society.

Somewhere in the mix of all this "well-intentioned" societal organizing, we forgot about the goal: fulfilling our primitive needs for food, shelter, and community. The desire to evolve, expand, and transcend are woven into the fabric of these needs.

These basic goals have sadly morphed into a mindset, rampant in the modern business world, that is driven by an algorithm I call the More Equation.

More = energy x consumption x growth x profit x power x prestige

This equation represents the endless yearning for more of everything. More houses. More cars. More TVs. More money to buy these things. More everything. These so-called middle-class aspirations the world over are based on an assumption that endless consumption is a requirement for a good life. Rarely do we hear the phrase, "I have enough," or even rarer, "I am enough."

IS THIS REALLY ME?

The Algonquin Nation uses the word *wetiko* to describe the mindset of the white men who landed on North American shores in the fifteenth and sixteenth centuries. In my understanding, it's just another word for The Wound.

More specifically, wetiko is cannibalism, and means simply "consuming of another's life for [one's] own private purpose or profit."[11] It is referred to as a mental virus, a disease of the mind, and reflects the view that one man is separate from the next, and therefore we regard each other as competition or prey. This is just another way of saying we are insatiable, we see our wound, and so frantically cover it with any bandages and distraction we can.

Historian Jack D. Forbes refers to wetiko as "the sickness of exploitation." And writer Paul Levy refers to wetiko as "malignant egophrenia," an unfettered ego driven by the malevolence of a cancer cell.

❝❞

The vast majority of the population suffers from some form of mental anguish

When people are infected with wetiko, instead of entering into relationship and sacred partnership with the world, they think of the world as an object separate from themselves to be used and exploited for their own benefit, a perspective that simultaneously turns them into objects as well. This results in them losing awareness of their interconnectedness with the web of life. To quote Alnoor Ladha and Martin Kirk from their article "Seeing Wetiko": "*Wetiko* short-circuits the individual's ability to see itself as an enmeshed and interdependent part of a balanced environment and raises the self-serving ego to supremacy." It is thus particularly dangerous when those who are taken over by wetiko are in positions of power.

As Forbes says, "If we continue to allow the wetikos to define reality in their insane way we will never be able to resist or curtail the disease."

The mythologist Richard Heinberg in his book *Memories and Visions of Paradise* talks about the "former sense of oneness" that has been lost over the past several centuries. He explains that early explorers left Europe, which was a mess, and hoped to find some sort of Utopian ideal, but this of course didn't last long. Just ask the spirit of Sitting Bull, who fought these Utopia-seeking explorers. The mantra we so often hear is about mankind "reaching for the stars," extending our limits of knowledge and technical superiority, blah blah blah. We often seek something greater than what we are, than what we already have. But this is not nature, it is simply a part of *our* nature.

❝❞

When people are infected with wetiko they think of the world as an object separate from themselves to be used and exploited

What is it we are chasing? Who exactly is driving this train? And, at the deepest level, what are we really saying? Even though we have made a mess of Earth, we're now rich enough to slow down the train. When we have the wounded dunce and schoolyard bully Donald Trump at one end of the wetiko spectrum and the wounded boy-genius, never-good-enough Elon Musk at the other end, what do we have? Views of the world that are completely wound-based—they are dominant versus receptive, masculine versus feminine. They are out of whack. Propping up these idols does a disservice to our children, who are born fair, creative, kind, and empathetic.

All of humanity's dominant belief systems have an origin story, and, in my view, that origin is The Wound. Instead of working together to heal The Wound—securing safety and health for as many people as possible—we embrace a mentality of "every country, person, community for themselves." These efforts to bandage The Wound have been a corrupting force that separates us further and further from our nature while The Wound beneath the paltry bandages festers and grows worse.

My experience has shown me that the ego is a structure of mind that allowed me to function in my daily life, the "doing" of "living," and yet it was a prison of sorts, keeping me trapped in a false belief system and a low-grade state of misery, confusion, and doubt. Years ago, my wise Jungian analyst even adopted a moniker for me, in a gently chiding voice and with a twinkling gleam in his eyes: "Oh Ye of Little Faith!"

The divine—whether it be God or Ayahuasca—that penetrates, reforms, and informs the limited ego can provide a pathway to other realms of consciousness that mediate between the "doing" ego and the "divinely infused" ego. So, for example, when I'm talking to someone standing in line at a coffee shop, or the person making the coffee, or a business colleague, I no longer see the role, or the physical. Instead,

I now see a multidimensional being, a soul, a spirit, just like me, who has chosen to make their way in the material realm doing what they do. I am not Buddha, nor am I enlightened, but it is fair to say I have been "lightened."

The darkness has lifted and given way to the miracle of understanding that despite outward appearances, there is no real difference between me and you.

HUMILITY NEEDN'T BE HUMILIATING

The morning after my third ceremony, I was finishing my vegan, lactose- and gluten-free breakfast, grateful for the endless supply of high-octane local coffee. One of the guys, once notable for his confident, muscular, athletic swagger, seemed pale, smaller, and somehow liquid in contrast to the concrete energy he had earlier in the week.

I asked him simply, "How you doing?"

He looked at me with a gentleness I had not seen before: "I think I need to work on humility." That was it. That said it all. Clear. Honest. Human.

The medicine had crushed his impenetrable exterior, revealing a kind-hearted, gentle soul who was still in the throes of hurtling through the abyss of self-awareness. Beautiful.

As the week progressed, the depth of the experiences everyone had undergone radically altered the dynamic of the group. Individually and collectively they had become more open, more heartfelt in their language and conversation, more engaged with one another, more human. And a couple even surreptitiously darted off into Tamarindo one afternoon during a break in the madness, returning with what I initially thought was new body hair. This was a hallucination. They were proudly sporting new tattoos to commemorate their deeply powerful experiences.

The uninformed egoic mind can only handle fear-based, survival motives. Ultimately, this small ego leads to a craving for entitlement, specialness, and exceptionalism. The leadership industry, and business in general, thrives on this craving; everyone wants to be at the top of their game. But it's just that, a game. The Buddhists might call this desire.

❝❞
What is it we are chasing? Who exactly is driving this train?

I have seen in myself—and so many of my peers in business—the gradual erosion of the "common touch" with the remnant surface being a layer of false importance, which I call "exceptionalism."

This exceptionalism can be extrapolated to the smallest detail of living, such as feeling that I should not have to wait in line for a taxi or fly economy in a crowded airplane. The underlying premise emerges in the form of a hierarchical thought that "I have an important title and position in my business, or among my peers, therefore I ought to have special treatment." This thinking spreads to every aspect of our lives until we need this special status continuously in order to reinforce our specialness. This becomes the external manifestation of what I call the dinosaur mindset (see Chapter 8): a voracious, roaming consumption that feeds the hunger for more.

My journeys with Ayahuasca substantially altered my perceptions of the role of true leadership, and my life review revealed an ugly truth about my own appetites and addictions. I use the term addictions in a broad sense, to include emotional patterns, justifying origin stories, and convenient rationalizations for shitty behavior. The underlying truth for me was the misguided need to be special, to be exceptional, and for everyone to know it and agree.

Role models for great leaders often fall in two realms: the realm of external achievement, which I term the realm of the "material mind," and the realm of inner or spiritual achievement, which I term the "divine mind." It turns out that leaders in both realms can fall prey to the desire to be "exceptional," and in both cases that desire can become toxic.

❝❞
I am not Buddha, nor am I enlightened, but it is fair to say I have been "lightened"

In regard to the material mind, great political leaders are often appreciated in the context of how they handled a crisis that was thrust upon them, but the crisis is often self-created. The world assigns certain characteristics or attributes to those leaders depending on the outcome of their crisis management, but we tend to forget how the crisis came to be.

Similarly, in business, great leaders are often defined as such by virtue of the financial returns generated by their businesses, with aggrandizing terms such as *visionary, epic, titan, mogul, guru, savant*—always used to convey a sense of uncommon giftedness, and by default, privilege. These terms are used to place the leader's abilities beyond the reach of the common person. At the same time, the core goal of the leadership business is to encourage and inspire the workforce to believe—with little if any hope or reason to expect it—that this business-centric enlightenment could actually occur for any of them.

In the divine mind realm are spiritual leaders—and their doppelgänger cousins, "thought leaders"—upon whom we bestow great respect and reverence, but whose lives we see as necessarily decoupled from our own. We look to these leaders as resources we can turn to in times of crisis, desperation, weakness, fear. The Dalai

Lama (meaning literally "ocean teacher"), for example, is a man who symbolizes the higher elements of humanity, compassion, love, humility, and humor, a man who is inspiring, beloved, and whose existence in the world brings us great comfort. Yet, for the most part, while these basic human attributes are accepted as being foundational to success in business, they are not necessarily widely observed or practiced, nor can they be taught at any leadership seminar.

The converse is often true: lying, manipulating, self-serving behavior is far more common than we like to admit. Sadly, current leadership in the US is demonstrably the archetype of this behavior, while perhaps serving a greater purpose by reflecting back to us our own deceptions.

IS IT LEADING OR MANIPULATING?

As mentioned earlier, manipulation and lying are foundational to social power. At this point in our history, we are now bearing witness to the embodiment of this principle at the pinnacle of leadership, which may in subsequent generations be known as the Trumpian Ideal. Rather than obsessing over the possible negative side effects of psychedelics and their hallucinogenic properties, our leaders would be better served trying to eliminate their own infinite capacity for hallucination.

The leadership industry has valiantly morphed over the past three decades, co-opting various teachings from the spiritual or psychological domains in an effort to humanize the business realm. This has happened without any meaningful recalibration of business goals across the economy. New mantras periodically emerge, pervading start-up pitch decks and evincing a new-found mindset underlain by the desire to "make the world a better place." And yet, the commercial goals have not changed. So, we have the unfortunate situation where lying and manipulating are essential leadership tools. Meanwhile, the leadership industry promulgates the idea, mainly to midlevel managers and wannabe unicorn start-up entrepreneurs, that service, compassion, and empathy—indeed a change in mindset—are vital traits for the successful leader in the current paradigm.

Like a child in a playground balancing on a teeter-totter, slightly shifting in either direction with a gust of wind, the leadership industry promotes the appearance of balance and strength, without any real or sustainable stability.

Trends come and go in the leadership world, spanning a vast array of ideas, some deeply considered and helpful such as leading by serving, changing the mindset, and *becoming* empathetic, some simply ridiculous. The magic number seven pervades this realm, no doubt pulling from the symbolic significance of the number seven in many spiritual traditions, a perfect example of co-opting serious principles for marketing purposes. Why are there just "7 Habits to Success"? Because it sounds mystical, that's why. While we valiantly try to find our balance under the shifting winds of the leadership industry and its branded enlightenment, we must jump off the teeter-totter entirely and ask: What tools can help create fundamental change at the deepest level of our humanity?

One outcome of my psychedelic experiences is the acuity of my own self-contradictions. Now, my all too frequent hints of looming hypocrisy erupt to the surface in a molten mass of self-disclosure. Should I blindly miss my own hypocrisy, and then suffer and endure the truth from another person, I am learning to simply say, "You're right." After meeting Mother Aya, I am still a human full of limitations, but my small ego, having receded into the ether, has given way to a more peaceful and, most importantly, humorous awareness and acceptance of my limitations as a human being. My sense of connection to a much greater consciousness constitutes divinely infused ego in action. I understand now that am not a big deal, nobody is. In fact, there is no "I" in the sense of the former "I" that strived so desperately to be special.

THE NEED TO BE RIGHT

Fear of failure, and therefore appearing to be less than exceptional, underpins much bad behavior in business.

Years ago, as part of a small team of geoscientists, I was privileged to play a key role in the discovery of a very large natural gas field in Pakistan. At the time, there were many unknowns and very few knowns. The prospect had been given an 8 percent chance of success. This was real wildcat exploration, to use a term from the early days of oil exploration. Wildcat exploration is where a basic idea or concept grows into a "tangible" project into which a company is willing to invest millions of dollars on something that cannot yet be proven, let alone explained with much scientific veracity. This sort of exploration lives in a realm of possibilities, not unlike Deepak Chopra's description of the soul as being a "field of infinite possibilities." In Chopra's world, which is not dissimilar to the psychedelic realm, there is no hierarchy to whichever possibility you settle on; they are all good if they are true and realized. In the business world, however, there is a strong hierarchy and it is binary: you become either a saint or a bum. While enlightenment places value on the search for truth, rather than what you find on your search, the business world is all or nothing: success, or in my case, discovery of some imagined oil field, is the goal.

To avoid the failure label, geoscientists in the oil and gas industry created a wonderful escape clause known as "technical success, commercial failure." It somewhat facetiously states that no failure is a failure if something was learned or some new technique was developed. This turns out to be completely true to life in general. Even if it was simply the case that "It was a pretty bad idea and we sure won't chase that one again," the chance of success, being typically less than 30 percent, means we were paid to fail. I routinely reminded my technical teams of this, but as I moved up the corporate ladder this became something not to be discussed, especially with staff and shareholders.

66 99

Fear of failure, and therefore appearing to be less than exceptional, underpins much bad behavior in business

Similarly, the answer "I don't know" is not often seen as acceptable, more likely leading to a quick, involuntary exit. So we learn to babble, backflip, bluff, and B.S. Why? Because of the obsession with being exceptional. Very commonly, when raising money, a simple question from an investor is "How big is the prize, and what will it cost me to get the prize, and what is the probability that I'll lose all my money?", which routinely leads to a circular buzz saw of technical, theoretical, incomprehensible jargon-laden half-truths, the impact of which leaves the questioner with an unusually large headache, approximating a concussion. And an unwillingness to invest. In my experience, the ability to simply lay out risks, uncertainties, and unknowns shows confidence, not the other way around. It establishes trust.

In one instance, I was standing at the front of a very large boardroom full of oil and gas experts from around the world. I was asked a question that was highly technical in nature and impossible to answer as there was no data to support any cogent response. The question was being asked by an arrogant, overeducated Oxford-trained geoscientist. He had a well-earned reputation for trampling over less-technical intellects, of whom I was definitely one, and he derived great satisfaction in causing distress, discomfort, shame, humiliation, and other ignoble human responses, which invariably left the unhappy recipient in a cortisol-laden stress coma. This type of intellectual bullying had always been a point of vulnerability for me. My typical response would be combative, aggressive, defensive, all in an effort to cover up my inadequacy.

This time was different, and it was not due to any newfound sense of enlightenment. "I don't know," I replied. I simply gave up the pretense. It was more akin to a giant "f*&k it." I gave up. I then dropped into a protracted pause, allowing the group to grasp the inarguable accuracy of my reply. My colleagues squirmed in their seats. But somehow I had a sense of peace because my response was true. In a moment of temporary, pre-psychedelic awareness, I felt a sense of relief in admitting I did not know something or, as it has later come to pass in the psychedelic chapter of my life, anything.

Following this meeting, rather than focus on the positive outcome of the meeting, my multicultural team focused on that single answer. Most of the team felt it reflected badly on me (and them), with a single exception. A British colleague with a PhD gleefully asserted that he found it "refreshing indeed" that for the very first time in his career he had witnessed someone admit they did not know something in a key meeting. Further, he commended me by saying, "That was indeed a showstopper. Well done!"

There is great power, and peace, in simply admitting we don't know something. My desire to be exceptional, in knowing all the answers, was clearly misguided. Leaders are terrified of this simple answer, which can be easily remedied with the addendum "but let's find out."

During the heady runup that preceded our calamitous failed IPO in the fall of 2006, we were actually exceptional. Unbeknownst to most of the business community in Calgary, we had been chosen by *Oilweek* magazine as the "Producer of the Year." A prestigious award in a region where, at the time, there were almost one thousand oil and gas companies operating in Western Canada. From a standing start with no assets and a few million dollars, over a six-year period, we had moved to the head of the pack in terms of helping pave a new way forward in a stagnant industry. While this was not new in many countries around the world, we had done it differently in terms of our transparency with stakeholders, innovative environmental, technical and operational solutions, and our "culture."

After all the interviews from *Oilweek* were done and the photos of our teams were taken, I was stoked. As one of the "big three" executives on the cover of the magazine that would sit prominently in the reception area of every company in Calgary, recognition had arrived at my doorstep.

❝ ❞
We learn to babble, backflip, bluff, and B.S. Why? Because of the obsession with being exceptional

It was similar to, though supposedly more prestigious than, the early days of McDonald's. A *Harvard Business Review* study years ago about employee motivators found that, in the early days of McDonald's, it wasn't money, but recognition that galvanized the company. The Employee of the Month award was a coveted holy grail. This is no different for senior leaders. We are basically still flipping burgers in the depths of our wounded egos while never getting paid "enough."

I was also very worried by the timing of the publication. This award was to be

THE PSYCHEDELIC CEO

presented in the fall, right around the time of the IPO. While all of our technical and operational achievements were real, I had a nagging fear that something might go wrong, as we were spending money at an unsustainable rate. This intuition turned out to be all too accurate, only in a much bigger way than I could have imagined.

66 99
There is great power, and peace, in simply admitting we don't know something

Fast-forward a few months, our IPO had failed, we were starved for cash, and I was sitting in the transit lounge of the Toronto airport on my way back to Calgary after begging for emergency debt funding in New York. The award was to be announced later that week, but I wasn't feeling celebratory. My cell rang and the soon-to-be-excommunicated CEO said, "I just got a call from *Oilweek*, and they've heard rumors that we are in financial trouble. They want to know if it's true? What should I tell them?"

I paused, and said reluctantly, "Well, it's true. We are." The pause was again deafening as we both grappled with this dilemma. The decision seemed binary. If we told the magazine that yes, we were in financial trouble, then they would not give us the award. All our hard work would go unrecognized. I finally said, "Give me some time, and I'll reach out to the team," which at the time consisted of seven vice presidents who all reported to me. I wanted their input.

My email was answered within minutes. They were basically split, with most abstaining from a strong view one way or another. However, an undercurrent came through this feedback: fear and embarrassment if we failed to rectify our financial situation.

The CEO said, "You make the decision, I'll make the call." Given there is no public record of our company having received that award, it should be obvious what decision I made. What is on the record is that the magazine turned around and immediately gave the award to our joint venture partner, a household name in Canada. This company had piggybacked on our innovative, bold, and ultimately very valuable leadership for several years. A huge kudo had been transformed into a massive gut punch with one phone call.

For at least ten years this decision haunted me, for I too shared the deepest desire to be seen as exceptional, to be recognized. I was embarrassed with how it turned out. And with the wisdom of hindsight, it was really a technical and operational award that belonged to all our staff and contractors who had worked so creatively and diligently for so many years. While it was true that the company was in financial trouble at the time, was it really true it wouldn't survive? It did survive for another thirteen years after I left.

My journeys with Ayahuasca revealed to me the depth of my wounding with respect to my own father and the impact of this on my professional life. My almost obsessive desire to be seen, acknowledged, and respected arose from that wound. My fear of being wrong and of punishment translated into a type of paralysis in business that prevented me from interpreting the context of a business crisis accurately. I made that decision about me and my wound, and not about my peers and my team. I lost perspective and gave up my own power. My people were denied what was theirs.

What would have been the correct reply to the magazine, one that was true but also empowered and confident, thereby honoring the hard work of both me and my peers?

"Yes, as you know, the IPO didn't happen, but we have plenty of financial wherewithal. Most importantly, we have the people to survive anything. We are honored to accept the award."

It is not so much the outcome of our efforts that is exceptional, it is the way we manage our internal reality, respecting and valuing ourselves and our accomplishments enough to advocate for ourselves, even when a threat looms large.

WHERE THE RUBBER MEETS THE ROAD

The truth is the daily life of modern humans has little to do with transcendence or self-awareness. We focus on riches, narrow definitions of success, and external validation. With very little introspection, most of us can see that there is no end in sight for these desires; there is no limit to our bank accounts, there is no amount of money or recognition that ensures happiness. Is it possible that a healthy desire to better ourselves has been perverted by our underlying wounds and egoic states? Is it possible that "enough" has been co-opted by "more and more"?

If we are merely animals, then what is the point of these aggrandizing definitions of success in society? The answer lies, I believe, in the concept of the transcendent. We hope to transcend our earthly bodies, to be truly exceptional, but we do so by playing games with earthly feelings and objects. Our focus on "exceptional" external achievements derives from a deep hunger to transcend our limited survival-based animal nature. The idea that this is possible through societal definitions of *success* is the great myth of modern man.

While only one of many realities, the material world is where we are taught to find achievement, exceptionalism, and success. Other realities—deeper, more amorphous, more personal—remain at the sidelines, and only when a crisis emerges, beyond our control, do we look to the heavens and cry out for a reason. In these moments we look for a greater explanation, and another reality that can assuage our pain, confusion, and grief.

But what if we could live in the two realities simultaneously? What if we co-existed on both planes, entering and leaving each one as the need arises? What would this do for us, as we march through the material world only to be derailed by illness, disappointment, or death? What if we were conscious, empathetic, and open? What if our dreams of greatness, while inspiring us to achieve, were accompanied by the belief that we have already arrived somewhere exceptional?

We are divine beings, able to be content in the knowledge that the paths we take in the material realm are simply adventures of the soul.

❝❞

The truth is the daily life of modern humans has little to do with transcendence or self-awareness

The spiritual idea of being "in the world but not of the world" has rattled around in my mind for decades, but I could never reconcile this very simple statement with the myriad drives, conflicts, and confused emotions that were the template for my inner world. Did the search for meaning necessitate that I quit the business, go off on a spiritual pilgrimage, and find my "true calling"?

This was often tempting, I'll admit. Amid the drudgery, the pressure, the unrelenting motion of leading a complex business, and managing conflicting agendas with stakeholders—investors, board members, landowners, employees, and regulators—there were many times I felt like running away to something "better." The key I missed in all of this was that my family were also stakeholders, as was my soul. While this is something that wise leaders intuitively know, I did not naturally make the same correlation, and when I finally did, the peer pressure to forget it once again within the business realm was immense.

I recall a time when we were lining up a big financing road show and my wife was ill with a chronic form of arthritis. She was having a bad spell, and my leaving for a road trip presented a huge dilemma. My fellow executives, the bankers, the funds, were all part of a large domino game, with the pieces lined up that could lead to an array of possible outcomes. But the first move, to trigger the game, was dependent on my being physically present in the room. Even so, I postponed the entire road show for a week, and I recall feeling the collective disappointment and not-so-subtle judgment of my business associates. Clearly, there was a perception that I was not committed to the company's success because I had prioritized my wife. And of course, my wife rightly questioned my commitment to her and the family by the ambivalence I displayed in grappling with the dilemma. And so, from there I began to see my wife's illness as an impediment to fulfilling my role as a leader. I felt guilty and weak and that I was not fulfilling my role as a leader. The subtle but real judgments from my team were not easy to deal with, even though they were for the most part decent, caring people who were simply subject to similar pressures in their worlds. This business-first mindset that drives the need to be exceptional is destructive to individuals, personal relationships, and families. And ultimately, our psychological and spiritual well-being. Many companies today have expanded their views of the human side of the business, and there is movement in this direction in many sectors. But these dichotomies continue to exist.

ᶜᶜ ᵓᵓ

There was a perception that I was not committed to the company's success because I had prioritized my wife

The insights gained from psychedelics can reveal to us what is truly exceptional about our own humanity, independent of our wounds and our stories. And while this offers no guarantee that we will always make the right decision going forward, the experience provides useful self-knowledge that can help us recognize any dissonance between our true nature and the artificial constructs of the material world.

YET ANOTHER PARABLE

"A creature from the late Cretaceous period smashed sales records on
Tuesday in an auction that also included works by Picasso, Pollock and Monet,
leaving auction watchers wondering which anonymous buyer now owned a
multimillion-dollar Tyrannosaurus rex. The T. rex skeleton, nicknamed Stan,
closed the 20th Century Evening Sale, nearly quadrupling its high estimate
of $8 million to bring in $31.8 million, with fees."
—The New York Times, October 6, 2020

One day a vine, a leaf, and a mushroom walked into a bar. They started reminiscing about the good old days when dinosaurs roamed the Earth trampling and devouring everything in sight.

"Whatever happened to those guys?" asked the vine.

The leaf shrugged, "I heard they just disappeared one day."

The mushroom, being the oldest of the group, piped up, "They're still around, you know."

The leaf and the vine looked up, confused.

"Where?"

The mushroom slowly scanned the room. The leaf and the vine looked around and all they could see were men and women of all ages and shapes, drinking heavily, laughing, high-fiving.

"I don't understand," said the leaf.

"They don't look like dinosaurs!" chimed in the vine.

"Well, let me tell you a story," said the mushroom.

"Back in the day, I think maybe the Jurassic, or was it the Cretaceous, or both, the dinosaurs ran the show. As you both know, us plants and fungi were sort of invisible, staying out of the way. We were blowing in the wind so to speak; hoping not to get eaten. We just kept to ourselves, working within our communities, and some of us were even underground.

"But we all shared something in common. Consciousness—an awareness of our surroundings and our communities. Compared to the dinosaurs, we simply chose to do different things with this blessing.

"Anyway, a big explosion wiped out the dinosaurs and the rest of us just dug in for the long haul. While the dinosaurs couldn't adapt, adaptation had been our strength all along. I think this is because we work with the Earth, not against it.

"Some of our plant brothers and sisters decided to undergo a transformation, which took a very long time. For hundreds of millions of years, these plants were buried under thousands of feet of rock. The heat, the pressure, eventually caused a transformation into a black sticky ooze we call oil, gas, and coal. Meanwhile the remains of the dinosaurs lay alongside these plants, and their consciousness morphed into one: a masculine consciousness of power that formed while lying dormant.

"In the not-too-distant past, a scrawny biped known as Homo sapiens came across the black sticky ooze and, for some reason, decided to see if it would burn. It did. The power of these plants and fossils became his fuel and his obsession. Make no mistake, these old plants didn't intend to do harm. They thought they were helping man stay warm, survive, and flourish. But man had other ideas. Armed with this black sticky ooze, man decided he could become a dinosaur again, roaming the earth, mighty and powerful, devouring everything in his way.

"Meanwhile, back in the forests of the Earth, we plants and fungi just went about our business, hanging around in trees, floating in the breeze, gossiping underground, trying to avoid these new dinosaurs.

"It turns out we had some secrets of our own that we were excited to share. We had our own consciousness, one of collaboration, community, and longevity for all. This is the feminine consciousness of creation, sustenance, community, and receptivity.

"So, we began to tug at the minds of the forest people, the people of the land. They are called indigenous today, which simply means "of a place." Some of these humans were already experiencing great suffering in their spirits, so we drew them to us. They were healers, helpers, and shamans. Once we got their attention, we showed these humans what leaves, vines, and fungi to pick, and how to prepare and ingest them. What we were really doing was showing them a way to stay close to us, close to our earthly community. We were showing them that while they might have the urge to become dinosaurs, it would be a dangerous path that wouldn't lead to safety or freedom. We could see that the dinosaur mindeset would someday lead to disaster on our earth, so our job has been to try to counteract this.

"You see, we know about cooperation, sharing, combining efforts to create something greater than ourselves, but first and foremost, we know we won't survive without our planet, without Mother Earth. Our job is urgent. We must get into the brains and minds of these dinosaur humans."

The vine and the leaf sat shocked, looking around the bar at the humans going

THE PSYCHEDELIC CEO

about their business, so concerned with the price of their clothes and the appearance of wealth. It was clear to the vine and the leaf these humans would stop at nothing—and to be sure, nothing can stop them—in order to prove to the world they are the rulers of Earth, just like the dinosaurs once were.

CHAPTER 8

THE DINOSAUR AND THE MUSHROOM

"We can say that the earth has a vegetative soul, and that its flesh is the land, its bones are the structure of the rocks ... its breathing and its pulse are the ebb and flow of the sea."

—Leonardo da Vinci

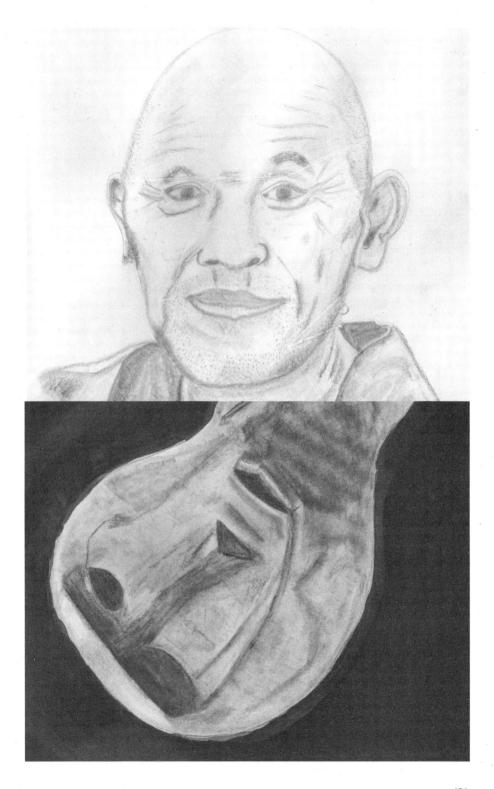

The terms masculine and feminine are not gender definitions. They are cosmic realities like plus and minus, electron and proton. They are energies, traits, characteristics, beliefs, and mindsets that shape our outlook on our lives and the world around us.

The *dinosaur* represents a wounded state of mind, which could also be termed a "masculine" or "patriarchal" state of mind. The dinosaur mindset still underlies the goals of the modern business and political landscapes, and largely undermines the sincere efforts of the many who toil in leadership and wellness industries. This effort to germinate and develop higher levels of consciousness more often than not fails. It's somewhat incompatible with the driving forces of our society.

The *mushroom,* or more broadly "plant medicine" in this context, connotes a "feminine" or "maternal" state of mind. Giving birth, providing nourishment, taking care of your own people and your world, and adapting to circumstances without pride.

Every human is a blend of these masculine and feminine energies, but for people who have been steeped in the masculine, plant medicine offers a chance to reconnect with the feminine and enjoy a new outlook on life and success.

A key insight from my Ayahuasca journeys is that humans are inseparable from nature. This pithy statement, bordering on trite in its simplicity, is a common theme, widely reported by psychedelic journeyers and yet is often dismissed as a temporary, hallucinatory state we might call "tree-huggeritis."

Standing outside the ceremonial room sometime before sunrise after one of my ceremonies, I stared at a giant tree and swayed to the soft sounds of ceremonial music still floating from the building. I sincerely hope the sight of an older bald man grooving to a track by himself in a garden did not traumatize any of the other participants on their journeys. I floated from side to side in time with the music and the tree swayed along with me. While many people understand our connection to the natural world, psychedelics allow us to *feel* that harmony. My rational mind decided to test this, believing I was truly hallucinating—doubting the harmony. I turned in a 360-degree circle, and all the plants and trees moved in sync with me. If I changed cadence or movements, the entire natural landscape changed with me. We were one, there was no difference, causing me to ask myself, *Is it possible we were merged temporarily into the same level of consciousness?*

Despite having been a lover of the wilderness, studying and exploring the forces of the Earth as a geologist for most of my life, I realize now that I still objectified nature in much the same way men have historically objectified women while also desiring to love and protect them. My attitude toward the natural world was goal-oriented, ego-driven, and competitive. Climb higher, ride longer, ski faster, drill more wells, produce more oil. But now, my awareness had shifted dramatically. I experienced nature, and the Earth, as a coeval force with humans. And so, you may ask, why should that be significant to me, or any leader for that matter?

DEER, BEAR, EAGLE

Over a year later, I still completely vibrate with nature in a way that I could not ever have thought possible. Rocks and mountains become faces and figures, animals and birds have characteristics beyond their simple form, and the land breathes with life and vitality. Very simply, there is no mental barrier between what I experience as "me" and the world around me. A good friend, a fellow musician and a member of the Stoney Nakoda First Nations west of Calgary, once taught me a song for deer. I asked him why he didn't say "the" deer. He explained that in his tradition, man and nature are indistinguishable from one another. Hence, he refers to animals without using the article "the." It is simply Deer. Bear. Eagle. It is a great deal of fun to be in nature doing absolutely nothing but observing and participating with an open awareness. Sadly, the realization that comes with this shift in awareness is that I see what we are doing to the Earth as a species as visceral, as if it were my own body.

This shift could be termed a change in consciousness. The term consciousness is rife with confusion, contradiction, disagreement, arising from the fact that it cannot be empirically studied or measured. But this is mainly just a limitation of language. It cannot be fully described within the limits of the human lexicon. And "it" has myriad meanings that wind their way through our belief systems like an invisible thread that holds us all together, yet we can't agree on its essence because we're so conditioned to measure and define our worlds, both inner and outer.

❝❞

Every human is a blend of these masculine and feminine energies

I define consciousness as a level of awareness that exists outside our thinking minds, outside our wounds and personal stories, and outside our limited egos.

Mindset—the leadership industry's castrated version of consciousness—is the common term used to describe how we view ourselves and the world around us. In another disempowering move, we're told that mindset can actually by taught. But we're never invited to question who is teaching this mindset. Are the teachers wounded? Is their mindset wounded? If so, then they will wound their students' mindsets as well. Techniques to shift our mindsets can certainly be taught, but we cannot be taught how to "be" without following a path of personal experience.

CONSCIOUS MEDICINE VERSUS UNCONSCIOUS DRUGS

When the Ayahuasca medicine enters our system, we are taken over by an elemental force of nature. Whether this is purely chemistry or something else is beside the point. The discovery by tribal shamans in the Amazon that a leaf and a vine combined create a powerful healing medicine can be argued to have arisen through trial and error. With the millions of species and subspecies of plants in the Amazon, this happy coincidence defies the odds of probability. If you view all things as having consciousness on some level, as the shamanic traditions do, you'd see that this particular vine and leaf consciously beckoned ancient healers in order to teach them secrets of the Earth, mainly man's intrinsic relationship with the spirits, and consciousness of the Earth.

❝❞

there is no mental barrier between what I experience as "me" and the world around me

The shamans were guided to mix the plants into a brew, ingest it, and understand its teachings. Western thinking and individualism prevent many of us from embracing such a submissive stance vis-à-vis nature—we don't like to give our power away. Our entire way of life revolves around the removal of ourselves from the natural harmony of the world. Plant medicine has the effect of exposing the idea that man can dominate nature as a complete and utter hallucination.

For the most part, the material mindset, being reductionist and addicted to self-gratification, roundly discounts this harmonious view of the world, because consciousness is not widely thought to be a scientifically understood fact. We haven't "proven" it exists yet, perhaps because we so badly want it to be an individual thing, ours, exceptional. But, the truth is, we may not have a say in the matter; our consciousness is shared.

WHAT ON EARTH?

We might be well served to look to the Earth for some assistance in healing our wounds, shifting our mindsets, and slowing down our race to the edge of another extinction.

In the minds of the many, the primary culprit in the mass hysteria around climate change is simply fossil fuels. But fossil fuels aren't bad. Actually, they are here to help. We misuse them like we misuse everything else. Man has developed methods to utilize this energy to raise the quality of life the world over. So far, so good.

It is not man's utilization of fossil fuels that is detrimental, but his mindset, which lets this use fall victim to exploitation and greed. Similarly, the mining of rare-earth minerals to create so-called renewable energy in the form of solar panels, wind farms, and electric cars will ultimately prove to be another non-terminating loop when it becomes abundantly clear that the supply outstrips demand. The energy that is being captured may be renewable, but the processes required to create the technology for this to occur is not.

We continue to look "over there" for an answer and a culprit, all the while desperately trying to maintain our standard of living. We have no stable understanding of contentment and self-sufficiency.

THE SIXTH EXTINCTION EVENT

The Gaia theory—developed in the 1970s by scientists James Lovelock and Lynn Margulis—states that, for much of the past 3.8 billion years, a holistic feedback system has played out in the biosphere. The theory proposes that organisms and their inorganic surroundings on Earth are closely integrated to form a single and self-regulating complex system, maintaining the conditions for life on the planet.

The view that the Earth is an interdependent, interconnected system lends incontrovertible support to the idea that the entire system can be permanently disrupted by the unconscious actions of one species alone. The word *unconscious* in this context accords well with the Cambridge Dictionary definition: "a state of not being awake, or not being aware of things around you." Humans are that species.

❝❞
It is not man's utilization of fossil fuels that is detrimental, but his mindset, which lets this use fall victim to exploitation and greed

More than two decades later, the situation had clearly become more dire, and in 1995, famed paleoanthropologist Richard Leakey stated that "homo sapiens might not only be the agent of the sixth extinction but also risks being one of its victims."

Much like the leadership industry, we are caught in a non-terminating loop. We know the way we are living is not good for the Earth, and by default it's not good for us either, but we seem unable or unwilling to change our behavior. We now find ourselves operating from a place of fear, victimhood, and blame.

The Earth has endured five extinction periods during the past 550 million years, each one due to changes in climatic conditions on Earth.

PERIOD	YEARS BEFORE PRESENT	GENERA (%) /SPECIES (%)	PROBABLE CAUSE	DIED OFF	THRIVED
End Ordovician	444 million	57/86	Climate Change	Marine Organisms	Sea Sponges
End Devonian	359–380 million	35/75	Climate Change	Fish, Corals, Trilobites	Tiny Tetrapods
End Permian	251 million	56/96	Climate/ Volcanos	Forests/ Vertebrates	Fungi
End Triassic	201 million	47/80	Climate/ Volcanos	Fish/Reptiles	Dinosaurs/ Crocodiles
End Cretaceous	65.5 million	40/76	• Meteor Impact? • CO_2 spike • O_2 Drop in Ocean	Dinosaurs	Mammals/ Birds
Present		Too many to count	• CO_2 spike • O_2 Drop in Ocean • Mindless Consumption	Man?	Mammals/ Birds/ Plants ...

Source: https://www.discovermagazine.com/the-sciences/mass-extinctions

These events were not instantaneous, they would sometimes take twenty million years—a slow, imperceptible decline toward mass extinction. Of the four billion species that have evolved over the history of the earth, 99 percent of those species are now extinct. Humans form part of the remaining 1 percent of surviving species.

One notable outcome of this seemingly endless geological saga is that species that survived these mass extinction events tended to thrive going into the next period of relative peace and prosperity. In many instances, it was the less visible, less obtrusive and humble species that somehow made it through to the next stage—a sort of *American Idol* for organisms. There is much to be said for the connection between humility and adaptability.

Fossil evidence supports the generally accepted baseline extinction rate of one species per million species per year. Today, the rate of extinction is calculated at up to one thousand times the rate of previous periods. The dramatic increase in the rate of extinction leads many to conclude that this is primarily due to human activities—

population growth, materials production, consumption, and disposal coupled with the concomitant requirement for increasing amounts of energy, mainly fossil fuels.

In case anyone doubts the impact humans are having on the earth, recent observations from seismologists are striking. When COVID-19 forced the global community to stay home, we stopped traveling, moving about, and heavy machinery use was curtailed. The constant vibration all this movement caused, called "anthropogenic noise" in the seismic world, has dropped significantly this year. In an article published in *Science*, seventy-six scientists from twenty-seven countries confirmed that the entire Earth had become quiet between the period March to May 2020. Areas of greatest population density typically experienced the greatest reduction in noise level as would be expected, but the impact of this noise reduction often radiated out for hundreds of miles from the epicenter. While imagining New York City as the epicenter of a human earthquake might seem like a sci-fi fantasy, the data tells us it's all too real. This does cause me to wonder about the impact of a Foo Fighters concert on global seismic activity.[12]

With this evidence firmly in hand, it's clear that our human footprints are perfectly capable of producing our own earthquakes.

It is no coincidence that we are also fascinated by the mighty dinosaur, as if it had a consciousness all its own that pervades our being. This mindset is unfortunately exemplified by leaders the world over, reinforcing the idea that selfishness, greed, and ignorance are indeed noble traits. And yet in the context of geologic time, the humble fungi, neither plant nor animal, adapted at least 250 million years ago, continues to do so, and works tirelessly underground to keep things afloat for the rest of us. The dinosaur, on the other hand, has become a museum piece, an animatronic movie star, forever relegated to the imagination. Do we want to move in that direction?

WHAT IF PLANTS ARE SMARTER THAN US?

How do we solve the problem of our lack of consciousness? Leaders of tomorrow have a duty to ask this hard question, and some answers to this question may again lie within the simple realm of plants.

Many psychedelics—including Ayahuasca, psilocybin, ibogaine, peyote, and mescaline—are natural plants found in many regions on Earth. While many participants in these forms of psychedelics would likely agree that the plants have messages for us, that they are conscious, intelligent beings, it's still a bit of stretch for the mainstream public and, in particular, the majority of the scientific community to align with such a paradigm-shifting claim.

One of the original scientific researchers into the mysteries of Ayahuasca, Dennis McKenna, a US ethnobotanist, maintains that Ayahuasca is intelligent. In an interview in *The Guardian*, he categorically affirms this:

"Yes, plants *are* intelligent. Not in the way that we are, but in some ways they're much smarter than we are. It depends on how you want to define intelligence, right? If intelligence doesn't require nervous systems, it doesn't require brains ... intelligence is when something reacts to their environment in a way that optimizes its adaptation. There's really compelling evidence that plants are capable of planning, remembering, dealing with other plants and other things ... Something else we're learning about intelligence: you don't have to have a brain. Brains are over-rated, you know. What you have to have is neural networks—very extensive networks of connections."

Researcher, scientist, and eminent mycologist Paul Stamets likes to point out a little-known scientific fact that humans share evolutionary pathways with fungi, as proto-fungi gave rise to animals, including the animals known as human. A new super-kingdom known as Opisthokonta has been created to join Animalia and Fungi together. In addition to the evolutionary connection between humans and fungi, archaeological and paleontological evidence has categorically concluded that fungi have played a key, albeit undetermined, role in the evolution of consciousness for over five thousand years. From Aristotle onward, spanning some two thousand years, it is further accepted in many circles that man's consciousness and intellectual achievements have been intimately intertwined with the use of psychoactive fungi—or psilocybin as we know it today. There is a reason they are called *magic* mushrooms.

❝❞

We know the way we are living is not good for the Earth, and by default it's not good for us either, but we seem unable or unwilling to change our behavior

Most of the mushrooms we eat are known as sapropelic, with powerful ability to decompose and recycle organic plant matter. In his book *Growing Gourmet and Medicinal Mushrooms*, Stamets passionately states, "Through the genius of evolution, the Earth has selected fungal networks as a governing force managing ecosystems. This sentient network responds quickly to catastrophia. I believe the mycelium is Earth's natural Internet, a neural network of communicating cells. All landmasses are criss-crossed with interspersing mosaics of mycelial colonies. With more than a mile of cells in a cubic inch of soil, the fungi are moving steadily, although silently all around us. This vast mass of cells, in the hundreds of billions of tons, represents a collective intelligence, like a computer honed to improve itself."[13]

The words *sentient, neural network,* and *collective intelligence* are thought-provoking when one considers that the average person either has an aversion to mushrooms or simply regards it as food, or mold, or both.

WHAT IS CONSCIOUSNESS ANYWAY?

"Looking for consciousness in the brain is like looking inside a radio for the announcer." —Nassim Haramein, physicist

Whether it's in facing childhood trauma, overcoming depression, addiction, or myriad illnesses, the main effect of psychedelics can be described with the blanket phrase, "a change of consciousness." A change of consciousness, in this context, simply describes that I now experience my self differently from before. Insofar as our personalities are comprised of stories, those stories, their meaning, and their context have now been altered. It does not end here, though. The Earth is a living, breathing, organism, of which I am only a small part—as opposed to a big rock floating in space.

❝❞
There is a reason they are called *magic* mushrooms

After my journeys, I began to investigate further the idea of consciousness, because I wanted to understand what exactly had changed "in" me, and in others who report similar changes after Ayahuasca ceremonies. I found that in many fields of study, consciousness was actually a rather elusive concept, and a brief overview of some of the current thinking suggests that among the silos of spirituality, philosophy, and science, there is indeed a common theme: this mysterious thing called consciousness can't be defined, only experienced. Let's take a quick dive into how these silos approach this mercurial topic.

SPIRITUAL TRADITIONS

Within spiritual traditions, the concept of a universal consciousness is pretty much a fact. In the Buddhist view, there are different levels—the sensory consciousness of ordinary wakefulness, the subtler consciousness when we dream, and the subtlest consciousness that manifests at the time of death. Further, the Dalai Lama stated recently, on his Facebook page no less, that:

"Sentient beings including insects are all the same in wanting happiness and seeking to avoid suffering. There's no dispute about this. We tend to rely on physical and sensory sources of pleasure, but without peace of mind, we won't be consistently happy. Material development has greatly improved our physical facilities, but peace of mind isn't manufactured by machines in some factory, we have to create it within."

Ancient Sanskrit teachings known as the Upanishads state that consciousness is not merely physical, but permeates physical forms; it is both within and without the physical form. According to this belief system, to measure it is inherently impossible. While complex in the extreme, the six major schools of Hinduism—Nyaya, Vaisesika, Samkhya, Yoga, Mimamsa, and Vedanta—all adhere to the existence of Atman: the essence of all things. According to these traditions, it can be experienced and perceived only through meditation.

The mystical Jewish tradition known as the Kabbalah asserts that there are five ascending levels of consciousness corresponding to various states of reality, all emanating from The Infinite One—Ein Sof—or God.

❝❞

I began to investigate further the idea of consciousness, because I wanted to understand what exactly had changed "in" me

Similarly, in traditional Islam, references to consciousness are no less prevalent. The Arabic word *taqwa* broadly refers to God consciousness. In the Islamic mystical realm of Sufism, consciousness exists at many levels. In a description that would much later be proven by quantum physics—which we will also touch on—Amir al-Mu'minin Ali says, "You think you are a small body, yet within you is wrapped the greater world."

Today, spiritual teachers such as author Deepak Chopra point out that higher consciousness is observational and experiential, just as advanced spiritual practitioners over the millennia have demonstrated that the mind can observe itself. Similarly, the elfin spiritual teacher Eckhart Tolle states that there is a level of consciousness known as the fourth state, which is "a dimension from where you can be aware of what your mind is doing without being totally trapped in what your mind is doing."

While the entire history of mystical experience has been rife with criticism, skepticism, ridicule, and in various eras, persecution and death, the materialistic scientific complex is beginning to open to the idea of other, unquantifiable realities.

Within the realms of modern scientific and philosophical investigation, the topic of consciousness is naturally being approached with the reductionist idea of determining objectively the nature of consciousness. We want to know where all the neurons go and why, and we hope when we know that we will understand what it means "to be."

PHILOSOPHY OF MIND

The term consciousness has been eternally problematic and hotly debated for generations by the cranially gifted elite specializing in the philosophy of mind and arcane disagreements with one another.

In the realm of material philosophy, for example, all matter and life forms are unconscious. That means they can be described and measured objectively. That which cannot be measured is said to not exist. It is *this* belief over the past five centuries that has driven man's behavior on the planet, and it has laid the foundation for his belief in his innate superiority over other life forms. If we categorize it and label it, it exists, if we don't, it does not.

Consciousness is commonly confused with "human thought," the physical output of the brain-centered "mind." The truth is, some of our neurons are several feet long, and neurons exist throughout our body. The divide between physical and mental is somewhat contrived; the division of mind and body might just be a mirage, a symptom of viewing our body from within our mind-body.

This was first broached in what philosophers define as "The Hard Problem." Originally set out by philosopher David Chalmers in his 1996 book *The Conscious Mind*, the central issue revolves around how the physical brain produces subjective experience. Chalmers suggests that consciousness is the "feeling of what it is like to be something." The Hard Problem is that according to materialism, it's unclear how a bunch of neurons and cells can give rise to subjective experience, or consciousness. An equal, if not harder problem, is that there are very polarized camps of philosophers and neuroscientists who simply cannot agree on the existence of The Hard Problem in the first place.

A compromise to the hard problem of consciousness is a theory known as panpsychism, yet another hotly debated topic in the innately polarized world of philosophy, in and of itself another hard problem. The word itself was coined by the Italian philosopher Francesco Patrizi in the sixteenth century and derives from the two Greek words *pan* (all) and *psyche* (soul or mind). Panpsychism states that consciousness pervades all levels of existence, or put another way, all things have a mind or a mind-like quality.

While there are those who argue for consciousness, others in the physical sciences argue against it, mainly because there are no objective predictions or explanations for what it really is. So the march goes on, while it becomes increasingly obvious that we will not be able to debate or study our way into a universally acceptable definition.

MODERN NEUROSCIENCE

New psychedelic research is beginning to expand our understanding of consciousness and the human brain. Neuroscience's focus on consciousness is based on the foundational premise that conscious experience in humans is dependent on "brain activity." Researchers, therefore, find it necessary to create subsets of consciousness, some of which bear empirical study, and some of which clearly do not.

The *Stanford Encyclopedia of Philosophy* explains that among the types of consciousness generally excluded from neuroscience investigation are "consciousness in audition, olfaction or gustation; disturbed consciousness in mental disorders such as schizophrenia; conscious aspects of pleasure, pain and the emotions; the phenomenology of thought; the neural basis of dreams; and modulations of consciousness during sleep and anesthesia among other issues."[14]

It should be clear to us that this excludes much of daily human experience. What is left after hearing, eating, smelling, feeling emotions, and dreaming?

❝❞

it's unclear how a bunch of neurons and cells can give rise to subjective experience, or consciousness

In an attempt to find something legitimate to study and measure, neuroscience distinguishes between "access consciousness" and "phenomenal consciousness." The former describes a state that "is accessible for use in reasoning, report, and the control of action" or in other words, it describes the measurable functions within the body. Phenomenal consciousness, on the other hand, is the subjective or internal state of experiencing what something is like. Phenomenal consciousness is further subdivided into generic and specific consciousness. Generic consciousness is explained as being aware of a hot surface or an angry feeling. Specific consciousness is explained as an internal perceptual state of experiencing something.

It is at this nexus that the philosophy of mind and neuroscience intersect, bringing to the surface the aforementioned Hard Problem of consciousness. It might help researchers earn grant money to parse out consciousness this way, but the Hard Problem still remains: how is it possible, viewing things materialistically only, that we are able to have subjective experience? This subjective experience, in which we are so interested yet also weirdly avoidant, is also the heart of the problem in studying psychedelics. We discount subjective experience as having little scientific value, and so do not know what to do with these natural substances that alter our consciousness in predictable and reliable ways.

BIOLOGY

The materialistic, dogmatic view of biology is that we are victims of our own predetermined genetic blueprint. This outdated but widely accepted view has coalesced into a state of mind centered around victimhood.

Biologist and author Bruce Lipton, however, elucidates the scientific evidence proving that this so-called biological fact is patently untrue. In doing so, he corroborates the ancient Buddhist teaching that *what we believe, we become*.

In the realms of the new study of biology known as epigenetics—which focuses on how genes are expressed—research reveals that it is the environment within which the cell lives that controls genes, and ultimately, mental and physical disease. Given what we know about meditation and spiritual practice, it's not outside the realm of scientific possibility that if you alter your mind, you can alter the way your body works. You can perhaps heal yourself.

Lipton also reframes this concept by stating that our consciousness is controlling our genetic activity. Our brains directly control blood flow to the body, and ultimately, our cells. The key element here is that the images we have in our minds control the physical actions of the brain, our blood chemistry. Lipton believes that the brain translates mind into chemistry, that the "brain is the chemist." Lipton's work demonstrates that feelings of love produce the chemicals dopamine, oxytocin, vasopressin, and growth hormone in our bloodstream, leading to increased cell growth. Similarly, fear releases stress hormones and inflammatory agents, which directly cancel growth at the cellular level. If we lessen or increase these chemicals, we will be healthier or unhealthier. This is presumably why people who are married tend to live longer.

❝ ❞

We discount subjective experience as having little scientific value

The behavior of the cell is controlled by proteins, receptors, and effectors. Receptors provide "awareness of the environment" and effectors convert the awareness into "physical sensation." So far, it might appear as if the brain is just mechanically affecting the cells, but here is where it gets really interesting. Lipton asserts that these receptor-effector complexes provide the "fundamental unit of belief" and that protein receptor units provide "the foundation of biological consciousness." He extrapolates this observation to make the broad claim that:

"By this understanding, evolution, the expansion of awareness would most effectively be modeled using fractal geometry. The fractal nature of biology can be observed in the structural and functional reiterations observed among the hierarchy of the cell, multicellular organisms (man) and the communities of multicellular organisms (human society)."

In layman's terms, this means that from the level of the individual cell, to a single human being, to society as a whole, our beliefs are a determining factor in our well-being.

Does this not represent what happens in the realm of the psychedelic experience, where a profound shift occurs in beliefs about ourselves and the world? Suddenly, with a changed biology, we can directly affect our own health and that of the world around us.

THEORETICAL QUANTUM PHYSICS

The topic of consciousness in the realm of physics has grown over the past decade or so from being the uncle you don't want to invite to dinner, to a tolerable guest, occasionally irritating, but nonetheless entertaining. One day he will be taken fully seriously.

Nassim Haramein, a groundbreaking physicist and author investigating the nature of reality, the universe, and consciousness, states the following. (It's a confusing mouthful but hang in there as it becomes clearer.)

"We have found that when considering the granular spacetime information-energy structure from which we demonstrate matter and mass arises, the phenomena of self-organizing systems that leads to self-awareness and consciousness is integral to—and a natural emergent property of the feedback-dynamics of spacetime information itself."

❝❞

The key element here is that the images we have in our minds control the physical actions of the brain, our blood chemistry

"Furthermore, the recursive information encoding feedback processes of the quantum spacetime micro-wormhole network, which we refer to as space memory, enables memory and learning in physical systems across all scales, resulting in universal evolutionary tendencies toward higher levels of ordering and complexity—foundational to evolution, sentience, and awareness."[15]

Thankfully, Haramein has the gift of simplifying for the layperson. He explains: "In order to be self-aware, you have to have feedback. Consciousness is a feedback between the external world and the internal world. That's fundamental to ALL things. So then ALL things are conscious. All objects are an extension *of* space not *in* space. We are consciousness."

He points out that the placebo effect is the exact phenomenon demonstrating the impact of consciousness on the physical reality of our body. Roundly ridiculed by the mainstream medical profession for decades, if not centuries, the placebo effect is in fact direct evidence of consciousness itself being utilized to perform a miracle.

MIND OVER MATTER

"Okay," it would be easy to say, "well, now I know I am consciousness, so what?" Well, it's one thing to read or talk about climbing a mountain, it's another thing entirely to actually do it. The experiences are not the same. Similarly, talking or reading about consciousness is not the same as the profound subjective experience of consciousness in a psychedelic journey. The fact that we don't always feel fully conscious, which is why we take psychedelics, may point to the neuroscientists being on to something. We seem to have a mundane consciousness that ignores great truths all day long, so we have brain space to pay the bills and feed the dog.

It turns out, the psychedelic state makes us more conscious; it removes the fluff of ego and mundanity that we need to survive in society. In the entropic brain theory, scientists claim, "The psychedelic state is considered an exemplar of a primitive or primary state of consciousness that preceded the development of modern, adult, human, normal waking consciousness."[16]

The more esoteric experiences caused by Ayahuasca, psilocybin, or other psychedelics have historically been kept out of mainstream scientific discussion. Science in its foundation is part of a global guild that emerged out of the male-dominated, post-industrial mechanistic mindset, and while changing slowly, this mindset still largely prevails today. There's simply not a lot of room for fluffy talk of feelings, ego, and metaphorical wounds.

Overtones of mysticism, entities, deities, energetic forms, spirituality, aliens, other realities continue to slip into the vortex of "woowoo," or "we can't measure it so it can't exist," or more commonly, "if we talk about this, we will not get the funding we need to actually study it."

In the scientific world, a subjective experience by definition cannot be validated by peer review. This limitation is held on to, despite the discovery that at the quantum level, *everything* is subjective. When will we be brave enough to extend the beautiful mystery of subatomic particles to our own minds and bodies? We are made of those magical particles after all.

Interestingly, in a guided shamanic journey, the shaman takes the medicine with the participants, and actively participates in the healing at the level of consciousness of the individuals. More often than not, the shaman sees what the participant sees, which raises interesting questions about subjective versus objective reality. In psychedelic journeyer parlance, this phenomenon is called "sync." This is the mysterious phenomenon where multiple people have the same visions, hallucinations, or experiences on psychedelics.

LEGALIZE IT

Psychedelics have come a long way in the past few years in terms of legalization and mainstream acceptance. Until recently, psychedelics were banned substances in most jurisdictions around the world, thanks to the rigidity of the International Narcotic Control Board (INCB), which in turn falls under UN jurisdiction. The mindset of these governing bodies is reflective of the dinosaur mindsets that has pervaded many of our corporate and public organizations over the past several centuries.

In a review of the INCB's 2010 Annual Report and its policies on plant materials, including Ayahuasca, researchers Kenneth Tupper and Beatriz Caiuby Labate concluded that the INCB "misrepresents widely diverse plant materials and their effects." Further, they stated that it "fails to distinguish between 'use' and 'abuse' of psychoactive substances and appears to assume that particular elements of culture—specifically, traditions involving psychoactive substance use—are, or should be, static, eternally frozen in time and place."[17]

In other words, the authorities who regulate drug use worldwide ignored cultural, sociological, and spiritual contexts for safe and therapeutic use of plant medicine, relegating many of these medicines to the same category as addictive and clearly harmful drugs.

❝ ❞

When will we be brave enough to extend the beautiful mystery of subatomic particles to our own minds and bodies? We are made of those magical particles after all

The primary transcendent molecule of Ayahuasca, DMT (N-dimethyltryptamine), is still illegal in most countries. Interesting exceptions *do* exist, led by countries where plant medicine has been part of the cultural and spiritual milieu for centuries. Presently, Ayahuasca is legal in Costa Rica, Brazil, and Peru, as one would expect, but also Italy and Romania. It is a controlled substance in Chile, and to some extent in Spain. Court rulings in the US and Canada over the past ten years have begun to grant certain exemptions to religious institutions.

In Canada, although DMT is classified as a Schedule III drug under the Controlled Drugs and Substances Act, in 2017 the Santo Daime Church Céu do Montréal was the first to receive religious exemption from Health Canada to use Ayahuasca as a sacrament in its rituals. Currently six churches have been granted special exemptions by Health Canada, four in Quebec, one in Ontario, and one in Manitoba.

While innovative research has been conducted selectively for several decades, the modern renaissance in psychedelics is widely attributed to the pivotal work done at the University of New Mexico between 1990 and 1995 by Dr. Rick Strassman. His work, funded by the US government, investigated the effects of DMT on humans with a sample size of sixty volunteers. Of the many groundbreaking findings from this research, more than half of the participants reported encounters with non-human beings while under the influence of DMT. This is of great interest to me personally, given my own experiences during the Ayahuasca ceremonies, coupled with the fact that roughly half of the sixty people in my first week ceremonies also reported "alien" encounters.

Strassman later published his findings in the popular book *DMT: The Spirit*

Molecule, followed by a documentary film of the same name in 2010. New research is now being conducted at reputable institutions across the globe. As the research and testing within established protocol regimes matures, further liberalization is expected to follow the path of psilocybin—or magic mushrooms.

Psilocybin is much further along the path of institutional public and corporate awareness and acceptance than is Ayahuasca. Psilocybin and MDMA have each been designated as a "Breakthrough Therapy" by the FDA in the United States. This designation speeds up the process of the development and review of drugs that address serious medical conditions, and for which preliminary clinical evidence suggests the new drug may be superior to those currently available. Decriminalization, and in some cases legalization, of psilocybin has occurred in many countries. Some cities in the US such as Denver and Oakland have decriminalized the plant.

In Canada during August 2020, four terminally ill patients were granted exemptions to the Controlled Drugs and Substances Act by Health Canada to pursue psilocybin therapy to assist in managing their anxiety and depression, common side effects of receiving a terminal diagnosis.

❝❞

Both psilocybin and MDMA have each been designated as a "Breakthrough Therapy" by the FDA in the United States

Our fears associated with dying are crippling and modern medicine does little to assuage this condition—it turns out a change in consciousness can improve our subjective experience even when we are nearing death or experiencing great pain. This highly progressive ruling is the first in Canada since psilocybin was made illegal in the early 1970s. In a sign of the rapidly evolving regulatory mindset, in 2020 Health Canada also granted a Vancouver-based company a license to produce and extract Psilocybe mushrooms for research purposes, and the company recently announced it has now successfully harvested the first legally grown crop of Psilocybe mushrooms in Canada. Most recently, under the same Health Canada provisions, a Calgary-based therapeutic group administered psilocybin to a terminally ill patient and helped him cope with his end of life anxiety.

CHAPTER 9

WHERE THE RUBBER MEETS THE TOAD

n daily life, I typically refrain from proselytizing about my experiences with Ayahuasca unless I encounter someone who has a sincere interest in the subject.

The line of questioning from a skeptic who has just heard my story invariably leads to a semantic cul-de-sac at the end of a tedious mental journey:

Skeptic: How do you know it's God talking to you?

Me: I didn't say it was God. I just can't say it isn't.

Skeptic: Are you saying you're *enlightened*?

Me: No, I just feel better.

Skeptic: So how do you know you're not just hallucinating?

Me: Well, I am hallucinating.

Skeptic: How do you know you're not just making it all up?

Me: All I know is the old me isn't making this up anymore.

Skeptic: Maybe it's just a chemical reaction, maybe it's not spiritual at all.

Me: Okay. Maybe. So what?

In this way, under the guise of logical, scientific reasoning, the modern mind will go to great lengths to avoid facing the amorphous, indistinguishable nature of reality and our thoughts. As shamans could have told you centuries ago: science will just have to catch up to what they already intuited.

The renaissance in cognitive neuroscience research into formerly prohibited drugs began with cannabis, and was closely followed by ketamine, both of which are entering the mainstream in the US, Canada, and Europe, among other regions. Closely behind are what are known as serotonergic psychedelics, a subclass of psychedelics that act on the neurotransmitter serotonin. The function of serotonin is complex, modulating mood, cognition, reward, learning, memory, and numerous physiological processes such as vomiting and vasoconstriction.[18] Serotonergic psychedelics include:

- psilocybin
- LSD
- Ayahuasca (DMT)
- mescaline
- 5-MeO-DMT—which besides being found in a number of plants, also improbably originates from the Sonoran Desert toad

Many of the "bad trip" stories and other controversies surrounding psychedelics are the result of inexperienced, untrained, and opportunistic people who pass themselves off as shamans and administer a brew from questionable origins in unsafe settings. Reputable sources, however, routinely pre-screen candidates to highlight those who are predisposed to mental health issues, and for whom Ayahuasca can cause anxiety, panic, mood, and other psychotic disorders. Pre-screening for medications is also essential, due to known, negative interactions between certain prescription drugs and Ayahuasca. There is no evidence that in a controlled, safe setting with proper pre-screening people experience any lasting negative effects.

BUT *HOW* DOES IT WORK?

Western researchers are not sure yet if the hallucinations are actually required to achieve the therapeutic effects. From personal experience, my instinct is that the hallucinations are the source of the healing. But science marches on regardless, seeking the active ingredient.

Aptly introduced by Michael Pollan in his book *How to Change Your Mind*, the research now being conducted by Imperial College London, Johns Hopkins, and other prestigious universities is demonstrably impactful and clearly groundbreaking. The ability to image changes in the brain using functional magnetic resonance imaging (fMRI) and to offer science-based explanations that advance our understanding of what is happening in the brain organ under psychedelics is helpful in terms of gaining funding and wider public acceptance. While much of the commercially oriented current research is focused on psilocybin, LSD, MDMA, and mescaline, Ayahuasca (DMT) research is rapidly moving into the mainstream as well.

❝❞

Under the guise of logical, scientific reasoning, the modern mind will go to great lengths to avoid facing the amorphous, indistinguishable nature of reality

The medical journal *Psychological Medicine* recently published the results of a randomized, placebo-controlled trial with Ayahuasca for the very first time. With a patient sample size of twenty-nine patients with treatment-resistant depression, it was found that 64 percent of patients receiving Ayahuasca experienced significant and rapid improvement in symptoms.[19]

Similarly, the *Journal of Psychoactive Drugs* published the results of a survey specifically to measure the overall well-being of regular Ayahuasca users. In assessing 380 long-term users of Ayahuasca in Spain, the joint survey concluded "that a respectful and controlled use of hallucinogenic/psychedelic drugs taken in communitarian settings can be incorporated into modern society with benefits for public health."[20]

Importantly, the baseline for this last study applied established criteria for diagnosing mental illnesses set out by the American Psychiatric Association. The researchers found no evidence of any patients developing substance abuse disorders, either in relation to Ayahuasca itself or other drugs.

Among the more empirically based research being undertaken, one of the most interesting is a 2017 study published in *Nature* which examined the effects of Ayahuasca on neurogenesis—the growth of new brain cells. Neurogenesis was once considered impossible, but it is now widely accepted to occur in mammals. Neural growth mostly takes place in the ventricles and the hippocampus areas of the brain under various conditions and stimuli. The hippocampus plays an important role in cognition, including learning and memory.

❝❞

There is no evidence that in a controlled, safe setting with proper pre-screening people experience any lasting negative effects

In this study, brain stem cells from mice were subjected to controlled dosages of the active chemicals in Ayahuasca, DMT and beta-Carbolines—mainly harmine, harmaline, and tetrahydroharmine. In the experiments, cultures comprised of neural stem cells from the hippocampus of adult mice were created, and the cell cultures were each then tested with three compounds: saline (the constant), harmine, and tetrahydroharmine. The goal was to test the effect of each compound on early, or young, neurons, as well as mature neurons. The authors found that there was a large and noticeable increase in neuron development. They concluded that harmine and tetrahydroharmine have "potent neurogenic properties."

In November 2020, researchers from Johns Hopkins University reported in *JAMA Psychiatry* the results of a study of twenty-seven people using psilocybin to treat depression. This study arose out of previous work with cancer patients, and the researchers then extrapolated the results to further investigate depression among the general population. Psilocybin outperformed antidepressant drugs by a factor of four. Participants in the study experienced positive effects within one day of receiving treatment, with the effects lasting up to one month. Two years prior, ketamine was approved by the FDA for treatment-resistant depression, and psilocybin has now been granted "breakthrough status," clearing a path to accelerated clinical trials. Lack of funding within the institutional realm is still a limiting factor, however, with the above study being partly dependent on crowdfunding.

It is now accepted that chemical and neural changes do occur in the brain, and that psychedelics have a direct impact on mental conditions that are known as internalizing disorders. These disorders partly originate in an area within the brain known as the Default Mode Network (DMN). This is a neural circuit in our brains where our daily thoughts are believed to reside. It is also within this circuitry that obsessive thinking, rumination, rigid thoughts, and beliefs hang out, and it is this cluttered never-ending freeway of thought that leads to depression and other mental illness and addiction.

This is how we live our daily lives. We get into ruts. We get depressed. We can't stop thinking the same way. Over and over. But there are ways to interrupt this circuit, with psychedelics being uncommonly effective in breaking our compulsive thought patterns.

The opposite of this rigid state of mind is entropy, a term used in this context to describe a state of disorder. Imagine a fifteen-year-old teenager's bedroom. This would be a state of entropy. The parents' bedroom, on the other hand, being spotless and tidy, represents the DMN. Very predictable, but boring and slightly depressing, and you wouldn't want to hang out there with your friends.

Active psychedelic compounds in psilocybin in effect cause the DMN to go into what is known as a state of entropy or disorder. Further, the DMN is decoupled from another part of the brain known as the medial temporal lobes. Our common thought patterns are interrupted, with new neural pathways temporarily forged, leading to many of the therapeutic, cognitive, spiritual, and perceptual outcomes cited throughout this book.

The state of consciousness that one enters under a psychedelic experience is a state of entropy. Momentary disorder, the breaking of routine thought patterns causes a reframing of our sense of ourselves and our realities, commonly referred to as ego dissolution or ego death. This effect in the brain has been imaged by high-resolution fMRI tools.

It is worth considering the following statement from a paper by neuroscientists at Imperial College in London, in the context of the shamanic view of wounding: "The psychedelic state caused by psilocybin, for example, is considered an exemplar of a primitive or primary state of consciousness that preceded the development of modern, adult, human, normal waking consciousness."[21] Could this also be the "pre-wound" state of the shaman, the home of the "restored soul"?

Further, the authors hypothesize that "disintegration of the 'ego' is necessary for the occurrence of primary states. The ego can be defined as a sensation of possessing an immutable identity or personality; most simply, the ego is our "sense of self." They go on to invoke Freudian metapsychology to further state that "the ego is not just a (high-level) sensation of self-hood; it is a fundamental system that works in competition and cooperation with other processes in the mind." This "system" might also describe the DMN.

The specific receptors—called 5-HT2A—sit on large neurons clustered within the cerebral cortex, which is part of the DMN. The molecules that form the basis of serotonergic psychedelics are serotonin receptor agonists. An agonist is a chemical (molecule) that binds to a receptor to produce a biological response. In this case, a psilocybin molecule binds to a 5-HT2A receptor, and at this point it is said to activate the receptor. This in turn "excites" the host neuron in the cerebral cortex, and the normal state of the neuron is then interrupted, or "dysregulated." This causes a chain reaction toward the state of entropy, or disorder, that leads directly to positive therapeutic and experiential outcomes.

❝❞

The state of consciousness that one enters under a psychedelic experience is a state of entropy

In early 2020, it was reported in *Cell* that scientists had solved the high-resolution structure of the compounds psilocybin, LSD, and mescaline when they are actively bound to the 5-HT2A receptor.[22] This breakthrough will allow further investigation into how these compounds might be synthesized into commercially available drugs in the future, although the researchers admit they don't yet know exactly what causes the hallucinations.

This entropic process is now understood to produce brain plasticity, both psychologically—described as "an enhanced capacity for change"—and also neurobiologically in the creation of new neurons and pathways.

HEAVEN AND EARTH

"We practice the medicine to return to the origin of creation and the origin of life."
—Taita Juanito

Shamanism has been around as long as mankind, and with remarkable similarities observed among shamanic practices the world over. The term *shaman* originally, and with no small measure of condescension, was coined by anthropologists to refer to "primitive" or "Stone Age" peoples. More to the point, it referred to those whose practices defied Western logic and reason and for which no tidy explanations could be made.

Generally thought to have originated from the Siberian Tungus people, shaman simply means someone who enters a trance by drumming or other ceremony, and then cures people. The shaman's job is to journey into the spirit world, or non-ordinary reality, getting advice and powers to maintain the balance between the natural and supernatural. Shamans most commonly accomplish this journey by

---

altering their consciousness through ritual methods such as drumming, dancing, chanting, and/or the use of psychotropic plants. In the Amazon, indigenous shamans use chanting, songs (known as icaros), and plants such as those that make Ayahuasca to achieve this altered state. Shamans are most often male, and are also called curanderos, medicine men, witch doctors, vegetalistas, and ayahuasqueros. For women who practice shamanism, it is considered to be an expression of their masculine side.

There are many types of shamans, but the distinctions can be critically important for the uniformed Westerner seeking a transformative experience:

Vegetalista: A shaman who works with various plant medicines, including Ayahuasca.

Palero: A shaman who works with tree barks that are another source of remedies.

Tobaquero: A shaman who works with indigenous tobacco, in its own right very strong medicine.

Brujo/Bruja: Brujo means sorcerer and bruja means witch. These people are typically motivated more by money and power rather than healing. Brujos are prevalent in Peru, a locus for Western Ayahuasca tourism.

Ayahuasca has been used by shamans, also known as curanderos, to alter consciousness for at least five thousand years in the Amazon, with around seventy-two known indigenous peoples using it as a regular part of their cultural and spiritual traditions. The word Ayahuasca, meaning "vine of the soul," originates from the indigenous Quechua people of Peru and Ecuador.

Traditional Ayahuasca use is concentrated in two regions in the Amazon, the western part of the Amazon basin, including the adjoining parts of Colombia, Peru, Ecuador, Bolivia, and Brazil, and the western part of Guiana Shield, which encompasses much of Colombia, Venezuela, Guyana, Suriname, and French Guiana. This broad region is the nexus of Ayahuasca use.

Other indigenous peoples including the Tsáchila and Chachi of the northern coast of Ecuador, the Emberá of western Colombia, and the Chocó of northwestern Colombia near the Panama border, and some Guaraní groups in eastern Bolivia may have adopted Ayahuasca in modern times.

The inhabitants of each area have their own unique Ayahuasca practices, including names for the brew such as Yagé, Yajé, Caapi, Natem, Pinde, Karampi, Dapa, Mihi, and Kahi, among others. The common element is the sacred ceremonial context within which the medicine is taken. Typically, the curandero has trained for many years to become expert in serving the brew and conducting healing ceremonies. This training can include long periods of isolation, celibacy, and severe dietary restrictions. Most modern Ayahuasca retreats suggest that participants similarly adopt a subset of these practices of abstinence up to a month before undertaking a ceremony as it is believed that impurities can unleash negative spiritual forces.

Taita is a title of reverence given to spiritual leaders of the Inga people in the Amazon. While my eight ceremonies were led by several skilled curanderos of various traditions, two ceremonies were notable. These two ceremonies were led by Taita Juanito Guillermo Chindoy Chindoy, who is an ethnobotanist and doctor in his community in the Colombian Amazon, from a lineage extending back many generations. As a young boy he started working with the medicine and the Ingano traditions, later studying the Siona ways with his grandfather, Taita Laureano, reportedly the oldest living shaman in the world at 109 years of age.

The Sionas are recognized as exceptionally powerful shamans, having been leaders in Ayahuasca traditions for centuries.

The critical importance of the role of a gifted shaman is well described by anthropologist David Maybury-Lewis: "If drinking Yagé (Ayahuasca) is so unpleasant and frightening, why do people persist in using it? Because they believe the terror is something a person must overcome in order to attain knowledge. Needless to say, the insights acquired through taking Yagé depend very much on the training of the taker. An experienced shaman can see many things while under its influence. A novice may only be suffused with panic or lost in ecstatic vision he cannot interpret."

In ceremony, the shaman will often see what the participant sees, in what is known as "synchronicity" or "sync." From this perspective, the shaman guides the participant and helps interpret their experience.

It is of critical importance to understand the difference between an ayahuasquero and a curandero. A person who is formally trained to "set the stage" for an Ayahuasca ceremony and administer the brew is known as an ayahuasquero. The ayahuasquero then steps back and lets the medicine do the work on the patient. They should not generally attempt healing on the participant, deferring instead to a skilled curandero.

The true healing shamanic skills are the purview of the curandero, who is also an ayahuasquero but not the other way around. Traditionally, in the Ayahuasca medical system, spirit (Source/God, etc.) is the doctor and the medicine, whereas Ayahuasca, the plant medicine, is the curandero's *tool* to connect to the spirit world. The curandero has learned to work with energies/spirits and guides the patient in managing this energy/spirit so it is no longer a negative influence. Importantly, the curandero protects the patient from outside spirits that can intrude during a ceremony. Ayahuasca opens up a person's energy and the protection offered by the curandero is critical to a successful journey. Some curanderos have additional skills in creating remedies for various ailments like candida, arthritis, herpes, and in some cases cancer. Curanderos will often ingest other plants in addition to Ayahuasca, and these plants become healing allies, working with the curandero in their healing work.

These terms *shaman*, *curandero*, and *ayahuasquero* have routinely been co-opted and intermixed by many indigenous locals and Westerners who purvey and monetize an expertise in plant medicine that may be ill-founded and often used to claim healing shamanic skills that they do not possess. When embarking on a journey into plant medicine, the uninitiated are well advised to ascertain the credentials of the person leading the ceremony.

While there are no objective certifications and requirements for administering plant medicine, the novice participant must proceed with caution and diligence. In addition to conducting rigorous pre-screening of mental and physical health conditions and medications, a credible shaman or therapist should be able to demonstrate a history of working effectively and safely with the medicine over a sustained course of practice. Testimonials and references from others who have worked with the practitioner are highly recommended to minimize the inherent risks of working with someone unqualified to conduct this type of experience. No less important than the qualifications of the ayahuasquero is what we bring to the experience, our mindset, also known as "set," and the "setting," or the ambience and surroundings within which one participates in the ceremony.

A recreational, party mindset in a loud, raucous EDM concert may be momentarily transformative, but carries huge risks to mind and body. In contrast, a sacred, healing intention in a nurturing environment under the care of a gifted healer invariably leads to positive, lasting outcomes.

http://www.ayahuasca.com/, *The Cosmic Serpent* by Jeremy Narby, *The Way of the Shaman* by Michael Harner, *Millennium* by David Maybury-Lewis

PEER PRESSURE

Scientific protocols are necessary and valuable, as they encourage and support the rigor required to validate an outcome as being dependable, fact-based, repeatable, safe, useful, helpful, or at least plausibly beneficial to the academic career path.

Admittedly, there is an inherent contradiction at some point in the continuum. In order to overcome the limitations of subjective experience, and to weed out the charlatans, the science industry has created such "gold standards" as the double-blind experiment and the much vaunted peer review process—which are highly useful and usually essential.

However, it's unclear if the very real effects of psychedelic trips can ever fit neatly into this paradigm. It seems a new Hard Problem of consciousness lies in the fact that scientific and philosophic worlds may add little to our understanding simply because the proof lies in the psychedelic pudding. Subjective experience might be the active ingredient.

The movement toward determining what causes the hallucinations, and then eliminating that effect from new molecular compounds, is predicated on the idea that hallucinations are a bad thing for many people and are separate from the therapeutic effects. This is because we are determined to prove that the way we think doesn't change the way our bodies and minds work. Arguably an overhang from the mechanistic mindset, this path of research is in its own right exciting and game-changing for mental health in the world today, but it does run the risk of eliminating the most valuable information contained within the realm of the hallucinations.

Strikingly, researcher Dr. David Nutt comments that "part of the core drug action seems to be to make people exceptionally sensitive to what lies beyond their ego boundaries, whether this be material percolating up from their inner world, e.g., in terms of emotions and memories, or coming into the brain from the outer world, e.g., in terms of therapist(s) present and music heard." Further, the research suggests it is the "emotional breakthrough" from a powerful psychedelic experience that predicts a successful outcome.

Although time will tell, I remain skeptical that taking psychedelics without hallucinatory effects will have the same profound healing effect on mind, body, and spirit. We must be vigilant in not allowing our Western minds to minimize or even negate the deep wisdom and knowledge that lies within these mystical realms.

TWENTY-FIRST CENTURY ZEITGEIST

Psychedelics are rapidly permeating our mainstream consciousness by virtue of by now routine coverage in most major media outlets. The focus is generally on the mental health benefits and associated commercial potential of psychedelics.

The degree to which the corporate world has woken up to the commercial potential of psychedelic medicine is highlighted in a recent, slightly perverse but revealing episode of the HBO series *Billions*. The series pits two deeply wounded and powerful leaders against one another, exemplifying the extreme predatory and destructive effects of the dinosaur mindset—one of the men represents unfettered greed and the other unfettered self-righteousness. Both are, however, clearly sociopaths. In this particular episode, the main hedge fund guru attends an Ayahuasca journey under the guidance of a shaman. As he and his business partner are highly intoxicated and in sync, expressing to one another their extreme ego dissolution and acceptance of their frailties, they come to a great realization: they can make tons of money from Ayahuasca. This scene alone shows that, like any powerful tool, Ayahuasca is not a panacea for the ego distortions of greed and self-interest. It has to be used correctly, and when done so, these gross distortions can be largely eliminated.

Powerful symbiotic relationships between reputable scientific researchers and commercial interests are exploding as new companies based around psychedelic therapies are being founded every day—and even going public. A recent public listing of a psilocybin company achieved a pre-revenue valuation of $1.4 billion. Many others are emerging in the public and private markets, with over $400 million in capital being raised in the past two years.

These companies are forging a clear path through the various regulatory hurdles around the world. Entrepreneurs can make things happen quickly outside of established, moribund institutional settings. The rapid escalation in clinical trials in the new industry of psychedelic medicine is a direct result of entrepreneurs raising capital, providing much-needed funding to research bodies in many countries, paving a path to market. This symbiotic relationship between business and science all but ensures the momentum that psychedelics are gaining in the mainstream will be unstoppable.

❝❞

Subjective experience might be the active ingredient

Typically, a company puts up money for research into certain defined psychedelics at a university known for its cutting-edge scientists, and in exchange, the company gets the commercial rights to manufacture and market any drug that emerges out of the lengthy and costly research and clinical trial process.

The power of this entrepreneur model is twofold. Creative out-of-the-box research is encouraged, and funding channels and timelines are cleared and accelerated. It is counterproductive for leading researchers to spend most of their time writing and defending proposals, when their true value and passion reside in hands-on lab work. Otherwise, researchers are routinely required to navigate Kafkaesque bureaucracies in order to receive funding. Add to that the fact that the limitations of oversize egos and dinosaur mindsets are no less prevalent in academia than they are in the corporate world.

The extraction of the "molecular" components from psychedelics is one direction that will invariably lead to dramatic new medicines. As is the case in all instances where plant remedies are being transformed into medicine, scientists must procure measurable active ingredients so that approved medicines contain only the molecules required to have the intended effect.

These new medicines, when they become commercially available—likely within the next five years—are expected to be highly disruptive to a variety of industries and academic disciplines. Indications from research studies worldwide suggest that very few dosages may be required to result in profound, lasting effects for patients, obviating the need for lifelong prescriptions. The dynamics of the pharmaceutical industry will be interesting, as larger manufacturers of pharmaceuticals recognize the very real possibility that new drugs may replace many of the more common commercial brands, which are a "repeatable" revenue stream (i.e., addictive or ineffective).

❝❞

A recent public listing of a psilocybin company achieved a pre-revenue valuation of $1.4 billion

I have become increasingly convinced that Ayahuasca is also a powerful tool in the context of leadership development and general well-being when used with the right intention in the right context. My hypothesis based on over thirty-five years in the male-dominated energy industry is that limiting mental conditions—usually undiagnosed and unexplored—tend to pervade most executive and leadership personalities. Business as a microcosm reflects the ills of society as a whole, so by placing psychedelics in the safe, arms-length realm of addressing "society's ills, but not my own," business leaders may run the risk of ignoring the true value of plant medicine.

In the same way that Ayahuasca tends to enter people's lives when they need it the most, so too will the availability of psychedelics enter the mainstream just as society—with its racial justice uprisings, routine recessions, political upheaval, and rampant mental stress—needs it most.

CHAPTER 10

THE INTEGRATION

"All sciences are vain and full of errors that are not born of
Experience, the mother of all Knowledge."

—Leonardo da Vinci

The yin and the yang represent the universal dynamic: dark/light, plus/minus, masculine/feminine. The idea is that "truth" lies in the dynamic between these two things, not in one or the other. It is only through integration and harmony between the poles that truth can be attained or even approached. Similarly, the dichotomy between "spiritual truth" and "scientific truth" is artificial; both are a type of truth that require one another. To move forward as a species, we must learn to integrate the incongruous parts of ourselves and our belief systems.

It's a misconception that all science-based endeavors are somehow able to achieve complete confidence and accuracy. In the oil and gas business, we routinely incorporate vast amounts of scientific knowledge to deploy extremely expensive projects with highly uncertain outcomes—if there is a mistake, or merely bad luck, the natural world, including people, can die in the process. A study in *The Harvard Business Review* found that 60 percent of business decisions were, in hindsight, deemed the wrong decision. This means that with all of our analytics and technology, we're still making the wrong decision the majority of the time.

Beyond the limits of what is objectively known and measurable lies our subjective, personal experience, and our instinct. This is the realm of our true power because after all the data and science are in, we have to decide whether we want to believe them or not. How do we integrate these two necessary realms?

For most of my professional life, I have managed scientific and technical teams. Invariably, the person who has worked the most with the data becomes considered "the expert." Typically, junior geoscientists, lacking what they feel is enough experience to make judgment calls on their own work, will fall into self-doubt since they can't back up their instincts with their data and experience.

As manager, I would assure them: "You are the one working with the data, you have internalized the most likely interpretation of the data, and you are therefore the expert. You simply need to develop a language to convey your ideas clearly and from the heart." This affirmation was designed to help them trust their own intellect and intuition, and to trust their internal processes rather than requiring immense or impossible amounts of external validation from peers or data.

Similarly, my experiences with Ayahuasca and psilocybin have a subjective aspect to them, as do all psychedelic experiences. I'm able to trust that, given the existing data around Ayahuasca and my own personal experiences, there is something revolutionary available in the cells of these special plants.

New scientific research into psychedelics has been winding its way down the backroads, navigating toward the mainstream of society, but it has a problematic passenger: scientific hubris. The scientific community, until very recently at least and with a few notable exceptions, routinely dismissed people's fantastical psychedelic experiences as subjective, unquantifiable, and therefore trips of imagination and fantasy with no scientific or practical value. But now the evidence has grown unignorable. The hubris manifests as distrust in people's self-reported, mystical, spiritual, and otherwise unmeasurable experiences. The nexus of these two will not likely ever be fully established, nor does it need be.

The established scientific community must carefully tread within the safe bounds of reason, data, quantifiable outcomes. These are typically focused on physical or chemical changes in the brain and can be measured or imaged, and therefore deemed *real*. Chemical changes in the brain, for instance, are observed to occur while on psychedelics.

The "problem" for scientists is that subjective experiences commonly include geometric shapes, visions, hallucinations, ego death, feelings of unity with nature, and that four-letter word that is the scourge of science and business—love. Because we can't fit love into these paradigms, such subjective experiences are set aside as an unwanted hindrance to the scientific process. Hence the definition of consciousness being surgically sliced up so as to avoid any talk of love, oneness, nature, and universal consciousness.

❝❞

To move forward as a species, we must learn to integrate the incongruous parts of ourselves and our belief systems

Oftentimes, when science does make an attempt to integrate these subjective experiences into the observable healing properties of psychedelics, it does so by invoking the placebo effect. But when scientists do this, they presume that the placebo effect means something "fake" is going on. The truth is, the placebo effect works. People who are visited by their priests in the hospital recover demonstrably faster than those who aren't. This shows not that priests have magical healing powers, but that a person who believes in something's magical healing powers can, in fact, actually get healed. This is really the point. The placebo is a belief. If belief affects our inner cell structures, as is confirmed by science, then the placebo is the most powerful drug on Earth.

The business reality of the scientific industry is no different from the leadership, wellness, or oil and gas industries. That is, commercial interests, peer recognition, and ego prevail. Funding is contingent upon presenting a field of study that falls within a window of "scientific acceptability," short-term for peer-proven, publishable, and patentable and commercial viability. The study of psychedelics poses interesting problems in this regard.

Before my ceremonies, I was skeptical about much of what I had read and re-searched on psychedelics. Specifically, I felt that the strongest proponents of psy-chedelics were generally unable to tell me exactly *how* the experiences had impact-ed their daily life. Grand notions of *gratitude, vulnerability, the divine feminine, ego death, oneness with nature* often struck me as fanciful, wishful, or magical thinking.

Being well aware of the high that follows a retreat of any type—we want to believe we have been instantly transformed—I was hesitant to attribute any immediate changes to Ayahuasca.

In her fascinating book *Eyes Wide Open*, anthropologist Mariana Caplan highlights some pitfalls of any spiritual journey: "There is a real danger in falling into what we call Spiritual Materialism—we can deceive ourselves into thinking we are developing spiritually when instead we are strengthening our egocentricity through spiritual techniques." For example, if I go to church every Sunday it does not mean I lead a spiritual life or am actually closer to God. Similarly, just because I saw spirit forms in an Ayahuasca journey, I am not suddenly connected to the divine in perpetuity. Am I?

❝❞
The truth is, the placebo effect works

Many of the proponents of psychedelics have been dismissed for this reason. Another common limitation of spiritual practitioners, which Caplan mentions, is known as Spiritual Bypass, which is when we rely on spiritual practice to avoid the meaningful, painful, and difficult work required to face our ego and our wound(s).

This can, and often does, manifest in an attitude of "I meditate regularly, and go to retreats, therefore I have transcended human frailties and no longer experience greed, lust, pride, or competitiveness."

During a particularly rigorous hot yoga class, I was overcome with rage due to my inability to hold my balance in Eagle pose. I wobbled like a drunken sailor, my face contorting like a demented circus clown. I was taken aback by these feelings. After cooling down and collecting my wits, I walked to the exit where the teachers sat, glowing with equanimity and love for their students, relishing the deep namastes and murmurs of gratitude from the adoring students. I sat down beside the instructor and confided, "I feel nothing but rage in the balance poses. Have you ever encountered that?"

She grimaced a faux smile as if it were an answer in itself, and then turned to greet another student. That was that. "Namaste." This was Spiritual Bypass, the inability to accept that negativity exists and is vital to experiencing positivity.

I have come to understand that integration does not mean elimination. The dark and the light, the positive and the negative, coexist necessarily, and it is folly to pretend this is not the case. After all, it is in our nature.

GETTING HIGH

There is also a danger in "chasing the high." While there is absolutely no evidence that psychedelics are physiologically addictive, any medicine or therapy—Ayahuasca, yoga, Xanax—turns from a medicine into a drug when its results are not integrated into a grounded life but are rather used for escape and avoidance.

Some people seek to maintain the elevated sense of being connected to divine energy, or spirit, without grounding the knowledge from the experiences and translating them to be of use in "waking" life. *Integration* means taking what one has learned and applying it in a practical, useful, tangible way so that we can benefit ourselves and those around us. There is always a tendency to fall back into old patterns after the psychedelic effect has worn thin, so the work revolves around continuously *integrating* the psychedelic experience into daily life, observing one's patterns, and with consciousness, empathy, and openness, confronting and transforming less desirable tendencies. It is the honest awareness of one's own humanity that leads to lasting transformation.

Much of the healing that Ayahuasca offers is not in the glowing and heart-opened experience and immediate aftermath, but in the folds and creases of daily life going forward. It is as if your brain forges new pathways that you can then access at any time—with or without the brew.

In the spiritual lexicon, mentalities are discussed as "high frequency" or "high vibration" when they are positive, and "low frequency" or "low vibration" when they are negative. Fear, anxiety, greed, and pride are low vibrational states. Love, humor, joy, gratitude, and forgiveness are high vibrational states. The question is not whether these vibrations are measurable in the "real" scientifically based world but whether you can experience these states in ways that are tangible and relatable. Certainly, you can think of people in your life at this moment and can categorize them as high or low vibrational people. These states can be sensed by anyone who cares to look. So, the inner experience of lower and higher states of being is real, as is the effect on those around us. Just observe someone who is saddened by grief, or depression, and you feel the low energy. And someone who is joyful emits a lightness.

Who do you want to hang out with? Who do you want to be?

The challenge for those who experience Ayahuasca, and psychedelics in general, is how to maintain a lighter sense of being in the context of our daily lives. Negativity and fear abound, and it is constantly purveyed though the media and blind idiocy of many of our leaders. Very real concerns of economic stability and health prevail in our world today, and the concerns of each human are real. So, the question becomes, is it possible to maintain a higher level of energy, hope, optimism, coupled with realism and general well-being?

❝❞

The work revolves around continuously *integrating* the psychedelic experience into daily life

The integration of psychedelic experiences into our daily lives is not easy. Following the advice of the staff at Rythmia, it is wise to take some time to digest the experiences before returning home. I spent a few days after the ceremonies in Nosara, a beach community south of Tamarindo. Some of my new friends from the retreat stayed in the area, and we met regularly for meals and conversation. A common concern seemed to center around how we would be able to reenter our lives and incorporate the insights, the power, the healing that had occurred. Would we be swept back into our old ways of being or would we be able to maintain some of the profound awareness that the medicine had delivered to each of us?

The world of plant medicine and shamanism is one that straddles a divide between the realms of day to day "reality," sometimes referred to as 3-D, and otherworldly dimensions or "realities" that exist in parallel but outside the realm of our normal everyday consciousness.

MY INTEGRATION

A month after arriving home, I had an appointment with a well-regarded psychic and spiritual counselor. Something in me—a residue of my old, familiar self-doubt—wanted to independently verify that Ayahuasca had really altered my psyche. She was as reputable as you can get in her line of work, having helped the RCMP—Royal Canadian Mounted Police—locate nearly thirty missing persons in Canada. One of her clients, after a session in which she was told the precise day, store, and lottery ticket number to select, won $7 million. You could dismiss these as coincidences, but the probabilities of several of these types of outcomes originating from one source is very low. She seemed to me very gifted in connecting with spirit.

I sat down, and she took my hands in hers, and gasped: "Your energy is off the charts!" She told me her arms went completely numb up to her elbows because I was vibrating at a very high frequency. I told her only that I had been to Costa Rica and done eight Ayahuasca ceremonies. She closed her eyes, breathed deeply, and began to tell me some of what I had experienced in various ceremonies, and there is no way she could have known any of it.

She confirmed my experience in the spirit world as real and summarized by saying that during my first week I was completely broken down and opened up, and that powerful and healing knowledge was transmitted during the second week.

While I fully admit this does not constitute a double-blind experiment, in the spiritual world, it certainly qualifies as peer review and empirical evidence.

Eight months after my ceremonies, I was driving down a frozen street in a Calgary winter. At a red light up ahead was a homeless man dressed as warmly as possible, but clearly freezing. He was winding through the traffic, a paper coffee cup in his frozen, mittened hand, hoping to receive a few coins from the warm and comfy drivers. My old small self would have gone through a process of judgment: *Get a job; not my problem; oh, maybe I should give him a toonie, is that too much? Maybe a loonie, or don't be so cheap. But I've worked hard for my money. I don't owe him anything.* This time, I reached into my pocket and saw a blue fiver. *Nah*, I said to myself, *give him something that'll at least make a difference today.* So, I rolled down my passenger window, reached over, and gave him $20. He was surprised, but still cold. I said, "Peace, brother." He looked me in the eye and said, "Peace, brother," and added a sincere, warm "Thank you." We were really brothers in that moment.

I drove on, weeping about the potential of connection between all humans. I wept not because I gave him a bit more money. Not because I'm a great person. But because we're the same person. He's there. I'm here. But there's no difference. Except external circumstances.

So, this felt like one direct, tangible outcome of the medicine. I was feeling more love. My continued, latent, explosive, integration of my plant experience is still ongoing. Compassion and love roar into my being at unexpected times, a rush of energy so powerful I feel I might collapse. This is a delicious movement into a realm of being where I am being loved, and it rushes through me into whomever happens to be in the path to receive it. I am not yet fit enough to *live* in this energetic realm full-time, as it is often accompanied by a deep restlessness, impatience, or thinly veiled peevishness with many of the things that occur daily in our lives—like traffic and waiting in line. These are only the ragged leftovers of my old ego self, but they are also part of what it means to be human. Still, every day my dips into higher vibrations are displacing the lesser energies with something bigger, better, and brighter.

The work of transformation and integration is indeed work. The medicine and ceremony comprise half of the work. The other half is integration into the world again and making it sticky. We were cautioned, wisely, that it takes months or longer to assimilate what has been gained from this experience. Over a year later, I am still experiencing the effects of my journeys.

From time to time, I microdose with psilocybin, paying close attention to differences in my internal and external experiences. Microdosing is when you take small amounts of psychedelics at regular intervals, for example every few days, the idea being that your brain chemistry is altered in imperceptible but substantive ways. Heightened sensitivity to the moods of others is a definite effect, rapid intuitive insights are common, as is a more uniform sense of peace and equanimity.

The owner of a yoga studio recently confided in me that her attention deficit disorder has been largely mitigated by microdosing psilocybin, allowing her to start two new businesses with complete focus and clarity.

Am I more cognitively functional? In a sense, yes. In another, no. The mitigation of negative emotional thought patterns has allowed me to be more present in whatever I am doing in the moment. I'm in a couple of bands, and my music gigs have taken on a life of their own, where it seems the music is really playing itself and I am a mere bystander.

66 99
Compassion and love roar into my being at unexpected times

Conversations have a distinct clarity and focus. It might be age, or it might be the medicine, but my prized memory for mundane facts, details, names has been obliterated. A friend who is much younger, but very involved in the deep therapeutic experience of Ayahuasca, tells me that other higher cognitive functions have probably been activated in me, and that we need only recall that which serves us in the moment. I find this to be an accurate description of my mind state much of the time, and at least it's a more acceptable explanation than just getting old.

In the same sense that when the medicine calls, things begin to shift, the same can be said after you have taken the medicine. My dreams have become inseparable from an Ayahuasca journey, and they can manifest any time of the day or night. Mother Aya continues her work. In my dreams, I feel the unraveling and healing of my wounds ongoing.

As I write this, it is now over eighteen months since my journeys with Ayahuasca, and something profound is certainly shifting in my life. Compassion, empathy, and right action are becoming more habitual, as opposed to my former life of pretense.

I have moved my ninety-two-year-old mother out from Manitoba to Calgary to live near me. I overcame my deep, selfish resistance to doing this, hardwired as I was to the self-serving refrain among my generation that "you need to take care of yourself first." While true in some sense, it does not mean shirking our duties to help where we can.

In this case, after years of resistance, I could finally experience my mother with compassion and love instead of through the lens of my childhood. She was lonely, and she needed help from an immediate family member. So, my life is now peppered with new duties: trips to the doctor, running interference between my mother and her hairdresser, who can't seem to do a proper shampoo, hospital visits, and endless cups of Tim Hortons coffee while we drive around the countryside looking at the Rockies and trying to forget about COVID. While I am far from a saint, and still resentful and impatient at various times, I am showing up every day to do my part. It is a blessing that I never expected to experience in my life. Mother Aya has placed my own mother squarely back into my life.

The world of Williams continues to unfold in strange and unpredictable ways. A few months ago, my youngest daughter signed on to 23andMe to get her genes analyzed. Somehow, through that network, she was contacted by a woman in Calgary who said she thought we were related on my father's side of the family. We all corresponded, exchanged details of our respective histories, and it seems I have had numerous second cousins living near me in Alberta my entire adult life. Even stranger, they are geologists, artists, writers, and musicians like me. They also have the Irish love of the drink, and of course a number of them are named William or Bill like my father and I.

Had I not experienced the vision I had of my father during my Ayahuasca ceremony—the deep healing of the lineage of my grandfather and father and my father telling me he wanted to be a writer—I would have dismissed this occurrence as mere coincidence. It is not. My life vis-à-vis my father and his ancestry has come full circle. It landed in my lap, so to speak. And now, as I write this book—something my father never did though he wanted to—my world of family, of home, of self is constantly expanding, and revealing itself to be much greater than I could ever have imagined.

Chasing the high by doing more and more ceremonies can be a misleading path for some. A dear friend of mine, a gifted energy healer, tells me she sees many clients who, upon returning from an Ayahuasca ceremony, are confused, upset, ungrounded, and unsure of what exactly they experienced. Invariably, these participants journeyed under less-than-ideal circumstances with ill-equipped albeit well-intentioned leaders.

With her loving guidance, she helps them to rebalance their energy so they can move back into their daily lives gracefully. Real shamans and therapeutic healers are deeply committed to the integration of a journey into one's daily life, invariably cautioning that it is not immediate, often taking months. This too has been my experience. I have said it before and I will say it again: Ayahuasca is not a panacea. Once it gives you the priceless gift of awareness, it takes active work, vigilance, practice, and time to learn to be "in this world, but not of this world."

CHAPTER 11

WOMB WITH A VIEW

"Overall, women are perceived as being slightly more effective and competent than their male counterparts in most of the measured specific competencies. Out of the 19 capabilities measured, women outscored men on 17 (e.g. takes initiative, resilience, self-development, drives for results, higher integrity/honesty etc.)."

—Jack Zenger and Joseph Folkman

Field, British Columbia, is a beautiful, timeless railway town that lies along the axis of a geological feature known as "The Great Divide." It is an area famous for the Burgess Shale, which provides hard evidence of life on the planet from at least 500 million years ago. Geographically, the Great Divide is the topographic axis, meaning the highest point in the area, which splits the Western Cordillera, "the Rockies," in two, although it's not immediately obvious to a casual observer. On the eastern side of the divide, all waters flow toward the Atlantic Ocean. On the western side, all waters flow to the Pacific Ocean.

In another context, this could readily be a metaphor for the wound, or the split, between the masculine and feminine energies.

Alberta, on the east, embodies dominant masculinity—with its oil and gas, ranching, and a belief that unbridled, entrepreneurial spirt and technological knowhow will solve all ills. The west coast of British Columbia has a calm, embracing, creative feel; the pace slows down, with the power of the feminine ocean being an overriding presence. You can see similar splits between West Coast and East Coast mentalities in the US. Over the past thirty years, I've explored the western coastline in my boat, playing music with great friends. I once owned a house on the beach, and my daughters and former wife reside there. When I'm there, I feel my desire to conquer the world evaporate, and I begin to question anything resembling external or ego-based achievement. This dissonance between the two geographic realms may be due to very real energies emanating from Mother Earth. Following this statement, I fully expect to be stripped of my professional geologist designation and declared an embarrassment to the scientific community. So be it—I embrace the power and importance of subjective experience.

As you know by now, Ayahuasca is a divine feminine presence. Within her deep embrace in ceremony we are given new life. She works through male and female shamans, equally, because in her world, men and women are equal. Masculine and feminine energies reside equally in both sexes. There is no distinction between a male or female's ability to lead a powerful healing ceremony. It is not a male or female thing.

I have attended ceremonies conducted by both male and female shamans. The men were loving, caring, gentle, and nurturing, powerfully exhibiting traits that men fear in the puerile world of the toxic masculine, for they are "feminine" traits. The women shamans were powerful, energetic, wise, and grounded, with extraordinary endurance that allowed them to lead and protect groups of between sixty and ninety people for up to twelve hours of intense vigilance and personal power, without once flagging.

In the world of shamanism, the masculine and feminine traits manifest according to the needs of the situation, and the people within the shaman's care. There is no differentiation between male and female roles or capability. Shaman is not politicized to "sha-woman," referring instead to the broader sense of mankind. The term is gender-neutral, much like the term doctor, and this confers balance. It is an internal dynamic, not a cultural or external one. It's simply the balance of masculine and feminine energies. Think of it as a type of energetic or even spiritual androgyny that we all possess. When we begin to experience this within ourselves, and then begin to perceive those around us in these terms, we develop a broader sense of humanity.

The concept that men and women both carry masculine and feminine energies within their consciousness is not new. In analytical psychology, Carl Jung used animus to describe the unconscious masculine side of a woman and anima as the unconscious feminine side of a man. He believed these were part of the "collective" unconscious, a vast realm that connects humanity, and the degree to which the two are integrated within our psyches is indicative of our level of what Jung termed individuation.

While familiar with these terms from my sporadic dives into Jungian therapy, I struggled to understand what this actually felt like, and how it might manifest in my life. My Yoda-like male analyst was highly adept at helping me activate my masculine side, which was infinitely helpful for my career—yet it didn't help my marriage, which continued to be a source of frustration, and ultimately failure. I spent an inordinate amount of time trying to think my way into my heart, with very little success. So much for dream interpretation. I needed to go deeper. I needed stronger medicine.

❝❞
I embrace the power and importance of subjective experience

In a previous company that I led, I was routinely ridiculed by one of my executives for using the word *feel*. He would preface a meeting with his drilling and operational team—best described as oily-handed sons of toil—with the disclaimer, "I've gotta warn you guys, Murray is going to ask you how you *feeeeeel* about things." This was always met with gales of laughter and derision.

How did I *feel* about *this*? Honestly, I felt confused. At one level I was okay with it, as I had inhabited this world my entire life, the world of macho, goal-obsessed males. The fact is, I liked and respected these men, as their roots were my roots, and mutual humiliation under the guise of humor is a cultural reality among many groups of men. But at another level, I wondered if I was weak, if maybe there was something wrong with me, with this desire to bring "feeling" into my workplace. Despite the fact that I knew intellectually their reaction was just a cover for their doubts about their own masculinity, and I laughed along with them, I was still wounded by it.

According to author and retreat leader Suzanne Kingsbury, the divine feminine implies nurture, intuition, and empathy, traits that both men and women are well served to develop within themselves.

❝❞

I had inhabited this world my entire life, the world of macho, goal-obsessed males

Masculine traits tend to be more commonly respected in business, and sought after, those being ambition, power, logic, conquering, and dividing. While under certain circumstances, these traits are valuable, and essential if fighting a tribe of cannibals while trying to shake a rabid gopher off your ankle, they have also led us where we are in the world today. On the other hand, the more feminine traits including creation, intuition, community, sensuality (feeling rather than thinking), and collaboration are still largely undervalued in business and leadership in general, while remaining enormously powerful and positive.

This internal courting, and ideally marriage, of masculine and feminine traits within an individual person might most accurately define the overused and misunderstood term *balance*.

PACHAMAMA AND "THE FEMININE UNIVERSE"

It can be instructive to revisit one's own myths and belief systems in the context of other systems, for no other reason than to examine whether we have all the answers. Every major religious or spiritual tradition has at its core a creation myth that shapes the social and cultural fabric of that particular culture. The common thread is always the relationship between Man and Woman.

The ancient belief system of the Andes and parts of the Amazon holds that the Universe is feminine and that Pachamama, wife of Pachakamak, is the great feminine spirit, the source of life itself, Mother Earth or Gaia. The name Pachamama is translated into English as Mother Earth since *pacha* is a word in both Quechua and Aymara that means earth, cosmos, universe, time, space, etc., in English and *mama* means mother. Aided by a skilled shaman, the experience of Ayahuasca is an encounter with Pachamama.

The following creation story provides a foundation for the belief that shamanism is fundamentally a masculine occupation, with the corresponding belief that women shamans are fully engaging their masculine side. The story comes from a book by Achiq Pacha Inti-Pucarapaxi, translated by Gayle Highpine.[23]

A creation story from Otavalo, Imbabura, Ecuador

After Pachakamak, the Great Spirit Bringing Order to the Totality of Creation, created this world and Man and Woman, he told them to rest and to come back calm and refreshed the next day, so that he would give to each of them the duties in this world for which they had been created.

The human beings rested well in their new Earth home, which Pachakamak said he gave them to receive. The Woman went to sleep immediately, and the next day quickly went to receive what Pachakamak gave. She rose and appeared together with the sun of dawn; she went and left the Man asleep. The Man had not gone to sleep immediately but had remained awake for a while to look at the world. Thus, today the woman is the one to arise very early.

The Woman arrived where Pachakamak was, to speak with him about the duties she would have in life, wanting thus to receive her destiny.

The Orderer of the Universe led her to see all that was growing. All the stones, all the mountains, all the beautiful maturing soil, rivers, lakes, all the happy plants and flowers, all the fragrances and colors he showed her. And also the work with the animals' lives, their behavior, what each one did, their skins, he showed her.

Thus they walked among all things that live and grow. The blue upper world was there, where Father Sun, in charge of giving food and power to all living things, makes his beautiful light and warmth. And at night the upper world was filled with stars, and with the moon who also feeds life.

The Woman was in awe of all the great beauty showed to her. Each new beautiful thing that appeared before her, she asked that it be hers, all the great beauty that Pachakamak had made to grow. She touched and felt the heartbeat of life of all the different beings of creation—all the varied stones in the world, the minerals, the hard rocks and the sparkling crystals that came from the fertile earth. Every insect and every animal attracted her enormously, their great variety, their whimsical and harmonious forms, their skin and the color of their fur. But she always looked down, and she was attracted most of all to the puppies and the defenseless beings. She took them into her arms and held them in the warmth of her lap, and a desire grew inside of her to have all of this in her domain, under her care, to keep them so beautiful, and maybe she could make them even more beautiful, and care for them, and protect the puppies and the defenseless beings.

Everything was so beautiful and needed her care, it seemed that she couldn't choose anything in particular to keep near her. Finally she decided, and said to the Great Pachakamak:

"Everything you have shown me is so wonderful. In the life of this world I want to work with and care for all that is so very beautiful, to obtain everything that is necessary to sustain their lives and that of my husband. I want Woman's domain to be over all that exists here, everything that is on Earth, to care for it and observe it daily."

The Woman's words seemed so powerful to Pachakamak that he gave everything that grows and lives on Earth to the Woman. Everything was left in the Woman's care.

"I put you in charge of life," said the Great Soul. "From then to now, the different things you see, you will give life to the different things. Your mission will be to give continuity to eternity; to give Time within eternity. The different things will be born from your belly; you will give bodies to the human beings and to all life.

"You will have understanding, love and tenderness in order to be able to fulfill your duty. Your desire will always be to clothe, feed, sustain and care for life, and to keep life in order. Yours will be beauty, harmony, balance, which are necessary for this task. You will be sensitive, loving, and benevolent, since the continuity of creation depends on you, and in this everyone will help you. You will be ready to give your life for that which you have desired, because the children who are born from you need your care in order to prolong their lives, and it may be that they demand of you the greatest extreme, to give your own life in order that they be born.

"You will always seriously see everything that is in the present. Everything that presents itself to you, you will transform into beauty. You will decorate things and you will care for everything that is beautiful and worthy. The spirits of Water and Earth will always accompany you, and the Moon with all her children, the stars, will be with you directing your life.

"All the Universe that you see is feminine; the whole field of life which you have chosen and which I give to you. I give you the responsibility to generate, maintain and protect life, nature, and the Man. Through you the Man will be able to live, and he will seek you because you will give him the strength to be useful and you will direct his strength. In your work, I will help you together with all the other Powers, so that as you mature you will continue in your desire to reach out to all life. To your children, you will give life, love, and wisdom."

Thus spoke Pachakamak and withdrew. The Woman was left happy. She took the responsibility that Pachakamak had given her, as she had wanted. All of Pachamama—Mother Earth, Mother Nature, Mother Universe—was hers. Something had only to appear and take form and presence, and the woman was its master and caretaker.

Then the Man appeared before the Great Pachakamak and said: "I come into your presence, now tell me what work in this world is to be mine."

The Great Pachakamak told him, "The Woman came first and desired everything that she saw. The Universe is now feminine, she has taken the responsibility to care for all life and has gained the honor of prolonging and sustaining life. So I have given to her everything that you see before your eyes."

The Man was surprised. But then he recovered his breath and asked, "If you have given everything that exists to the Woman, what work is left for me?"

The Great Pachakamak assumed his state of wisdom and said: "The Woman has taken on everything that is visible in this world. You will not take the responsibility for what is visible. Everything that is visible is the responsibility of the Woman. But your place will be everything that is hidden from sight. I see that you will dedicate yourself to the 'invisible world' of the Creation.

"Everything that exists and appears, everything that has form and presence, everything that leaves a 'footprint' upon the Earth is the feminine world. Everything that does not exist or does not yet exist, everything that is invisible in the field of the world, everything that cannot be seen, everything that is hidden from the normal look of light and form, is your world. Here you will find the world of the future, of projections and plans, of dreams and ideals that hope to appear one day. You will go to that world in order to bring those things, you will make them appear, and you will put them into the hands of the Woman, and she will give them life. Yours will be the world of death, of transformation, of renovation. Yours will be the world of causes. You will not look at form but at what originates and gives form, its causes. Yours will be the world of mysteries, which will call you to resolve them. In this universe, the days of the future will be yours. Your work will be to think of what will come after the present day. You will be able to look beyond the visible world of the present and past. You will bring about the future. You will be a creator, and your knowledge will be of the depths. If you cannot find these depths, you will be a sterile and useless being and everything will be against you. But if you discover the mysteries of the depths you will be a great yachak (shaman)."

The Man was taken by Pachakamak to the world of laws, to the processes of transformation, to the internal world of thought, to the world of creative imagination, to the world of decisions, to the world of death. The Man descended into the depths of human passions, meeting hell and rising to unknown heavens.

"You will be a seeker, an explorer. You will have the curiosity and restlessness to discover what does not appear. Thus, you have dominion over the invisible, which will permit you to organize and govern the visible. You will seek wisdom, which will give you strength and authority.

"If you do not have wisdom, you will be useless to others. That which you seek and find does not belong to you. If you want to be a worthy Man, a son of Pachakamak, then you must share everything that you gain. The more that you share, the more will return to you.

"Yours is the field of magic. You will make it appear through your wisdom.

You will give life to things that do not exist, but the moment that they take on existence, they no longer belong to your domain, but to the domain of the Woman. Because of this you will always be together with her, and from this joined action the universe will continue forward."

The great Pachakamak reunited the human pair and felt satisfied and proud of his children.

THE BOYS' CLUB

If it walks and talks like a duck, it likely is a duck. The leadership industry falls flat in addressing essential elements of humanity because the Western business world is masculine and simplifies any hope at balance into concepts like "work-life balance," which fail to create any deep or meaningful dialogue and change.

Since most companies still walk and talk with masculinity, they are by definition masculine.

There is no question that in the business and government realms, some progress has been made in terms of women being represented in the upper echelons, but the ratio of women to men on boards is still alarmingly low. Furthermore, you might notice that women with strong masculine attributes tend to rise to the top. That isn't a value judgment, it's just a comment on the rules of our economic game; it doesn't reward balance, it rewards imbalance, mostly toward the masculine.

In Canada, among the 31,266 director seats in Canadian corporations, 18.1 percent were held by women.[24] In 2017, the majority of boards were composed entirely of men (61.2 percent), and only 8.5 percent of the highest-paid positions in the top 100 Canadian companies were held by women.[25] In the US, the data governance company Equilar analyzed gender representation on the boards of directors at companies in 98 percent of all publicly traded US companies and found that as of 2019 women held a paltry 20.2 percent of board seats.[26]

These distributions are routinely pointed to as improvements at first glance, but the reality for many women on boards, based on my personal first-hand knowledge from conversations with female former colleagues, is that it is often extremely difficult to be heard or treated with the same degree of credibility by an overwhelmingly male board. So, one could argue that it's all still window dressing.

In 2013, a study by *Harvard Business Review* stated: "Although boards say they like diversity, they don't know how to take advantage of it. [...] Women told us they were not treated as full members of the group, though the male directors were largely oblivious to their female colleagues' experience in this regard."[27]

In a private comment to me, a highly talented corporate controls expert who routinely works for boards of directors stated that the dream of "old white guys" is to sit on boards with their friends, play golf, and get paid to look the other way. While initially seeming inflammatory, her comments based on direct experiences, which are broad, deep, and highly credible, are revealing.

She also confided in me that the other side of this coin is that women are hesitant to support, promote, and stand up for one another. There is a certain level of envy of men's ability to at least superficially like and support one another in the mysterious realm of their buddy system. I have heard this many times from my female friends and former colleagues. This is the boys' club we hear about. In how it leverages personal friendships for business success, it is a powerful, valuable support network among men. In business, the lack of entry into such a network can be highly detrimental to women and pretty much anyone who finds themselves in a non-dominant group.

A recent discussion with some business associates on the topic of board composition confirmed that we still have a long way to go. One of these men, a dinosaur, said simply, "Women add no value to a board." This was a conversation stopper and despite an intervention by me and a much younger male colleague, this dinosaur could not be convinced to leave the late Jurassic. This type of bias toward women that underlies the attitudes of male leaders is still widely prevalent, and I routinely see it and hear it in my business and personal dealings. Men hold these feelings without any awareness that it is the feminine in themselves they are rejecting—this is part of the circle of madness that re-wounds people.

As I write this, I admit with no small degree of embarrassment that I have not been on any boards with women, and I neither did I advocate strongly for more balanced boards. When I began to examine my own assumptions about gender, which were not pretty, I began to understand how harmful misogyny is for all parties. It usually comes out as an unconscious bias and plays out in the typical male psyche as follows:

The objective statement is: "Of course, I think women should be on boards. I am a progressive business leader." But the subjective reality is: "I don't want my mother, my wife, my daughter, etc., on my board, telling me what to do. I have enough of that at home."

This is of course not socially acceptable to say, unless we are with other men. This attitude is rampant among men, despite outward gestures to the contrary, and I too have been part of this "locker room talk."

During one of my ceremonies, a female, Egyptian form emerged from the void of my consciousness. I do not know her name, nor do I wish to guess, but her message is branded in my mind to this day: "The Egyptians had it right," she said as she held up an ankh.

In the past few months, I have come to understand that the Egyptians worshipped both male and female forms in a complex system of belief that while predominantly pantheistic, revolved around the divine feminine, incarnated nature herself.

The Egyptian goddess Isis is a deity that appears as the principle of natural fecundity among nearly all the religions of the ancient world, including Christianity, where she appears as the Virgin Mary. Also associated with knowledge and wisdom, this ubiquitous divine feminine may have appeared even earlier in the ancient Mayan civilization of Central America, thought by some scholars to be older than the Egyptian, in the form of Queen Moo.

Given the historical context of the divine feminine, weaving her way into mystical, spiritual, and religious belief systems over our entire recorded human history, and the reverence which she is accorded, one might ask whether Mother Aya is not simply another manifestation of this divine feminine wisdom.

❝❞

Men hold these feelings without any awareness that it is the feminine in themselves they are rejecting

A direct outcome of my Ayahuasca experiences is the acute knowledge of the degree to which the power of the feminine has been suppressed within my own psyche. It manifests as fear associated with "losing my power" to a woman, and the degree to which I carried a socialized attitude of being a liberated male, while hiding behind a wall of fear. This is not psychobabble. I have been through enough analysis to know the difference. This is a stark truth.

Plant medicine has a way of forcing ugly truths to the surface, despite wily attempts by the ego to justify doing otherwise. Furthermore, the split that occurs, separating the masculine from the feminine energies, further divides us within. From this divided state, we proceed to build our organizations, invariably to reflect a male-dominated world. As Jan Eden likes to point out, "You know, it's not a question of competence, it's a question of confidence. Men are just more confident in what they don't know."

The real point is that both men and women have work to do to balance their inner worlds so they can meet one another squarely in the middle. The divine feminine works to bring all of us into balance, male and female alike.

THE ORGANIZATION AS ORGANISM

In business, man is working from a mindset focused on survival: the mindset of the dinosaur, fight or flight. A company—or a body corporate, a corporation—is also derived from a mindset, or a collection of mindsets, that in the aggregate are survival-oriented and growth-oriented. The company must show survival and growth to be valued.

What's at heart here is *how* we qualify and quantify the health of this organism. The body corporate, being a manifestation of the mindsets of its people—but primarily its leaders—falls in a broad spectrum of wellness, as does any organism. If the organism is wounded—psychologically or physically—this impacts its ability to succeed in a competitive world.

What if instead of aligning a corporation around survival and never-ending competition, we aligned it with homeostasis, stability, and comfort? This would allow it to adapt to changing conditions while still taking what it needs to survive and flourish, to some extent, without taking more than is required for this flourishing. I know—it's sacrilege to propose we self-regulate company growth in exchange for stability. However, it's sacrilege only in regard to the unspoken truth that businesses see value exclusively in money, therefore they see their well-being exclusively in money and to limit their money is to limit their well-being.

But the truth is, corporations are not people, people are people, and their well-being should be the ultimate concern of any organization composed of well-meaning people. There is value beyond money—let's dive into what that looks like.

WHAT IS YOUR INTERNAL RATE OF RETURN?

Business is anchored in acronyms that have become mantras. The measure of the health of a business devolves into monetary metrics such as net present value (NPV), rate of return (ROR), profit investment ratio (PIR), and internal rate of return (IRR). In writing this book, it occurred to me that this last term in particular would bear redefining. In the economic sense, IRR tries to address the question: What is the value today of something you will do in the future? It is an indicator of profitability, efficiency, quality, or yield of an investment.

While companies usually deal with IRR in regard to money, what would happen if we expanded the concept of value to include the human lives that are involved, and the value they might get in return? Employees *invest* their time and their lives into the success of the corporation, but if the corporation's main focus is always grow, grow, grow, no matter the cost, people will get left behind, ethics will bend, stability and humanity will be (and is often) forgotten. This shift in value judgments ought to be foundational for leaders of tomorrow.

What is the value in the future of what I am doing today? Is what we are investing in today likely to positively impact not only our bottom line but also the peace of mind and safety of our colleagues, staff, and communities? This shift might fall under the principle of living from the standpoint of the divine feminine of Mother Aya.

Investors and board members could benefit from a deep personal examination of their own motivations. The so-called leadership cycle revolves around three primary nodes: investors (people who put money in), boards (people who are hired to protect the investors and support and guide management), and senior management (charged with spending the money and making the money). The extent to which this group of individuals is wounded in their views of themselves and the world around them is directly correlated to the type of organism a company becomes.

❝❞
What is the value in the future of what I am doing today?

This is not a grand "save the world" concept. It is small, modest, effective, and in that sense, satisfying. Integrating feminine energy into the masculine business world will not come without a fight, and will not come without some drastic change, but it will come with great rewards, both for the types of companies that succeed and in how much they succeed, and also for the sanity and health of the billions of people investing their time, energy, and lives into these corporations.

CHAPTER 12

THE PSYCHEDELIC CEO

The Psychedelic CEO doesn't refer to an actual chief executive of a company—
it's a state of mind. Conscious. Empathetic. Open. These are attributes you can
expect from someone who has explored the deep path of self-discovery. Psychedelic
CEOs have arrived at a broader understanding of what it means to be a whole
human who feels in control and at peace with their harmonious life and decisions.
While there are many paths to self-discovery, psychedelic medicine—specifically
Ayahuasca—is possibly the most efficient, powerful healing technology on the planet.

CONSCIOUS

"Each one of us is potentially Mind at Large. But in so far as we are animals, our business is at all costs to survive. To make biological survival possible, Mind at Large has to be funneled through the reducing valve of the brain and nervous system. What comes out at the other end is a measly trickle of the kind of consciousness which will help us to stay alive on the surface of this particular planet."
—Aldous Huxley, The Doors of Perception

As we have seen, consciousness has seemingly endless meanings that depend primarily on the perspective and intention of the person experiencing it. On the purely neurological side of the spectrum, we can consider it a biological awareness of attention that emerges from neuronal activity. On the purely spiritual side of the spectrum, we can view it as the undefinable presence that infuses all life and matter in the universe.

The degree to which we become conscious is the degree to which we have integrity. I don't mean integrity as in morality, I mean structural integrity. Being conscious means you have scanned the parts of yourself that make up "you," and understand how you're constructed. This is an ever-evolving journey; no one is simply conscious of everything about themselves and remains fully conscious through time. You don't attain consciousness and integrity, you *retain* it; we are constantly changing organisms, so this is why the path is always changing.

I spent my life exploring for and building structures. In business, I explored for geological structures, geometric arrangements of rocks that contain energy. In my personal life, I explored my own psychic structures as best I could. But underlying all this exploration was a structure whose foundation was flawed, bolted in place by wounds, with no doors or windows, and this structure eventually collapsed. I thought this structure was me, but it turns out I didn't need it.

If we are conscious, then we are undivided, we have internal structural integrity, and we are much more likely to directly impact those around us in a way that is sane, humble, and loving.

EMPATHETIC

"I do not ask the wounded person how he feels, I myself become the wounded person."
—Walt Whitman, "Song of Myself"

Legend has it that when you meet the Dalai Lama, he will invariably oscillate between crying at one person's misfortune and laughing uproariously at some other event. Back and forth, he has immediate and strong reactions to every interaction. If you didn't know the Dalai Lama as an elevated spiritual leader, you might be forgiven for thinking him mentally ill. The reality is that he meets each person in a state of pure presence, compassion, and empathy. He doesn't just imagine that he feels their pain or joy, his brain seems to actually feel it, and his body responds as if these feelings were his own.

At the deepest level, below our wounds and our protective shells, both physical and metaphorical, we are all extraordinary. No exceptions. Empathy means knowing deeply that despite having different roles in life, we are at our core the same peaceful beings in need of love and capable of giving love. Responsibly taking psychedelics and doing the work to integrate the experiences into your waking life will almost necessarily result in an increase of empathy in your life.

〔〔 〕〕
We are constantly changing organisms, so this is why the path is always changing

Empathy does not, however, imply lack of discernment; it doesn't mean you accept and let everyone into your life. Rather, you simply observe clearly where other people are in their evolution as humans, and with that in mind, you work with them empathetically in the spirit of mutual cooperation. While we will always still fall into a negative, judging mind, we can even then discern the difference between feeling a judgment and the judgment actually being true. People rarely deserve the harsh judgments we lay upon them. The corollary is to perceive with empathy where another person is at in their life, and work from that place to find common ground and compassion.

The role of a true leader is to help another evolve on their journey. Empathy is not weakness. It is strength. Ayahuasca reveals that a lack of empathy for others always arises from a wounded self, not a complete and empathetic self.

OPEN
"When pain transforms into love, healing is happening."
—Taita Juanito

Openness is perpetual courage to jump into the unknown. Open people risk metaphorical death, if not an outright change in consciousness, for the chance to emerge as a more fully integrated, heart-centered human being. Openness requires a harmonious flow of energy between the heart and the head. Instead of one always dominating the other, they work together to increase opportunity and joy all around. Openness transforms the silo of self-absorption into the power and beauty of learning from and sharing with others, no matter who they are.

Openness means understanding that you don't need to identify your thoughts or actions with your *self*; openness means it's okay to be mistaken about who you are, or who other people are. Openness allows for change because you're no longer stuck to old stories.

Beyond understanding that there are other viewpoints internally and externally worth considering, being open means being able to receive other sources of knowledge and information beyond the empirical, material realm. What we find offensive or distasteful in another person is always an opportunity to examine what we find offensive or distasteful within ourselves, and that our own negative life experience in life may be serving a much higher purpose for *someone else*. We are not simply here to meet our own selfish desires.

❝❞

At the deepest level, below our wounds and our protective shells, both physical and metaphorical, we are all extraordinary

Openness is a close friend of love. But not the kind of love that is simply a four-letter word muttered through our mouths. Openness is the kind of love that allows our hearts to be seen and felt, and allows the intelligence of our hearts to inform our thinking and our actions.

It means being open to the truth that while we are in essence divine, we are a mundane sort of divine. That is, God is in everything, and I am part of it, but I am no more or less God than any other person, animal, plant, or object.

DRINKING THE KOOL-AID

What is clear to me now is that the idea of the mind is itself a limiting belief. In order to survive, of course we must limit our beliefs and perceptions to what is near and pertinent. Without this, we'd forget to eat, but this is not where our journey should end. In the same way people shouldn't do psychedelics every day, people should also not "do" their limiting beliefs all day every day.

This disconnect between what we want to do, who we want to be, and who we are becoming is why we so often look to spiritual gurus, business leaders, or digital influencers to give us answers. Unfortunately, other people can only ever be a guidepost, as we are in the driver's seat, and we are the only ones with the answers to *our* questions.

Enormous confusion exists around the questions of life purpose, calling, and vocation, leadership, and even "changing the world." Further, the idea of balance, while quite simple, is similarly misconstrued. We cannot simply think or wish ourselves into idealized states of mind. Whether it's with Ayahuasca or other psychedelics—a highly effective shortcut—or another type of contemplative or meditative practice, the answer lies in getting to know yourself deeply by experiencing your own divine nature; you've got to understand your undivided essence. From this reference point we can positively impact our sphere of influence.

In this pure sense, we are all leaders. We have a responsibility to ourselves and our community to make sure there is harmony between our calling and our purpose.

In this new world, it's important that you know that you are your own leader, your own CEO. Your job description is to become more conscious, more empathetic, and more open. A true leader owns their own path, their own experience, and has the courage to arrive at their own truth. It is not a career path, it is a life path. It is not easy, but it is priceless, and it is your purpose. You can't step down from this position, it's yours for life, and it's a prestigious title: You. More prestigious than any executive name plate.

Whether everyone who reads this book goes to partake in an Ayahuasca ceremony or not, the spiritual and cognitive issues plaguing many businesses, industries, governments, and organizations are still having tremendously negative effects on all living things, including humans. The power to overcome this dinosaur mindset that is ruining our lives and our planet resides in our leaders of tomorrow. Leaders must learn to trust the Earth, its wisdom, its feminine energy, and themselves. But the power to overcome this outdated mentality is also equally incumbent on the increasingly fossilized boomer generation. This dinosaur generation, of which I am a card-carrying member, can exhume the deep traditions of the elders and lend support, guidance, and wisdom on this new journey toward a more conscious, empathetic, and open future.

It's all hands on deck. How will you help?

THE FINAL PARABLE

"When I look back at '88, surprisingly to me, it wasn't competing that resonates the most—it was the opening ceremony. I was in the second row of athletes walking in, and the feeling of the energy rush from the crowd as a physical form— like, we felt the energy from the crowd—that is a memory and an experience I've never had before. It was goose bumps, it was tears, it was joy. I definitely can't find the words to express it, except that it was truly a force of energy that you could almost feel pushing against you and propelling you."
—Kerrin Lee-Gartner, Olympic gold medalist, downhill skiing

In the not-too-distant past, 1988 to be exact, there was a ceremony. A giant Olympic ceremony that opened the world's eyes to the power of the collective. Bursting with youthful pride—and ego—the citizens of this small city known as Calgary volunteered their time and talent to make this happen.

A young man, full of ambition, drive, and pain, desperately wanted to be on the playing field, so he volunteered for the opening ceremony.

A Hollywood spectacle was planned, a ceremonial opening to one of the great events on Earth.

A giant inflated mountain the size of a football field was to grace the stadium, and around this inflated balloon would be a parade of towering dinosaurs, floating thirty feet high, anchored by ropes held by a cadre of eager volunteers. The young man was tasked with holding on to one of those ropes.

On the day of the ceremony, minutes before opening, unbeknownst to the billions of viewers, Mother Nature appeared with a vengeance. Gale force winds known to the locals as chinooks roared across the foothills and tore apart the artificial mountain. The tattered remains were hustled off the field with minutes to spare, and the show went on.

Instead of a prehistoric landscape, what the world saw bobbing up and down in the wind were only dinosaurs out of context, looking as if they were roaming the modern world. The young man held on for dear life and had no idea that he would hang on to this dinosaur for decades to come. Like many others, he was holding on to a mindset that Mother Nature wanted to destroy to make way for new creatures and thought forms.

Decades later, in this once young man's final Ayahuasca journey, he was taken back to this scene, back to Calgary. It was made clear to him that Calgary has enormous latent spiritual energy, but it has yet to fully mature into a new idea of itself. Besides its deep technological and intellectual talent, its people have the ability to mature and develop a new understanding of consciousness, empathy, openness, and identity. Might this not also be the case for anyone, anywhere? To be a leader in the world today, we must let go of our dinosaur and return home with fresh eyes.

ACKNOWLEDGMENTS

In my research into the leadership industry, I could not find anyone who had graduated from a name-brand executive training program and who had built a successful executive development business from scratch. Little did I know at the time that I was being guided to find that person so she could guide me.

In late 2019, I mulled over the idea of writing a book. While having coffee with a business friend, I mentioned to her that I thought I needed help, which was a huge admission for me. I could not get behind myself and continued to talk myself out of the idea of a book. I told her that although I had never had a coach, or adviser, in my business career, I felt I was ready to try it on this next project. But I was very specific. I needed someone of sufficient wisdom and psychological maturity in whom I could confide my weaknesses, with the breadth and depth to understand me as a human, and most critically, someone who had enough hard-won business knowledge to be helpful to me. I wondered if this person even existed.

Her eyes opened wide, staring at me with an electric surge of manic enthusiasm, as she blurted out, "You need to meet Jan!"

And so, I met Jan Eden. Without her, this book would not have been written. She appeared out of the ether, sent by the mysterious force of Mother Aya. The embodiment of a modern business shaman, she exemplifies the divine feminine by holding space purely for my own development. She has been advising, developing, and helping executives, entrepreneurs, business owners, and managers for over twenty-five years. She has no formal leadership training, having started her business from her kitchen table as a divorced mother of four. She possesses a unique gift with people and in business. Her intuitive sensibility coupled with a Mr. Spock–like focus on business and strategy is unique. Her contacts and breadth of experience are humbling, and her support of me on this journey has been of the highest order.

I could never have imagined, while plodding along my dinosaur tracks, that the feminine would emerge in my life in so many mysterious ways. Look for her, she is everywhere.

Out of the mysterious realm of synchronicity, during a random internet search for an editor, I came across Josh Raab. Something about his bio suggested he was my guy, but there was nothing to indicate his deep interest and knowledge of Ayahuasca, still be a primordial concoction of meandering thoughts in the journal of a dinosaur. And to his amazing publishing team: Amélie Cherlin, Andrew Bell, Ariel Davis, and Kim Peticolas.

Research into Ayahuasca was directed by the academically and energetically gifted Ashley Eden, who both challenged and inspired me to reach further than I originally intended. Research assistants Stephanie Law and Christine Novitsky provided concise, comprehensive background on the leadership industry.

To my friends from Rythmia who took the time to answer my questions with candor and love, thank you! In particular my friends Johnny Messner and Avril Lang, who have provided constant support, encouragement, and friendship along the way.

To all my colleagues, associates, employers and employees, too numerous to mention, my life has been enriched by your participation in my journey.

To my parents, my relatives, and my friends, thank you.

To my daughters Katya and Andrea for your support, integrity, and inspiration.

And to all the women in my life, past and present, who have helped shape and guide my journey that has lead me to where I am today, thank you.

To my friends from Rythmia who took the time to answer my questions with candor and love: Alysa, Bob, Catherine, David, Davis, Dorianna, Geri, Jeremiah, Kevin, Kristy, Lawrence, Linda, Louise, Mike, Pitzy, Sandra, Scott, Sharon, Wendy. While we could not fit all of your incredible comments into the book, they are forever etched in its essence. Thank you.

To Karen Duncan for your wisdom, thank you.

To my brother Johnny Messner, who I met standing in line to take the medicine for the very first time, your courage, heart and healing continue to inspire me.

To my sister Avril Lang, your divine feminine presence has been a gift, both during and after our shared ceremonies. To you both, your constant support, encouragement and friendship along the way is priceless. Thank you.

To all my colleagues, associates, employers, employees, and teachers, too numerous to mention, my life has been enriched by your participation in my journey. Thank you.

To all the women in my life, past and present, who have helped and continue to help shape and guide this journey that has lead me to where I am today. Thank you.

To my parents, relatives and my friends for your unconditional support and love. Thank you.

To my daughters, Katya and Andrea, for your love, support, integrity and inspiration. Thank you.

To Elizabeth, for showing me what balance between the masculine and feminine really means. Thank you. And finally, to Gerry Powell at Rythmia, for creating a sanctuary of safety, sanity, and salvation. Thank you.

With love to all.

SELECTED REFERENCES

The challenge with sharing deeply personal, subjective experiences such as I present in this book is that they can be discounted for exactly that reason. My long career at the intersection of business and science has ingrained in me a deep appreciation for "looking over the fence" to see what others are learning, or what the research shows, and how that can inform, or strengthen an idea that is often rooted in subjective belief or intuition. The testing of subjective experience against objective research is always useful. This might be termed the yin and yang of learning.

The following section provides an overview of the some of the pertinent objective research in both the leadership and psychedelic industries. While not exhaustive, these references are intended to provide a concrete, credible basis for some of the personal experiences and conclusions I present in the book. I hope that those readers who wish to delve deeper will find this section useful in gaining a deeper appreciation for the amount of research that underlies the premise of this book.

WHY LEADERSHIP DEVELOPMENT TRAINING DOESN'T WORK

1. In the 2007 article "The Arts & Leadership: Now That We Can Do Anything, What Will We Do?" in *Academy of Management Learning & Education*, researcher Nancy J. Adler examines how companies are increasing their use of artistic processes in their strategic day-to-day approaches to leadership. Adler writes: "Twenty-first century society yearns for a leadership of possibility, a leadership based more on hope, aspiration, innovation, and beauty than on the replication of historical patterns of constrained pragmatism." This requires creativity, passion, and artistic processes—people in the arts are positioned perfectly for this task. "The time is right for the cross-fertilization of the arts and leadership," notes Adler. Many leading business schools and programs are adding more arts-based courses to their curriculums, as old processes are becoming out of date and not working.

The following are five defining trends leading to our increase in artistic processes:
a) Increased global interconnectedness: With this comes increased and ongoing change requiring new and innovative ideas and creativity.
b) Increased domination of market forces: As power shifts to the private sector,

government intervention and welfare are decreasing. Leaders from all sectors search for partnerships and new creative ideas.

c) Increasingly turbulent environment: There's more ambiguity, uncertainty, and turbulence surrounding our business environments (take COVID-19 as an example). Relying on old hierarchies and outdated models is no longer feasible. Continuous change is no longer good enough—completely new products "redefining normal" are required. Meaning that organizations need leaders who are constantly being innovative, not just merely analytical.

d) "As Advances in Technology Decrease the Cost of Experimentation/ Organizations' Scarcest Resource Becomes Their Dreamers, Not Their Testers": The challenge is no longer the expense of testing ideas; it is to dream up new ideas.

e) Success is no longer enough: Modern society now wants wholeness and meaning; we don't want just another classic success story but instead to make a real difference. Essentially leaders need to lead with their hearts.

2. In Robert J. Allio's 2018 interview with Harvard professor Barbara Kellerman, "There's a Better Way to Train Leaders" in *Strategy & Leadership*, Kellerman explains how leadership development is a moneymaking business, which claims it can teach how to properly despite clear signs and surveys indicating that many leadership development programs fail to provide lasting change or prevent dissatisfaction among employees. Kellerman adds that there is little evidence indicating the leadership industry has made any meaningful change for society as a whole, with research indicating about 50 percent of leaders are still judged as falling short in terms of leadership following these programs. Says Kellerman: "Despite such signs that dissatisfaction with the leadership industry has been growing, our investment in the business of educating, training, and developing leaders continues to increase." The leadership industry seems to ignore the complex and reciprocal relationship between leaders and followers—thereby not addressing the other side of the equation.

Research shows that for leadership development programs to truly be effective they must do three things: educate, train, and develop. In terms of education, Kellerman argues that leaders should be trained with as much care and competence as in other prestigious fields such as medicine and law. Further, even hairdressers and other skilled jobs require specific training, whereas leadership is not professionalized and is not trained to any specific standard. She argues that leadership must become a "profession" where there is a curriculum, core skills required, and even credentials or licenses mandated. For leadership to be effective, it must be considered more essential and important, as training all leaders to a certain standard will improve society.

Bad leadership is not studied, as it is a moneymaking industry, but by studying bad leadership we could learn a lot. We ignore bad leadership, as it's unable to be separated from bad followership, while good leadership and followership are easily separated, therefore making them easier to study. Leaders and followers interact at all intersections; to train leaders means to study and to take into account followers. We cannot begin to understand the leadership system without looking at the whole picture.

3. In his 1991 article "Learning Some Basic Truisms About Leadership" for *National Forum*, psychologist Warren Bennis set out two laws illustrating what he learned about leadership upon deep reflection.

    a) "Routine work drives out nonroutine work and smothers to death all creative planning, all fundamental change in the university—or any institution."
    b) "Make whatever grand plans you will, you may be sure the unexpected or the trivial will disturb and disrupt them."

If followers and leaders themselves focus on the superficial, it disrupts all contributions to the true advancement of knowledge. There's a difference between managing and leading—leading requires looking wider, going bigger, considering new and unique ways of doing things, and questioning the status quo and routine. Wrote Bennis: "Leaders are people who do the right thing; managers are people who do things right." Leaders must be allowed to pursue novel goals without being roadblocked by bureaucracy. Leadership development may not work because it is a problem with our entire knowledge advancing system. A good leader must be one who pushes the limits.

Bennis also outlines four effective leadership competencies:
    a) Management of attention through a set of intentions.
    b) Management of meaning through strong communication of vision.
    c) Management of trust, through being reliable.
    d) Management of self, meaning staying true to your circle of competence and deploying your skills effectively.

In a 2007 issue of *American Psychologist*, Bennis claims we are lacking consensus on how to define leadership. In the modern world, the study of leadership is becoming more important as cultural changes have shifted our leaders and how people think of them and their roles. Leaders have the ability to shape our lives in large ways—think president, prime minister, corporate leaders, policy makers. He argues that an essential attribute which leaders must possess is creativity.

We also lack consensus on which traits define leaders and in what situations leadership exists and how it affects followers. Without this knowledge, we can't begin to address and attempt to "train" leaders without a solid foundation. Counter to popular opinion, we often choose our bad leaders, they don't just appear (e.g., Donald Trump). Through this lens, studying followers becomes even more important.

Leadership is not an individual phenomenon, however industry and research often treat it in this way. Media also plays a key role between our leaders and followers, as messages are perceived differently and shift. Media distributes stories, so the study of leadership development again must account for extraneous variables that don't seem to be considered currently.

A novel perspective Bennis takes is how leadership is overlooked as performance art. Leaders must communicate a vision and convey this in an inspirational way—this is often referred to as inspirational leadership. Looking at our past leaders, many of the greatest ones were well-spoken, centered within, exhibiting powerful language.

4. In their 2017 *Harvard Business Review* article "Turning Potential into Success," researchers Claudio Fernández-Aráoz, Andrew Roscoe, and Kentaro Aramaki assert that although 66 percent of companies invest and are interested in leadership development, roughly only 24 percent of leaders find the programs to be successful. Leadership failings are not due to a lack of talent. Predictors of successful leadership are: having the right motivation, curiosity, insight, engagement, and determination. Even knowing these identified competencies, many leaders struggle to develop and often change jobs.

These researchers suggest four ways to create more effective development programs:
   a) Determining the most important competencies in the specific leadership role (considering context).
   b) Rigorously assessing potential leaders on the above competencies.
   c) Creating a growth map demonstrating how each leader's strengths align with their competencies.
   d) Providing proper development opportunities (e.g., promotions, job rotations, coaching).

The authors further discuss eight leadership competencies predicting how an individual will progress as a leader. These competencies are: results orientation, strategic orientation, collaboration and influence, team leadership, developing organizational capabilities, change leadership, market understanding, and inclusiveness.

5. In their 2013 *Consulting Psychology Journal* article "Leadership Development: The Failure of an Industry and the Opportunity for Consulting Psychologists," Robert Kaiser and Gordy Curphy note that over the past fifteen years, organizational

spending on leadership development has grown by over $7 billion. However, this spending doesn't seem to be producing better leaders; in fact leadership seems to be declining in ethical standards specifically. Kaiser argues that there is an important place for consultant psychologists to help remedy this problem in the industry.

They note several key problems with our leadership industry:

a) The evaluation of leadership development programs is not standardized and often not measured. Further, the impact of development programs is not measured nor considered.

b) The leadership industry operates on a faulty definition of leadership. Just because someone is in a position of power or prestige and in charge of others does not make them a leader. We seem to lack an overarching agreed-upon definition of leadership and the goal of leaders.

c) Leadership development programs neglect group dynamics (i.e., organizational culture, workplace climate, etc.) while focusing only on leader competencies and personality traits.

d) Leadership development programs overlook the followers. It's interesting in itself to look at the differences among followers and how these dynamics play a part.

e) These programs neglect the needs of the leader—why is the leader needed, what goals is the group trying to accomplish? Programs must consider how to improve the team as a whole.

f) A major fallacy is that anyone can move into a leadership position and learn the skills needed, but not everyone is meant to be a leader or has the proper skills for it. Promotions are largely set up around advancing to a leadership position; this is not realistic and needs to change.

g) The influence of power that comes with leadership often corrupts leaders— development programs do not take this into account.

6. In her 2012 Brookings Institute article "Cut Off at the Pass: The Limits of Leadership in the 21st Century," Barbara Kellerman calculates that 77 percent of Americans agree that we have a leadership crisis, as confidence in leadership is quickly decreasing. Going back to leaders in the past such as queens and kings and philosophers (e.g., Socrates, Plato, Confucius), they were considered role models with strong virtues, emulating wisdom. Fast-forward to our current leadership and you'll see it is not the same—leaders are not considered virtuous role models, and rarely are considered ethical. Further, with increased revolutions, the outsider became the choice over the insider. Writes Kellerman: "Young over old, of newly engaged black voters over traditional white voters, of newfound grassroots power over old-fashioned party

power, and of new media over old media."

It also became hip in popular culture to disobey authority, making leadership that much more difficult. Leading by commanding is out, while leading by cooperating is in. Hierarchies no longer exist, while empowering and engaging and equality are taking over. As it becomes a team effort, it's important to consider the followers in the leadership system. As new norms come into place, leaders need to be taught how to navigate their position—to lead with authority but also cooperatively, to ensure they are heard but also listen. There is a paradox that exists for leaders and no guidelines for them to follow.

Importantly, as culture has shifted to depend heavily on technology, traditional wisdom is no longer valued as highly—this is apparent in many industries. The relationship between leaders and followers is heavily influenced by the web, so this culture shift must be considered. Kellerman cites Thomas Friedman: "We're going from largely one-way conversations—top-down—to overwhelmingly two-way conversations—bottom-up and top-down." We require a new paradigm.

Earlier, in her 2005 *Leader to Leader* article "How Bad Leadership Happens," Kellerman explained that it's clear why someone would want to be a leader (i.e., for power, autonomy, control) but not so clear why followers follow, especially why they follow bad leaders. It's been put forward that followers follow out of basic needs as individuals and as members of a group. Historically these needs were for safety and order, but now the situation has become more complex.

Kellerman splits bad leadership into two categories: ineffective (failing to produce the desired change) and unethical (right vs. wrong). She writes, "It is often assumed that one size fits all—that what applies to leaders and followers in one situation applies as well to leaders and followers in another situation." Although we know this to be true, in practice it falls through the cracks. Leadership development programs are often "one size fits all," ignoring important contextual differences. All components of the leadership web (leader, follower, context) must be taken itno account.

She suggests ways to protect against bad leadership. Leaders should:
   a) limit their tenure
   b) share power
   c) remain authentic
   d) stay balanced
   e) compensate for their weaknesses
   f) be reflective.

Followers should:
   a) empower themselves

b) be loyal to the whole not just the leader

c) be skeptical

d) be a watchdog

e) take a stand

f) find allies.

Finally, in her 2007 *Harvard Business Review* article "What Every Leader Needs to Know About Followers," Kellerman explains that we are so focused on good leadership and developing leaders through workshops, books, and trainings, that we pay no attention to what makes a good follower. Subordinates' actions and behaviors are constantly explained away through how the leader acts; the problem is that this is not a one-way catch-all relationship. Large differences in types of followers exist, affecting how the leadership system progresses and how the leader leads. Leaders must put effort into understanding their followers better. Researchers over time have attempted to classify followers into different categories (e.g., dominant, submissive, independent, challenger, etc.).

Kellerman suggests a new topology regarding followers' level of engagement: "I categorize all followers according to where they fall along a continuum that ranges from 'feeling and doing absolutely nothing' to 'being passionately committed and deeply involved.' " It seems engagement is the main determinant of the leader-follower relationship and the dominance versus submission. On her continuum there exist isolates, bystanders, engaged, activists, and diehards.

7. In his 2009 *Journal of Change Management* article "The Good, the Bad and the Ugly: Leadership and Narcissism," Malcolm Higgs discovers that the overwhelming focus in the related literature is on "good" or effective leadership, while bad leadership has gone unnoticed and is glazed over. Focusing solely on good leadership causes a leader-centric and limited view of what really encompasses the leadership phenomenon. This paper explores bad leadership with an emphasis placed on the effects narcissism has on leaders. Writes Higgs: "The more recent examples of dramatic, and indeed sometimes illegal, corporate implosions (Enron, Lehman Brothers) have clearly raised concerns about the nature and impact of 'bad' leadership."

A recent article by the Centre for Creative Leadership identified causal factors contributing to bad leadership: skill deficiencies; burnout; being insensitive to others; being cold and aloof; arrogance; betraying trust; and being overly ambitious. While they were all contributors, the personal flaws were larger contributors than skill deficiencies. In the literature, the major themes describing bad leadership are the following:

a) abuse of power

b) inflicting damage on others

c) overexercise of control to satisfy personal needs

d) rule breaking to serve own purposes

"The ability of leaders to engage in 'bad' behavior is seen to arise from their positional power," the article notes. Research shows that bad leadership can result in short-term performance increases or gains but in the long run causes performance to decrease, as well as having very adverse effects on followers: decreased job satisfaction, decreased psychological well-being, and decreased commitment. A few different views have been suggested as to what the antecedents are for poor leadership, the most pervasive one being that personal shortcomings are exacerbated by power. This article focuses specifically on how an excess in narcissism relates to bad leadership. Excess narcissism can cause toxic organizational cultures, increased blame, and unethical behavior. However, there is research suggesting proper amounts of narcissism may be productive for an organization.

8. In the 2018 article "Leadership Development Strategy: The Missing Links" (*Development and Learning in Organizations: An International Journal*), Shilpa Kabra Maheshwari and Jaya Yadav discuss the missing links in leadership development strategies. Maheshwari and Yadav conducted a qualitative study with 127 leadership development participants from 17 organizations. The participants partook in nine-to twelve-month programs consisting of 360-degree feedback, coaching, and action learning projects. The researchers found that 24 percent reported a lack of a clear leadership development strategy, 100 percent found 360-degree feedback and coaching effective but found the action learning and business exposure ineffective, 52 percent emphasized a need for networking and increased leadership opportunities, and career progression, job rotation, and succession-planning were found inadequate. Importantly, social recognition and personal aspiration fulfillment were identified as key motivators. It was concluded that among other themes, aspiration alignment is extremely important to leadership development programs—attention to individual identity and aspiration is crucial for the individual to meaningfully develop. People must feel responsible for their own growth and seek out the proper opportunities for their leadership behaviors to develop and flourish.

9. In the 2003 *MIT Sloan Management Review* article "Why Leadership-Development Efforts Fail," Douglas A. Ready and Jay A. Conger researched dozens of companies, finding that three pathologies were the root cause of the failure of many leadership development programs.

a) The "ownership is power" mindset: Older ways of managing are coming head-to-head with new realities in organizations. Leadership development efforts fail when executives approach leadership with an ownership or power-oriented mindset rather than a more inclusive accountability mindset. The approach an organization takes reflects its culture—a strong culture being the cornerstone of a healthy and well-performing organization. Further, HR or any other area in an organization should not be assigned the "ownership" of leadership development, as coordination often becomes an issue.

b) The productization of leadership development: Leadership development efforts are often not aligned with organizations' strategic goals. People want quick fixes and turn to development programs not suited to their needs. Leaders may become obsessed with the program itself rather than what really needs fixing. At times, leaders may misuse programs if not clear on what the problem really is. Overall, leadership development does not happen overnight or after attending a one- or two-day seminar.

c) Make-believe metrics: The metrics organizations use to measure their leadership development lead them astray. As we try to quantify specific activities and behaviors, this does not always work or have any meaningful relevance. There is a pervasive view that initiatives that don't have quantifiable measures have no value—this isn't true.

The researchers suggest three ways organizations can recover from these pathologies:
   a) Share ownership and demand accountability.
   b) Invest in processes, not products.
   c) Measure what matters.

They conclude: "Although leadership is a hot topic at present, without thinking more deeply about it, many companies will get burned by old world thinking about ownership, a product-focused mentality that focuses on quick fixes, and make-believe metrics that measure activity analysis rather than capability building. The risk is that by getting burned, companies will stop investing in leadership development and passively wait for leaders to emerge the old-fashioned, misguided way ... by letting the 'cream rise to the top.' "

9. In her 2016 *Harvard Business Review* article "Why Leadership Development Isn't Developing Leaders," Deborah Rowland presents research showing that one in three employees do not trust their leader, despite all the money spent each year on leadership development. Rowland argues that our current method of developing leaders is antithetical to the leadership we want and need. Our programs focus on

teaching feedback, leadership thinking, etc., when what leaders really need is to develop their emotional intelligence.

Rowland outlines four factors at the center of practical leadership programs:
a) Making it experiential: Development can't begin in leaders' heads but in their behavior and bodies. We learn by doing; breaking a habit requires more than reading information.
b) Influencing leaders' "being" not just their "doing": Leaders must learn to regulate their inner world and emotions before attempting to tackle the outside world. Inner stillness and mindfulness are a necessity.
c) Considering the wider systemic context of their leadership: We must attend to the organization as a whole.
d) Enrolling faculty/followers who act less as experts than as Sherpas: We must attend to the required skills individuals need for the specific leadership position and consider their characteristics.

Additional articles on the subject:
- Nancy J. Adler, "Finding Beauty in a Fractured World: Art Inspires Leaders—Leaders Change the World," *The Academy of Management Review* 4 (2015).
- Nancy J. Adler, "Global Companies, Global Society: There Is a Better Way," *Journal of Management Inquiry* 11, no. 3 (2002): 255–60.
- Warren Bennis, *The Unconscious Conspiracy: Why Leaders Can't Lead* (New York: AMACOM, 1976).
- Warren Bennis and Robert J. Thomas, "Crucibles of Leadership," *Harvard Business Review* 80 (2002).
- Warren Bennis, *Why Leaders Can't Lead* (San Francisco: Jossey-Bass, 1989): 118–120.
- Harvey Eisner, "WTC: This Is Their Story: FDNY Battalion Chief Joseph Pfiefer," *Firehouse*, Sept. 2, 2002, https://www.firehouse.com/leadership/article/10567892/911-interview-fdny-battalion-chief-joseph-pfiefer.
- Claudio Feser et al., "What's Missing in Leadership Development?" *McKinsey Quarterly* 3 (2017): 20–24.
- Pierre Gurdjian et al., "Why Leadership-Development Programs Fail," *McKinsey Quarterly* 1, no. 1: 121–126.
- Gill Robinson Hickman and Laura E. Knouse, *When Leaders Face Personal Crisis: The Human Side of Leadership* (Routledge, 2020).
- Barbara Kellerman et al., "The Recent Literature on Public Leadership: Reviewed and Considered," *The Leadership Quarterly* 12, no. 4 (2011): 485–514.
- Barbara Kellerman, *Bad Leadership: What It Is, How It Happens, Why It Matters*

(Harvard Business Press, 2004).

• Barbara Kellerman, "Leading Questions: The End of Leadership–Redux," *Leadership 9*, no. 1 (2013): 135–139.
• Joseph W. Pfeifer, "Crisis Leadership: The Art of Adapting to Extreme Events," March 2013, Harvard Kennedy School Program on Crisis Leadership, https://www.neilbakerconsulting.com/uploads/2/6/2/4/26245708/pfeifer_crisis_leadership--march_20_2013.pdf.

EMOTIONAL INTELLIGENCE IN LEADERSHIP

1. In their 2003 essay "Leadership at the Top: The Need for Emotional Intelligence in Organizations" in the *International Journal of Organizational Analysis*, Victor Dulewicz and Malcolm Higgs found that strong emotional intelligence (EI) is extremely important for top executives to possess. As more than fifty years of research has failed to propose a clear model for proper leadership development programs, alternative explorations into the emotion paradigm are well overdue. One study assessed managers on forty competencies and found that sixteen were relevant to different aspects of EI. The EI competencies that were eventually created by Higgs include: self-awareness, emotional resilience, motivation, interpersonal sensitivity, influence, intuitiveness, and conscientiousness.

The importance of EI is emphasized by many researchers as well as business leaders:

Warren Bennis: "In those fields I have studied, emotional intelligence is much more powerful than IQ in determining who emerges as a leader."

Roger Gill: "Managers need planning, organizing, and controlling while leaders need emotional intelligence and behavioral skills."

Sir John Egan: "It is really inspirational leaders who stand out in a crisis ... emotional intelligence is a big plus in hard times."

2. In their 2010 essay "Emperors with Clothes On: The Role of Self-Awareness in Developing Effective Change Leadership" in the *Journal of Change Management*, Malcolm Higgs and Deborah Rowland argue that the contextual factors of leadership development are often ignored in complex organizational systems. Leaders along with programs must address this issue, as their individual efforts may not make a difference if the broader context of the organization is not understood and/or addressed. In this study, leaders from thirty-three organizations were interviewed and asked about stories of organizational change within their leadership role and three questions were examined:

    a) What tends to happen to change initiatives when leaders are either blind to, or fail to challenge, the current organizational systems (both the legitimate and shadow systems)?

b) To what extent is a leader's self-awareness an important enabler of the ability to challenge current systems and to incorporate this challenge process into their behaviors and practices?

c) How can leaders work in a way that does challenge the established systems and thus moves the change forward?

It was found that leader "blindness" to organizational systems damaged the success of the change, whereas leaders considering the system displayed high self-awareness and were able to be agile in the moment considering multiple changing factors. Essentially, self-awareness is key for organizational change to be successful.

2. In their 2018 *Harvard Business Review* article "Self-Awareness Can Help Leaders More Than an MBA Can," Rasmus Hougaard, Jacqueline Carter, and Marissa Afton tell the story of a new CEO who was elected at New Resource Bank. Although he brought about amazing changes and progressions for the company, employees felt dissatisfied and had low engagement and low morale. Over time, the CEO was forced to come to terms with the fact that his leadership was not what he thought it was, that doing it by the books may not be the best way. He had to "ask questions about who he was, what he valued, and what it really meant to be a leader."

What he lacked was self-awareness—something not taught in many professional programs, such as MBAs. Recent research has found that MBA training may not be enough to lead organizations toward long-term success. Along with this training, leaders require self-awareness skills, understanding of others, and the ability to learn how to foster healthy cultures. Importantly, research finds that strong self-awareness is the starting point for good leadership. To increase self-awareness it is suggested to begin a daily mindfulness practice, take regular breaks, and listen attentively.

3. In their 2019 *Harvard Business Review* article "Research: Women Score Higher Than Men in Most Leadership Skills," Jack Zenger and Joseph Folkman explain that, overall, women are perceived as being slightly more effective and competent than their male counterparts in most of the measured specific competencies. Out of the nineteen capabilities measured, women outscored men on seventeen (e.g., takes initiative, resilience, self-development, drives for results, higher integrity/honesty, etc.).

Although women scored higher than men, they displayed lower confidence in their self-ratings, while men displayed overconfidence in their ratings. It is not until age forty that ratings merge. This has implications for women regarding which jobs they choose to apply for, how well they do in interviews, etc. Seemingly, it is a lack of opportunity to pursue leadership positions that is holding women back rather than their innate capability.

Additional articles on the subject:

- Suparna Chawla Bhasin, "To Become a Great Leader, Disover Your True Nature: Deborah Rowland," *People Matters*, September 2018, https://www.peoplematters.in/article/leadership/to-become-a-great-leader-discover-your-true-nature-deborah-rowland-19242
- Tomas Chamorro-Premuzic and Cindy Gallop, "7 Leadership Lessons Men Can Learn from Women," Harvard Busines Review, April 1, 2020, https://hbr.org/2020/04/7-leadership-lessons-men-can-learn-from-women.
- Jay A. Conger, "Can We Really Train Leadership?" *Strategy+Business*, Winter 1996, issue 2, https://www.strategy-business.com/article/8714?pg=0.
- Victor Dulewicz and Malcolm Higgs, "Leadership at the Top: The Need for Emotional Intelligence in Organizations," *International Journal of Organizational Analysis* 11, no. 3 (2003).
- Malcolm Higgs and Paul Aitken, "An Exploration of the Relationship Between Emotional Intelligence and Leadership Potential," *Journal of Managerial Psychology* (2003).
- Malcolm Higgs and Deborah Rowland, "Change Leadership That Works: The Role of Positive Psychology," *Organisations and People* 15, no. 2 (2008): 12.
- Joel Kurtzman, "An Interview with Warren Bennis," *Strategy+Business*, Third Quarter 1997, issue 8, https://www.strategy-business.com/article/18276?gko=0e7a4.
- Dori Meinert, "Emotional Intelligence Is Key to Outstanding Leadership," Society for Human Resource Management, February 23, 2018, https://www.shrm.org/hr-today/news/hr-magazine/0318/pages/emotional-intelligence-is-key-to-outstanding-leadership.aspx.
- Parker J. Palmer, "Leading from Within," in *Insights on Leadership: Service, Stewardship, Spirit, and Servant-Leadership*, ed. Larry C. Spears (Wiley, 1998): 197–208.
- Parker J. Palmer, "Leading from Within," Center for Courage & Renewal, http://www.couragerenewal.org/parker/writings/leading-from-within.
- Frank Rouault, "Leadership Can Be Learned: The Warren Bennis Theory," 2017, http://www.frankrouault.com/leadership-can-be-learned-the-warren-bennis-theory.
- https://learningforward.org/wp-content/uploads/sites/40/2018/04/palmer292.pdf
- Deborah Rowland, "Change Starts with a Leader's Ability to Look Inward," *LSE Business Review* blog, January 11, 2017, https://blogs.lse.ac.uk/businessreview/2017/01/11/change-starts-with-a-leaders-ability-to-look-inward.

FUTURE TRENDS IN LEADERSHIP DEVELOPMENT

1. In the 2006 *IEEE Engineering Management Review* article "Leadership in the Twenty-First Century," Kathleen E. Allen et al. argue that the purpose of leadership in the twenty-first century is as follows:

    a) "To create a supportive environment where people can thrive, grow, and live in peace with one another."

    b) "To promote harmony with nature and thereby provide sustainability for future generations."

    c) "To create communities of reciprocal care and shared responsibility—one where every person matters and each person's welfare and dignity is respected and supported."

The challenges to attaining this are the following: globalization, increased environmental stress, increased speed, and dissemination of technology and scientific and social change. These challenges directly interact with the ethical and spiritual dimension of humans, provoking questions such as: "Can humans develop the self-discipline to choose how they currently interact with each other and the environment? Can we develop the ability to live in peace with each other? Can we learn to live in harmony with nature?"

With these new challenges modern leadership must:

    a) recognize diversity as a positive asset.

    b) design, support and nurture flexibility.

    c) understand the fast-moving pace.

    d) show initiative and practice a systems perspective.

    e) consider equity, justice, economic, and ecological concerns.

    f) encourage and support continuous learning.

This new leadership approach is termed "collaborative leadership," with one important feature of committing to ongoing self-development.

2. In their 2014 *Leadership Quarterly* article "Advances in Leader and Leadership Development," on the history of leadership theory, David V. Day et al. explain that the advances in leadership have become intrapersonally focused for individual leaders and interpersonally focused for enhancing leadership capacity.

Issues in these realms include:

    a) Experience and learning: "Although there is a long-held assumption on the part of both practitioners and researchers that experience plays an important role in developing effective leadership, research suggests that the empirical evidence for this assumption is far from definitive."

b) Specific skill types: A variety of studies say certain specific cognitive skills, interpersonal skills, and technical skills are important for leadership with many studies disagreeing on which matter most and why. However, many studies agree that "identity, meta-cognitive, and self-regulation processes are thought to be crucial to the refinement of knowledge structures and information processing capabilities associated with leadership expertise."

c) Personality: Conscientiousness is agreed to be related to effective leadership performance.

d) Self-development: Work orientation, mastery orientation, and career growth orientation are found to play key roles in leader self-development.

e) Social mechanisms: Researchers "highlighted the importance of leaders creating positive learning environments in which learning about other groups occurs, innovation is supported, and cultural communication competence is encouraged."

f) Authentic leadership: Positive modelling is found to be the primary mechanism through which leaders create authentic followers, resulting in heightened engagement, increased trust, and increased well-being for all.

There are process issues of leadership development. One modern and popular assessment used is the 360-degree feedback. If used properly, it seems to be effective in helping leaders develop by gaining self-awareness, but if used poorly it may hinder development or even damage the organizational culture.

In their 2019 *Harvard Business Review* article "Educating the Next Generation of Leaders," Mihnea C. Moldoveanu and Das Narayandas explain that while the leadership development industry has blown up, it has unfortunately brought meek results for organizations and their leaders. They write: "Chief learning officers find that traditional programs no longer adequately prepare executives for the challenges they face today and those they will face tomorrow. Companies are seeking the communicative, interpretive, affective, and perceptual skills needed to lead coherent, proactive collaboration."

The authors argue that there three main reasons for the problematic state of leadership development:

a) Gap in motivations: Organizations pay for development for long-term benefits, whereas the individual leaders use it for short-term benefit and to advance their careers and may leave the organization.

b) Gap between skills taught and skills organizations require: Many development programs lack the teaching of interpersonal skills

c) Skills transfer gap: Few leaders actually apply what they learn in development programs

New trends emerging with providers include: an increase in Personal Learning Clouds (PLC) leading to lowered costs and more customizable development, a decline in standard classroom programs, and an increase in customizable learning environments. This digitization allows for increased efficiency, more forum communication, and lowered price in individual skill development. Further, these new programs are leading to disintermediation, meaning, according to the authors, "companies can go online to identify (and often curate) the highest-quality individual teachers, learning experiences, and modules—not just the highest-quality programs. Meanwhile, instructors can act as 'free agents' and take up the best-paying or most-satisfying teaching gigs, escaping the routines and wage constraints of their parent organizations."

PLCs have four important characteristics: learning is personalized, learning is socialized, learning is contextualized, and learning outcomes can be transparently tracked. In terms of what our future holds, costs will become lower per learner, each learner will benefit from more targeted offerings, learning will be better mapped out, action learning will increase, there will be better participant monitoring, and there will likely be a significant increase in behavioral change as learning becomes more applied.

Additional articles on the subject:
- Nancy J. Adler, "Global Leaders: A Dialogue with Future History," *Management International* 1, no. 2 (1997): 21–33.
- Malcolm Higgs, "How Can We Make Sense of Leadership in the 21st Century?" *Leadership & Organization Development Journal* (2003).
- Nick Petrie "Future Trends in Leadership Development," *Center for Creative Leadership* white paper 5, no. 5 (2011).

AYAHUASCA RESEARCH

OVERVIEW
Many of the studies conducted to date with Ayahuasca have been small and lacked appropriate controls. Although the adverse effects on humans have often been reported to be relatively mild, people must not take its use lightly, and should be aware of the unpleasant effects associated with use of Ayahuasca and of potential adverse effects described in several references in this review. Consistency of the dose and makeup of the Ayahuasca brew are serious matters to be considered, as are potential interactions with other drugs the subject is taking.[28]

Currently, the data are insufficient to support the use of Ayahuasca in a clinical setting. The clinical research involving Ayahuasca, which includes promising preliminary results for the treatment of depression, is limited by several factors, including lack of chemical analyses to confirm the exact ingredients in the Ayahuasca drink used in the studies. A multitude of additional compounds have been described across indigenous preparations, including, among others, caffeine, nicotine, cocaine, and scopolamine. In assessing the aforementioned studies, one must be cognizant of the fact that Ayahuasca was administered as a non-standardized concoction. Randomized clinical trials using pharmacologically pure compounds are necessary to advance our knowledge about the therapeutic potential of Ayahuasca.[29]

ADDICTIONS

In the right circumstances, meaning within appropriate supportive settings and social milieus such as Brazil's União do Vegetal (UDV) church, regular and long-term Hoasca (the Portuguese word for Ayahuasca) use may result in profound, lasting, and positive behavioral and lifestyle changes. The most dramatic example is the finding that, prior to their joining the UDV church, most members who were interviewed had histories of alcoholism, substance abuse, domestic violence, and other maladaptive behaviors and lifestyles. These dysfunctional behaviors resolved themselves on subsequent induction into the UDV and regular use of the Hoasca sacrament. The Hoasca study also indicates that Ayahuasca treatment, within an appropriate psychotherapeutic context, may also be applicable to the treatment of alcoholism.[30]

A preliminary observational study of Ayahuasca-assisted treatment for problematic substance use and stress was conducted in a rural First Nations community in British Columbia, Canada. The "Working with Addiction and Stress" retreats combined four days of group counseling with two expert-led Ayahuasca ceremonies. This study collected pre-treatment and six months of follow-up data from twelve participants on several psychological and behavioral factors related to problematic substance use, and qualitative data assessing the personal experiences of the participants six months after the retreat.

Statistically significant ($p < 0.05$) improvements were demonstrated for scales assessing hopefulness, empowerment, mindfulness, and quality of life meaning and outlook subscales. Self-reported alcohol, tobacco, and cocaine use declined, although cannabis and opiate use did not; reported reductions in problematic cocaine use were statistically significant. All study participants reported positive and lasting changes from participating in the retreats.

The conclusion was that this form of Ayahuasca-assisted therapy appears to be associated with statistically significant improvements in several factors related to problematic substance use among a rural aboriginal population. These findings suggest participants may have experienced positive psychological and behavioral changes in response to this.[31]

Gabor Maté, a Canadian physician, researcher, speaker, and columnist, held multiday "Working with Addiction and Stress" retreats, which included four days of group therapy and two expert-led Ayahuasca ceremonies in 2009 and 2010. The team holding the retreat included Ayahuasca ceremonial leaders from Peru and Canada, and the participants were from the general Canadian public. In this small study, data indicated reduced alcohol, tobacco, and cocaine use from six-month follow-up self-reports, but not for marijuana or opioids.[32]

Ayahuasca appears to be beneficial in treatment of addictions, and when used appropriately does not appear to carry risks of abuse or dependence. Ayahuasca may enable sustained abstinence from alcohol, barbiturates, sedatives, cocaine, amphetamines, and solvents, though most continue to use marijuana.

Adolescents from a Brazilian Ayahuasca-using church had less recent alcohol use (32.5 percent) compared to adolescents who had never used Ayahuasca (65.1 percent). Oliveira-Lima et al. showed that in mice, Ayahuasca inhibited some of the early behaviors that were associated with developing alcohol addiction.

Harmaline has been shown to lead to significantly reduced cocaine and morphine self- administration in rats. While cocaine increases dopamine efflux and reuptake inhibition in both the shell and core of the nucleus accumbens, harmine only augments efflux in the shell of the nucleus accumbens, perhaps demonstrating one mechanism of harmine that is similar to cocaine that can be useful in treatment and has far less addictive potential. As mentioned above, a Canadian study by Thomas et al. showed that Ayahuasca holds promise as a potential treatment for cocaine dependence, with a statistically significant reduction in use (by self-report) that is greater than the reduction in either tobacco or alcohol use.[33]

With research still in the early stages, four hypotheses have been put forward to explain Ayahuasca's proposed anti-addictive properties:[34]

1. Ayahuasca reduces brain dopamine levels or activity in the mesolimbic dopamine pathway, decreasing the reward associated with an addictive substance. DMT is a known 5-HT2A receptor agonist and 5-HT2A receptor agonism is known to inhibit dopamine release in the mesolimbic, nigrostriatal, and mesocortical pathways. Reduced brain dopamine also fits with elevated prolactin levels with Ayahuasca use. The opposite is also true as illustrated by atypical antipsychotics, which have 5-HT2A receptor antagonist activity and exhibit reduced dopamine blockade (70 percent to 80 percent blockade) compared to typical antipsychotics (90 percent), which have little action at serotonin receptors.
2. Reduced dopamine in reward pathways impairs the synaptic plasticity involved in addiction development and maintenance.
3. The introspection, self-realizations, and healing of past traumas afforded by an Ayahuasca experience offer better understanding of consequences and

improved decision-making, empowering the individual to abstain.

4. Ayahuasca facilitates transcendent experiences; the authors give the example of Bill Wilson, founder of Alcoholics Anonymous, having such an experience (not Ayahuasca-induced) and being able to give up alcohol.

PAIN/OPIOID ADDICTION

Beta-Carbolines may prove useful in treating opioid addiction. Harmine and harmaline act as imidazoline type 2 receptor agonists I2. Harmane and harmine have both been reported to reduce the symptoms of morphine withdrawal. Miralles et al. assessed the affinity of various beta-Carbolines for the I2 binding site in brain and liver and also found that norharmane prevents the stimulatory effects of opioid withdrawal as measured by withdrawal symptom severity, and attenuated L-3,4-dihydroxyphenylalanine (L-dopa) synthesis normally associated with withdrawal.[35]

In both studies, Ayahuasca users showed significantly lower scores than controls on the ASI Alcohol Use and Psychiatric Status subscales. The jungle-based Ayahuasca users showed a significantly higher frequency of previous illicit drug use but this had ceased at the time of examination, except for cannabis. At follow-up, abstinence from illicit drug use was maintained in both groups except for cannabis in Study 1. However, differences on ASI scores were still significant in the jungle-based group but not in the urban group.[36]

ANXIETY

In an open label trial in an inpatient psychiatric unit, scientists found that a single dose of Ayahuasca has rapid acting anxiolytic and antidepressant effects in patients with recurrent depression. A review of several clinical trials on Ayahuasca, psilocybin, LSD, and their effects concluded that all these drugs could be beneficial in treatment of depression (especially in treatment-resistant subjects), as well as anxiety and alcohol and tobacco dependence. The results also seemed to confirm that both the DMT and the beta-Carbolines in Ayahuasca show promise as effective depression and anxiety treatments. They highlighted findings that 5-HT1A receptor agonists have shown antidepressive and anxiolytic effects in both humans and animals, and 5-HT2A/2C agonists had antidepressive and anxiolytic effects in animal studies. In addition, 5-HT1A/2A/2C receptor agonists have shown anti-inflammatory properties, and there is growing evidence that inflammation is another process implicated in the pathogenesis of anxiety and depression.[37]

It is suggested that DMT action at a trace amine receptor may produce an anxiolytic effect. Anxiety, like depression, is another disorder that has been linked to oxidative stress with Ayahuasca being a possible treatment of potential use in a review of plant-based medicines for anxiety. A double-blind study showed a statistically significant reduction of hopelessness and panic-like parameters using standardized questionnaires, the Beck Hopelessness Scale and the Revised Anxiety Sensitivity Index, upon acute Ayahuasca ingestion. Furthermore, it has been suggested that DMT acts in a manner similar to serotonin, and 5-HT2 receptor activation has been shown to alleviate panic symptoms. It is important to note that some beta-Carbolines may have a possible anxiogenic effect, given their inverse agonist effect at the benzodiazepine receptor site of the GABA-A receptor.[38]

All volunteers reported getting benefits from regular Ayahuasca use. These included healing body and mind, self-knowledge, fear and anxiety reduction, improvement of personal relationships, more contact with nature, and cultivating compassion.[39]

DEPRESSION

Coupled with these positive psychological and behavioral changes was an unexpected finding. Apparently, regular Ayahuasca use results in a long-term modulation of serotonin systems in the brain; specifically, populations of serotonin transporters exhibit an elevated density in platelets and in the brain, an effect that may be due to one of the h-Carbolines in the Ayahuasca mixture.[40]

Several studies of harmine have shown an antidepressant effect. One known mechanism through which harmine and harmaline may exert an antidepressant effect is reversible inhibition of MAO-A, resulting in increased neurotransmission. Their reversibility for MAO-A inhibition makes them safer than the traditional nonselective, irreversible MAOIs. Fortunato et al. have conducted several animal studies assessing the antidepressant effect of harmine. Using the forced swim test, it was shown that the animals treated with harmine had decreased immobility and more swimming and climbing, and they had increased levels of brain-derived neurotrophic factor (BDNF), which has an antidepressant effect in the brain. Harmine was also able to reverse the anhedonic effects of the chronic mild stress test. Harmine acts to decrease synaptic glutamate via increased GLT-1/EAAT2 expression and subsequently increasing glutamate transport.

DMT activates sigma-1 receptors. Other antidepressants, though not all, of the SSRI, MAOI, and TCA classes have been found to do so as well. These receptors are found throughout the nervous system, and are concentrated in the hippocampus, frontal cortex, and olfactory bulb, consistent with a possible role in depression. Past experiments have shown an antidepressant-like effect in mice administered sigma-1 receptor agonists and attenuation of these effects with sigma receptor antagonists. Agonists of the sigma receptor are being studied as potential antidepressant drugs. More work into the functions of sigma receptors and their role in depression treatment is needed. A possible connection lies in the inhibitory effect of DMT on the NMDA receptor through sigma receptor activation.

Both I1 and I2 imidazoline receptors have been associated with the pathology of depression. I1 sites are decreased in brains of depressed suicide victims, notably in the hippocampus and prefrontal cortex. I1 binding sites are found throughout the human brain, and the highest-density areas include in the striatum, pallidum, hippocampus, amygdala, and substantia nigra. I1 receptors are thought to be involved in the central inhibition of sympathetic outflow, which can be altered in depression and hypertension. Interestingly, the number of I1 binding sites are reported to be increased on platelets of patients experiencing depression and premenstrual dysphoric disorder. This effect was highly correlated with severity of symptoms, but there was a consistent return to normal levels following treatment with fluoxetine, citalopram, bupropion, desipramine, clomipramine, imipramine, and lithium, even though several of these drugs act through different mechanisms, which suggests platelet I1 density could be used as a possible biological marker of depression. I was also explained an unpublished finding that in nondepressed patients, desipramine failed to produce the same effect. Therefore, platelet I1 sites could have potential as a biological marker of depression, as well as a measure of response to treatment. A downregulation of I2 binding sites has been found in frontal cortices and hippocampi of depressed humans postmortem. Harmine and harmaline have high affinity for the I2 binding site in rat brains. In terms of clinical use, the selective I2 ligand BU224 showed antidepressant-like activity in rats and increased 5-HT levels in the frontal cortex and hypothalamus. Antidepressant treatment caused upregulation of I2 sites in rat brains. Most I2 selective ligands have been found to be allosteric inhibitors of both MAO-A and MAO-B.

Evidence is now suggesting that reactive oxygen species may be involved in the pathogenesis of depression and anxiety. Harmine has shown to be of benefit as it increased levels of both superoxide dismutase and catalase enzymes, and attenuated oxidative stress parameters of lipid and protein oxidation in the rat brain hippocampus, a structure involved in mood regulation.

General mid-term adverse effects were not observed in this study, although some secondary acute reactions were observed in some individual cases (e.g., anxiety) and will be reported in a separate paper. Additionally, from a clinical point of view, there was a substantial decrease in psychiatric symptomatology after the first use of Ayahuasca, which persisted until the six-months follow-up. The most evident improvements were found with regard to depression. These improvements in depression found after performing clinical interviews were also demonstrated by the psychiatric rating scales. Better scores for depression were also observed among long-term users when compared with Ayahuasca-naïve users at baseline.[41]

Investigators noted that the most significant antidepressant effects were observed for expressed sadness, pessimistic thinking, suicidal ideation, and difficulty concentrating.

Positive findings in the earlier study were replicated in the second study, but because neither study was randomized, double-blinded, or placebo-controlled, the results must be viewed as preliminary.[42]

COGNITIVE FUNCTIONING

The longevity, physical vigor, and mental acuity evidenced by many ayahuasqueros in Peru has long been noted as remarkable. Many of these shamans living in developing nations are well into their seventies, eighties, and nineties and yet appear to live out their years in a state of physical and mental health that would be the envy of many in the so-called developed countries.

Psychological screening tests and evaluations have found no evidence of long-term mental or cognitive impairment in long-term Hoasca drinkers (UDV members). In fact, most members performed slightly better than control subjects on measures of cognitive function, verbal facility and recall, mathematical ability, motivation, and emotional well-being and personality adjustment.[43]

Cognitive processes related to Ayahuasca use were investigated by two case-control studies with experienced Ayahuasca users.[44]

DISEASE

Another piece of evidence that has emerged is more anecdotal than scientific, but is nonetheless intriguing. This is that Ayahuasca may have significant immunomodulatory effects. A number of users of Ayahuasca in North America have reported that they have experienced remissions of cancers and other serious illnesses in conjunction with regular use of the tea.

At least nine case reports regarding the use of Ayahuasca in the treatment of prostate, brain, ovarian, uterine, stomach, breast, and colon cancers were found. Several of these were considered improvements, one case was considered worse, and one case was rated as difficult to evaluate. In conclusion, the data available so far is not sufficient to claim whether Ayahuasca indeed helps in cancer treatment or not.[45]

RELATIONSHIPS

At baseline, urban Ayahuasca users scored better on a Family/Social Relationships subscale and worse on an Employment/Support subscale.

The benefits that participants received were characterized principally in terms of increased self-awareness and personal development. Insights into one's life, access to deeper levels of the self, and strengthening the higher self were significant benefits. The desire for more general enlightenment into the human condition as well as one's own life and directions were often stated.[46]

MISCELLANEOUS RESEARCH

Depression

Abstract of "Rapid Antidepressant Effects of the Psychedelic Ayahuasca in Treatment-Resistant Depression: A Randomized Placebo-Controlled Trial"[47]

Recent open-label trials show that psychedelics, such as Ayahuasca, hold promise as fast-onset antidepressants in treatment-resistant depression.

Methods

To test the antidepressant effects of Ayahuasca, we conducted a parallel-arm, double-blind randomized placebo-controlled trial in 29 patients with treatment-resistant depression. Patients received a single dose of either Ayahuasca or placebo. We assessed changes in depression severity with the Montgomery-Åsberg Depression Rating Scale (MADRS) and the Hamilton Depression Rating scale at baseline, and at 1 (D1), 2 (D2), and 7 (D7) days after dosing.

Results

We observed significant antidepressant effects of Ayahuasca when compared with placebo at all-time points. MADRS scores were significantly lower in the Ayahuasca group compared with placebo at D1 and D2 ($p = 0.04$), and at D7 ($p < 0.0001$). Between-group effect sizes increased from D1 to D7 (D1: Cohen's $d = 0.84$; D2: Cohen's $d = 0.84$; D7: Cohen's $d = 1.49$). Response rates were high for both groups at D1 and D2, and significantly higher in the Ayahuasca group at D7 (64% v. 27%; $p = 0.04$). Remission rate showed a trend toward significance at D7 (36% v. 7%, $p = 0.054$).

Conclusions

To our knowledge, this is the first controlled trial to test a psychedelic substance in treatment-resistant depression. Overall, this study brings new evidence supporting the safety and therapeutic value of Ayahuasca, dosed within an appropriate setting, to help treat depression.

Well-Being and Public Health

Abstract of "Ayahuasca and Public Health: Health Status, Psychosocial Well-Being, Lifestyle, and Coping Strategies in a Large Sample of Ritual Ayahuasca Users"[48]

Assessing the health status of Ayahuasca users has been challenging due to the limitations involved in randomized clinical trials and psychometric approaches. The main objective of this study is the implementation of an approach based on public health indicators. We developed a self-administered questionnaire that was administered to long-term Ayahuasca users around Spain. The questionnaire was administrated face-to-face to participants ($n = 380$) in places where Ayahuasca ceremonies were occurring. Public health indicators were compared with Spanish normative data, and intergroup analyses were conducted. Long-term Ayahuasca use was associated with higher positive perception of health or with a healthy lifestyle, among other outcomes. Fifty-six percent of the sample reported reducing their use of prescription drugs due to Ayahuasca use. Participants who used Ayahuasca more than 100 times scored higher in personal values measures. The main conclusion of this study is that a respectful and controlled use of hallucinogenic/psychedelic drugs taken in communitarian settings can be incorporated into modern society with benefits for public health. This new approach, based on the use of health indicators that were not used in previous Ayahuasca studies, offers relevant information about the impact of long-term exposure to Ayahuasca on public health.

Empathy and Creativity with Psilocybin
Abstract of "Sub-Acute Effects of Psilocybin on Empathy, Creative Thinking, and Subjective Well-Being"[49]

Creative thinking and empathy are crucial for everyday interactions and subjective well-being. This is emphasized by studies showing a reduction in these skills in populations where social interaction and subjective well-being are significantly compromised (e.g., depression). Anecdotal reports and recent studies suggest that a single administration of psilocybin can enhance such processes and could therefore be a potential treatment. However, it has yet to be assessed whether effects outlast acute intoxication. The present study aimed to assess the sub-acute effects of psilocybin on creative thinking, empathy, and well-being. Participants attending a psilocybin retreat completed tests of creative (convergent and divergent) thinking and empathy, and the satisfaction with life scale on three occasions: before ingesting psilocybin ($N = 55$), the morning after ($N = 50$), and seven days after ($N = 22$). Results indicated that psilocybin enhanced divergent thinking and emotional empathy the morning after use. Enhancements in convergent thinking, valence-specific emotional empathy, and well-being persisted seven days after use. Sub-acute changes in empathy correlated with changes in well-being. The study demonstrates that a single administration of psilocybin in a social setting may be associated with sub-acute enhancement of creative thinking, empathy, and subjective well-being. Future research should test whether these effects contribute to the therapeutic effects in clinical populations.

ENDNOTES

1   Malcolm Higgs, "The Good, the Bad and the Ugly: Leadership and Narcissism," *Journal of Change Management* 9, issue 2 (2009): 165–178.

2   Raymond Williams, *The Long Revolution* (London: Chato and Windus, 1961): 57–70.

3   "The New Leadership: An Interview with Gianpiero Petriglieri," Thinkers50, accessed Jan. 12, 2021, https://thinkers50.com/blog/new-leadership.

4   "Fresh Perspective: Barbara Kellerman and the Leadership Industry," *Integral Leadership Review* (June 2012).

5   Gianpiero Petriglieri, "Are You Sacrificing for Your Work, or Just Suffering for It?" *Harvard Business Review*, August 28, 2018, https://hbr.org/2018/08/are-you-sacrificing-for-your-work-or-just-suffering-for-it.

6   Rafael Guimarães dos Santos, José Carlos Bouso, and Jaime Eduardo Cecilio Hallak, "Ayahuasca: What Mental Health Professionals Need to Know," *Archives of Clinical Psychiatry* 44, no. 4 (2017).

7   Gianpiero Petriglieri, "The Psychology Behind Effective Crisis Leadership," *Harvard Business Review*, April 22, 2020, https://hbr.org/2020/04/the-psychology-behind-effective-crisis-leadership.

8   Christopher Timmermann et al., "DMT Models the Near-Death Experience," *Frontiers in Psychology* (August 15, 2018).

9   *Oxford Reference Standard Edition* XIV: 146–58, at 147.

10 Steven J. Lynn et al., "What Do People Believe About Memory? Implications for the Science and Pseudoscience of Clinical Practice," *Can J Psychiatry* 60, no. 12 (2015): 541–47.

11 Jack D. Forbes, *Columbus and other Cannibals* (New York: Seven Stories Press, 2008).

12 "Global quieting of high-frequency seismic noise due to COVID-19 pandemic lockdown measures." *Science*, September 11, 2020, Vol. 369, Issue 6509, pp. 1338–1343.

13 Paul Stamets, *Growing Gourmet and Medicinal Mushrooms* (Potter/Ten Speed/Harmony/Rodale Kindle edition): Kindle locations 245–249.

14 Wayne Wu, "The Neuroscience of Consciousness," *Stanford Encyclopedia of Philosophy* (Stanford University, Winter 2018 Edition), https://plato.stanford.edu/archives/win2018/entries/consciousness-neuroscience.

15 Nassim Haramein, William David Brown, and Amira Val Baker, "The Unified Spacememory Network: From Cosmogenesis to Consciousness," *NeuroQuantology* 14, no. 4 (December 2016).

16 Robin L. Carhart-Harris et al., "The Entropic Brain: A Theory of Conscious States Informed by Neuroimaging Research with Psychedelic Drugs," *Frontiers in Human Neuroscience* (February 3, 2014).

17 Kenneth W. Tupper and Beatriz Caiuby Labate, "Plants, Psychoactive Substances and the International Narcotics Control Board: The Control of

Nature and the Nature of Control," *Human Rights and Drugs* 2, no. 1 (2012).

18 Simon N. Young, "How to Increase Serotonin in the Human Brain Without Drugs," *Journal of Psychiatry & Neuroscience* 32, no. 6 (November 2007): 394–99.

19 Fernanda Palhano-Fontes et al., "Rapid Antidepressant Effects of the Psychedelic Ayahuasca in Treatment-Resistant Depression: A Randomized Placebo-Controlled Trial," *Psychological Medicine* 49, no. 4 (2019): 655–63.

20 Genís Ona et al., "Ayahuasca and Public Health: Health Status, Psychosocial Well-Being, Lifestyle, and Coping Strategies in a Large Sample of Ritual Ayahuasca Users," *Journal of Psychoactive Drugs* 51, no. 2 (2019), 135–45.

21 Carhart-Harris et al., "The Entropic Brain."

22 Kuglae Kim et al., "Structure of a Hallucinogen-Activated Gq-Coupled 5-HT2A Serotonin Receptor," *Cell* 182, no. 6 (Sept. 17, 2020).

23 Achiq Pacha Inti-Pucarapaxi (Luz Maria de la Torre), *Runapaqpacha Kawsaypi Warmimanta Yuyay, Yachaykunapash*, as translated by Gayle Highpine, "Thoughts and Knowledges About Women in Indian Universe and Life," Ayahuasca.com, January 25, 2017, http://www.ayahuasca.com/psyche/shamanism/thoughts-and-knowledges-about-women-in-indian-universe-and-life/.

24 Statscan released data in early 2020 that was obtained under the Corporations Return Act for the years 2016 and 2017.

25 According to the Canadian Women's Foundation.

26 "Equilar Q2 2019 Gender Diversity Index," https://www.equilar.com/reports/67-q2-2019-equilar-gender-diversity-index.html.

27 Boris Groysberg and Deborah Bell, "Dysfunction in the Boardroom," *Harvard Business Review*, June 2013, https://hbr.org/2013/06/dysfunction-in-the-boardroom.

28 Colin M. Reiff et al., "Psychedelics and Psychedelic-Assisted Psychotherapy: Clinical Implications," *American Journal of Psychiatry* 177, no. 5 (2020): 391–410.

29 Jonathan Hamill et al., "Ayahuasca.," *Current Neuropharmacology* 17 (2019): 108–128.

30 Dennis J. McKenna, "Clinical Investigations of the Therapeutic Potential of Ayahuasca: Rationale and Regulatory Challenges," *Pharmacology & Therapeutics* 102 (2004): 111–129

31 Paulo Cesar Ribeiro Barbosa et al., "Health Status of Ayahuasca Users," *Drug Testing and Analysis* 4 (2012): 601–9.

32 Jonathan Hamill et al., "Ayahuasca.," *Current Neuropharmacology* 17 (2019): 108–128.

33 Gerald Thomas et al., "Ayahuasca-Assisted Therapy for Addiction: Results from a Preliminary Observational Study in Canada," *Current Drug Abuse* Reviews 6, no. 1 (2013), 30–42.

34 Jonathan Hamill et al., "Ayahuasca.," *Current Neuropharmacology* 17 (2019): 108–128.

35 Dennis J. Mckenna, "Clinical Investigations of the Therapeutic Potential of Ayahuasca.," *Pharmacology & Therapeutics* 102 (2004): 111–129

36 Josep Maria Fábregas et al., "Assessment of Addiction Severity Among Ritual Users of Ayahuasca," *Drug and Alcohol Dependence* 111, no. 3 (2010): 257–61.

37 Jonathan Hamill et al., "Ayahuasca.," *Current Neuropharmacology* 17 (2019): 108–128.

38 Jonathan Hamill et al., "Ayahuasca.," *Current Neuropharmacology* 17 (2019): 108–128.

39 Eduardo Ekman Schenberg et al., "Acute Biphasic Effects of Ayahuasca," *PLOS ONE 10*, no. 9 (2015): 1–27.

40 Dennis J. Mckenna, "Clinical Investigations of the Therapeutic Potential of Ayahuasca.," *Pharmacology & Therapeutics* 102 (2004): 111–129

41 Daniel F. Jiménez-Garrido et al., "Effects of Ayahuasca on Mental Health and Quality of Life in Naïve Users: A Longitudinal and Cross-Sectional Study Combination," *Nature Study Scientific Reports* 10, no. 4075 (2020).

42 Colin M. Reiff et al., "Psychedelics and Psychedelic-Assisted Psychotherapy." *American Journal of Psychiatry* 177, no. 5 (2020): 391–410.

43 Dennis J. Mckenna, "Clinical Investigations of the Therapeutic Potential of Ayahuasca.," *Pharmacology & Therapeutics* 102 (2004): 111–129

44 Paulo Cesar Ribeiro Barbosa et al., "Health Status of Ayahuasca Users." *Drug Testing and Analysis 4* (2012): 601–9.

45 Eduardo Ekman Schenberg et al., "Acute Biphasic Effects of Ayahuasca," *PLOS ONE* 10, no. 9 (2015): 1–27.

46 Michael Winkleman, "Drug Tourism or Spiritual Healing? Ayahuasca Seekers in Amazonia," *Journal of Psychoactive Drugs* 37, no. 2 (2005): 209–218.

47 Fernanda Palhano-Fontes et al., "Rapid Antidepressant Effects of the Psychedelic Ayahuasca in Treatment-Resistant Depression." *Psychological Medicine* 49, no. 4 (June 15, 2018): 655–63.

48 Genís Ona et al., "Ayahuasca and Public Health." *Journal of Psychoactive Drugs* 51, no. 2 (2019): 135–45.

49 Natasha L. Mason et al., "Sub-Acute Effects of Psilocybin on Empathy, Creative Thinking, and Subjective Well-Being," *Journal of Psychoactive Drugs* 51, no. 2 (2019): 123–34.